Master Passions

Master Passions

Emotion, Narrative, and the Development of Culture

Mihnea Moldoveanu
Nitin Nohria

The MIT Press
Cambridge, Massachusetts
London, England

© 2002 Massachusetts Institute of Technology

This book was set in Sabon by Achorn Graphics.
Printed and bound in the United States of America.

Library of Congress Cataloging-in-Publication Data

Moldoveanu, Mihnea C.
  Master passions : emotion, narrative, and the development of culture / Mihnea Moldoveanu, Nitin Nohria.
    p. cm.
  Includes bibliographical references and index.
  ISBN 0-262-13405-5 (hc: alk. paper)
  1. Emotions—Social aspects. 2. Ambition. 3. Envy. I. Nohria, Nitin, 1962–
II. Title.

BF531 .M65   2002
152.4—dc21

2001044327

For Angelica
—Mihnea Moldoveanu

For Sumantra Ghoshal, my friend and mentor, who stokes the master
passions
—Nitin Nohria

Contents

Preface

In an unguarded moment, introspection can show up the stories we tell ourselves and others about ourselves *as* stories. In their stead stands revealed a coterie of motives that may appear so vulgar, evil, or extravagant as not to merit close consideration as alternative explanations for why we did what we did. We may sweep them aside or shrug them off. "It's not out of envy of his mistress and physique that I fired him," we might say reassuringly. "It cannot be out of ambition that I married her," one might say while looking at her naked vanity exposed before a mirror.

Suppose, though, we did not shrug away our deepest suspicions and we stared them down instead and played with them. Suppose we tried to understand them and their relation to us; that instead of blinking we looked on; that instead of running away we stopped and reflected. What then? That is what the book you are about to read tries to get you to do—neither to fight nor flee but to look and listen.

On one level, the book is an exercise in introspection. It takes the reader through a series of thought experiments and tries to build the reader's capacity to experiment with that most precious of his or her possessions—the self. Running in parallel, however, is a commentary on modern organizational culture, which appears simultaneously as a product and a progenitor of our social sentiments. Friedrich Nietzsche and Sigmund Freud opened up a vast horizon of inquiry with their uncovering of wish and will behind facts, propositions, and truths. They focused on the creative power of the psyche and its propensity to concoct worlds that seem real—as will we. But they did not to the same extent focus—as will we—on the effect of our creations on our own minds, on our entrapment by our own culture, and on the mechanisms by which culture entraps individual minds into individual thought patterns.

The ambitious mind, for instance, is flooded by images of glory that in turn amplify the wish to succeed. In turn, this wish generates the energy required to create greater dreams, more persuasive images, and goals and purposes of even greater scope for one's desires. To see how the mind creates problems, scenarios, therapies, and plans out of ambition, which in turn commit us to continue living ambitiously, we provide a hermeneutic of ambition: What is it? How does it work? What desires does it produce? What are the myths by which these desires are rationalized?

To understand culture, we cannot use merely the standard explanatory devices of the natural sciences: we must live it within our own world of desires because it is through our desires that culture replicates itself over time. The psychological project of providing a set of lenses on the self and the sociological project of providing an explanatory or interpretative lens on culture merge: we experience the self through the many lenses of culture, just as we experience culture through the passions of the self. By bringing together the master theories of Karl Marx, Max Weber, Adam Smith, and Freud with the phenomenology of the self and its desires (which become transparent through introspection, reflection, and self-experimentation), we aim for a phenomenological understanding of the "master theories" that have gripped our sociological imagination for the past two hundred years.

If passions are the masters of reason—as David Hume (1960) believed—then they have done a remarkable job at getting us to believe in their benign nature—their outright subservience to reason. Deception and self-deception are as critical to the narratives that the emotions wield as blood is to a tragedy. Critical also is the fear of being "caught"—in one's "true colors," one's real emotional state. Falling prey to one's passions—wearing one's heart on one's sleeve—is often considered imprudent, dangerous, and inconsiderate—a flaw. At all costs, the passions in our culture stand ever in need of repression, suppression, or the therapeutic influence of reason. What we cannot explain must often remain hidden. Hence, the student of passions should take the stance of a detective or a spy, seeking to expose the tranquilizing mechanisms of the "reasonable temperament."

The workings of what we now call reason spring from a primitive emotion—our anxiety at being alive and thrust toward an end past which we cannot see with any of our senses. The impulse to explain is the impulse to freeze the elusive moment into an immovable concept. But for conceptual maps that shape our perceptions, we would be free—and on our own—to face the unknown that lurks from behind every leaf and every smile. But for the justifications that ground these conceptual maps into other ideas, we would be free—and on our own, again—in doubting the maps that give the mind comfort in the fact that the world is intelligible, predictable, and known. But for the logic that underlies these explanations, we would be free to doubt the very foundations of any explanatory act.

The fact that logic is timeless—untensed—is not a coincidence: it is the tenselessness of logical explanations that makes them attractive to a mind so impressed with its own temporality. The impulse to explain and to give accounts is also the telltale sign of the desire to impress by expressing—to control other minds through erudition, wit, and eloquence. We can seize others "by their minds" with our justificatory strategies. We get them to see the world "our way," and we can hope to thus tame the unknown that lurks in other minds and to harness these minds for our ends. Impeccable justification is the hallmark of successful persuasion.

Much of modern science bears the mark of the ambitious who needs to conquer other minds through far-reaching "theories of everything." He aims to conquer in mind-space what Alexander the Great, Napoleon I, and Adolf Hitler tried to conquer in world-space—"the world." "I want the world," we hear sexy heroines declare to their anxious lovers in popular movies. "The world" is a popular subject of desire: many of us want "the world" most of the time. And passions that come to rule our lives and shape our construal of reality—such as ambition and envy—are born of our inability to achieve the world, a fact that makes some turn either bitterly destructive, delusively constructive, or hotly maniacal.

"I am a maniacal 'toon,'" screams Dr. Doom in Steven Spielberg's *Who Framed Roger Rabbit*. His eyes are red and sinister and pop out of his head. His dream is to build the modern highway, with restaurants and gasoline stations pouring their contents into millions of gas- and food-guzzling Americans speeding along. He would like to wire his will into the lives of millions—by creating a structure that will constrain their behaviors according to his wishes. He is the ambitious demon of our age—one whose incarnation in the Carnegies and Rockefellers and Morgans of the American century has produced the infrastructure underlying the "everyday" in North America today. The lust for "cosmic power"—popularized but not exorcised by the evil genie in Disney's *Aladdin*—is alive, well, and ever present in the everyday: just look closely at your boss, wife, husband, and mother in their domineering moments. But we've become increasingly better at disguising this lust: "Do you want your eggs fried or boiled?" we ask, instead of first making it clear that the poor creature *must have eggs,* no matter what his or her wishes might be.

"Destruction—aught with evil bent—that is my proper element," says Johann Wolfgang von Goethe's Mephistopheles. His will—to repay "spite with spite," as John Milton would put it—draws its breath from the passions of envy and jealousy. Destruction wreaks envy upon matter—sometimes stoking it, sometimes exorcising it. So Mephistopheles destroys. He cannot create—even though he is a genius. He can dream of great fires but cannot, like his creator, invent the spark that causes a fire. Nor can he cause causation to "happen." Instead of looking inward to see the flaw, the shortcoming, the difference between himself and God, he curses and rebels; he leaks profanities wherever his athletic body takes him. And it usually takes him toward the beautiful and the damned—those who crave recognition and respect from others and are willing to give up their authenticity to receive it. Gratefully the mighty evil one obliges them, fondles their entrails with the pleasures of satisfied vanity in exchange for further considerations. He is the envious demon of our age—the great inspirer of the people who brought us the Gulag labor camps and the Communist heaven.

Master passions—passions that create our world and are in turn proliferated by these very creations—are ubiquitous. But ubiquity is a privilege that accrues to those who can make themselves invisible. So the master passions orchestrate their own disappearing acts. To be successful, they *must* be invisible. They help us create the myths and stories that will render them invisible. "The greatest trick the devil has perpetrated," says Kevin Spacey's character in *The Usual Suspects,* "is to convince people there is no such thing as the devil." The master passions thus can erect their own smoke screens. When in their grip, we get to choose between deception and self-deception. Either you truly believe that you are firing your friend for the good of the firm, or—if not—you might realize that you are doing it so you can have greater power within the organization, and you must lie to him about the true motive of your behavior. Self-deception is often the easier and more comfortable path.

This book seeks to begin a dialogue with the reader on the subject of the passions and in particular those passions that most powerfully shape turn-of-the-millennium social and organizational culture. We speak to readers being—like them—anxious, striving, and emotive. We do not aim to persuade but to inquire. You, the reader, are our medium for inquiry as well as the subject of inquiry. You are—as we are—will be the subject of thought experiments aimed not at corroborating hypotheses but at opening vistas and perspectives on the thinking and feeling subject. If the master passions have us, then who can behold them? How can they be beheld? By what mechanisms? And for how long?

Chapter 1 (Prelude: Shadows of the Master Passions) attempts to create a genealogy of the socially oriented passions, starting from a simple thought experiment—a crucial day, the day of a decision that will change a life in some irreversible way. We document various attempts to flee the anxiety about "what will come" through action, reflection, the pursuit of other glorious exploits, or running narratives that seek to encompass all of human knowledge and experience. We can seek to destroy and diminish those around us, annihilate the foundations of the social world, or make a virtue of the absurd—as many modern writers and artists have enjoyed doing. Alternatively, we can dissolve in obsessive rituals or sink slowly into the blue clouds of depression.

In the remainder of the book, we focus on the ambitious and envious escapes from anxiety—to which we can always return to contemplate the unknown. We explore the ways in which ambition and envy help us construct possible worlds and enact them—the world of the political anarchist, the world of the jealous lover, the world of the military dictator, the world of the corporate climber, the world of the tortured and the torturer, the world of the ambitious academic, the world of the yes man, and the world of the consummate political animal. We show how ambition and envy color our realities inescapably and marshal reasons and reason itself to their ends. At the end of the journey, we attempt to take in the human spectacle we have created and ask, Can it be escaped?

Chapter 2 (An Orwellian Abduction: The Rationalization of the Passions) asks the obvious questions: Why have we for so long missed the causal power of the passions in our social theories and everyday explanations of phenomena? Why do we talk in terms of reasons, principles, and laws when—as much of social and cognitive psychology teaches—we act on the basis of proclivities for self-therapy, self-presentation, self-aggrandizement, and the control of others so powerful that we feel them as "needs" rather than "desires"? The answer may be that the passions are dangerous not only as actors—because they are so causally potent—but also as subjects of conversation. Envy, for instance, has long been considered a social taboo—associated by Milton with the devil, pilloried by writers such as Helmut Schoeck as the motivator of manic teenage girl murderesses. Envy is something one *cannot* admit to—even to oneself. Similarly, ambition is terrifying to the immediate other—who sees his own freedom threatened by the ever greater needs of the ambitious for causal powers over everything that surrounds him.

Reasons—by contrast—are cool, quiet, placating. They are civilized, antiseptic, and sedate. They are the jewels in the crown of our Western heritage, developed by those who developed the Aristotelian idea that reason could always effect a miraculous synthesis or harmonization of the "lower" faculties and appetites. In reason all the ways of being of different beings could come together: their synthesis would be as harmonious as the arches of a Greek temple. Aristotle's followers did not conceptualize reason in the context of a world in which naked jealousy and envy would drive some people to put other people in gas chambers and turn on the taps on the basis of a "master theory" or of a world in which Gulag would be justified by the promise of a heaven on earth for future generations based on Marx's inexorable "logic." They seemed to have been unwilling to confront the underbelly of life, the powerful undercurrents of consciousness that expressed themselves in periodic and powerful outbursts throughout the centuries that provided us in equal measure with catharsis and the perspective of hell on earth: Heraclitus, Heinrich von Kleist, Niccolò Macchiavelli, Ludwig van Beethoven, Friedrich Nietzsche, Gustav Mahler, Emil Cioran, Michel Foucault, Georges Bataille, Jean Baudrillard.

Reasons and the uses of reason provide apparent truces—happy respites from the labor of the emotions. They can provide legitimate "outs" for nixing a lover, firing a friend, screwing a business partner, or bombing a country. When we use reasons and manage to create the impression that reasons—and not passions—are the causes of our actions, we become apparently predictable, comfortable to be with, reassuring. The illusion of predictability borne of structuration and regularity is what makes certain forms of rationality so appealing and the discourse of reason a warm place to come home to.

But as conscious beings we can ask: Is it all true? Are we truly reasonable creatures? Or are we, after all, slaves of the passions? The second chapter proposes a series of mechanisms by which the passions have seduced us into believing in reasons and trusting in reasonable people. It is a therapeutic mechanism. The modern commitment to instrumental and technical rationality is a collective attempt at self-therapy. The picture of a world rent by passions whose quiet everydayness could vanish any day without notice can bring on obsessive rumination about ends, about meaning, and about sense and reality themselves because accepting the world as wild and unpredictable means that we have to ready ourselves to give up all we "have" on a moment's notice. This is often too great a burden to bear for the mind— better, perhaps, to be deceived than to live in the cauldron of questions that "the truth" may reveal.

Chapter 3 attempts an interpretation of Anxiety: We aim to lead up to the Heideggerian notion that "anxiety is at the heart of everything." Thought experiments will be our binoculars. Just as discovering your wife's panties in another man's glove compartment can provoke a crisis of identity, so the admission that there is always a "reasonable doubt" about our deepest intuitions about the world produces a tension that can temporarily be escaped through hedonism, alcoholism, or detached reflection. But the fact remains that we are confronted with the nameless and the unknown at every turn of our lives.

Every moment is plausibly a first and possibly a last. Every plane we set foot on is the next possible Pan Am disaster over Scotland. Every oven we use could be a fake oven, wired by an evil genius to explode in our faces. There is no way of excluding these possibilities by a logical argument. There is no logical basis for inductive inference—and this is not a trick that philosophers of science play on us out of meanness for they, too, might like to know *for sure*. We require a leap of faith unto trust of the world to find the confidence to go on.

Anxiety is at the heart of everything because anxiety *is* everything: it is the "stuff" of which actions and words are made. Every word is an attempt to make the unknown known, to name the nameless, to bring the free and hence mysterious other (child, lover, teacher, pupil) under our own jurisdiction. Every action is an attempt to bring the unknown "out there" under our control, carried out under the impression that what is inside us is known.

Out of anxiety (or, more precisely, to deliver us from anxiety) come master passions such as ambition and envy—the positive and negative spirals that carry us along to lives of structured, orderly achievement or destructiveness, chaos, and glee at the systematic destabilization of others. They are master passions because they have us rather than the other way around. When in the grips of a bout of envy we think up the images and propositions that will further stoke our envy. When gripped by the will to achieve, we see other people—as we do other objects—as means to our ultimate end. The master passions help us lose our own tracks in the flight from anxiety.

Chapter 4 (Ambition as Desire and the Will to Power) is a journey into the lifeworld of the ambitious—an exploration of the ambitious spirit of capitalism that conflates worldly achievement with spiritual elevation and provides the impetus for the modern "American dream." Capitalist activity is the playing out of a passion that is much more ancient than the market—the desire for ever greater causal powers, mirrored, through money, into matter. We travel into the worlds of lovers who try to manipulate each other to obtain each others' recognition, into the world of sadists and masochists who enact their repetitive rituals of willful submission and reluctant domination, into the world of the twentieth-century scientist who may believe that she finally has truth and reality by their entrails and that it's just a matter of time before nature will lie exposed before the bespectacled gaze of the scientist. We travel also into the lives and worlds of assembly-line workers for whom immediate control over their actions—and the thought that they have eluded the gaze of the ever present master—are more important than material benefits; and into the life and world of a dictator who, haunted by the ghosts of people who saw him for a fake, kept executing people who reminded him of his indictor.

Chapter 5 (Envy and Jealousy: The Master Ratchets) attempts an interpretation of envy—of the need to become better in one's own mind by rendering the other worse, poorer, or more unfortunate than oneself or than the other currently is. It is a paradoxical story of betterment by diminishment, of constant comparison in terms of brain sizes, breast sizes, and IQ sizes, of murder among teenage girls, mayhem among the goddesses who stood to be judged by a mortal. It is a story about the emotion that breathed life into Marx's theoretical writings, helped turn them into the realities of Joseph Stalin and Nicolae Ceauşescu, and moved readers of *The Communist Manifesto* to bloodshed, lest "the capitalist" should eat their lunches and soil their women with their reproductive fluids while the workers work the mines. It is also about the feelings that come to the fore in an egalitarian society in which, paradoxically, *proximity* of social and material position breeds envy and resentment.

Chapter 6 (Want, Will, Wish, Would: The Predicaments of Desire) is an essay on types of desire told as a tale about two men fated to want in very different ways—one ambitiously, the other jealously and enviously. It examines the many moods of Narcissus—alone on the edge of his pond, aloof and ever concentrated on the image that has just forever fled, despairing of holding up time, yet hoping always and secretly that the image he so jealously guards is there the whole time and that the wrinkles that appear, the bitterness of the eye, and the twisted corners of his mouth are but figments of his own imagination.

It also examines the thoughts of Sisyphus—alone with the rock he pushes to the top of the mountain, as certain of the rock's will fall back into the valley as he is of his inability to make it stop or to stop the spectacle of his life from unfolding as it does. That he feels no fatigue—as he cannot, for he is already in hell and needs not be reminded of hell's presence by the normal procedures—only heightens the appearance of absurdity of his task. He finds meaning and energy in his work in spite of its absurdity—in spite of the fact that he is not pursuing this work for any particular purpose. "What is the purpose of having a purpose?" he would ask, eyes smiling, those who stop to ask him why he is doing what he is doing.

Chapter 7 (Self Against Self: An Aesthetic of Rage) delves further into the phenomenology of desire to seek out the roots of rage—of desire turned on itself with a vengeance. We try to show that from the simple and primitive irritation of a middle-age man stuck in traffic, whose cusses slowly turn into howls and curses thrown upon his wife, children, and various bosses, to the rejection by the metaphysical poet, anarchist revolutionary, and nihilist philosopher of truth, language, universe and humanity, there is but a step, a step we shall try to take.

Chapter 8 ("The Truth Is Always Incredible": Deception and Self-Deception) takes a step back from the melee to ask, How is such a smooth-running civilization possible against a background of such inner turmoils? Either the inner life is not what it is purported to be by the poets and the phenomenologists, or it must be well camouflaged. We explore the hypothesis that it is well camouflaged rather than nonexistent or tame and proceed to examine the mechanisms of deception and self-deception. The task proves to be remarkably easy—as easy as getting our readers to recognize the indelible presence of lingering doubt about every fact of their lives and also the thirstlike desire to get rid of the doubt by telling "a story."

That we sometimes live our lives dangling between deception and self-deception is something that Robert Solomon (1993) has presciently pointed out by his anecdote of a woman who picks a fight with her husband every time they are just about to go out to a movie. Queried, she seems quite forthright in her anger: "He really *did* forget to buy detergent today!" But the repetition of the ritual before every movie suggests another explanation, which she will aver only in a moment of unguarded introspection and perhaps only to herself: she hates the movies her husband picks and must choose between feigning anger to deceive her husband and deceiving herself into being angry. She chooses self-deception over deception.

So does the worker who tries to convince himself that he is happy doing what he is doing to avoid lying about it to his friends and resenting them afterward. So does the young married woman who has begun to love someone new and who must now convince herself of her love for her husband to avoid having to deceive him after telling herself the truth: "He's boring." So does the ambitious corporate climber who litters his trek to the corner office with the demotions of those whom he has declared (and convinced himself that they are) criminals. To admit otherwise would be to lose the force of moral conviction and to turn into a self-conscious hypocrite, which does not generate the mental energy necessary to sustain an upward climb through the corporate world.

Chapters 9 (The Moral Tyrant) and 10 (The Rational *Causeur*: The Subordination of Reason to the Passions) delve further into the picture of ideas and theories as masks for the emotions and creations of the passions and attempt to show that rational discourse and moral discourse are effective tools for hiding the inflammatory passions that drive us to act. "Isn't reasonable, isn't fair, have to seek consensus, have to get approval, have to change some processes to get this done" are ways in which we place the responsibility for our actions or nonactions on other people, on institutions, or on impersonal principles.

The logic of explanation beats out the logic of understanding when the purpose is to hide the passions that move us to act. It is easier—emotionally speaking—to explain than to understand because a statement can be refuted or modified by some logically compatible appendage, but what do you do with a feeling? How do you refute a feeling? Root it out? We do not yet have a language that captures the dialectic of sentiments, and our work is a first step toward creating such a language. A good place to start creating such a language is the thought experiment that is extreme (to counter indifference) and vivid (to avoid ambiguity), and to this end we delve into the moral calculus of a torture chamber, with real blood and real torture instruments, where the tortured gets to torture the torturer by carefully staging her smiles and whispers.

Chapter 11 (Soliloquies of the Candid Villain: Catharses of the Master Passions) is an account of the widely ignored phenomenon of catharsis—of the moment in which we become free to let ourselves be. These are dangerous moments—the melting kiss of two lovers who have suppressed their feelings for each other to save their families from ruin; the sudden, irrepressible realization that your boss is a creep, your wife is a fake, and your child is a fool; the immediate perception of your own desires to advance in the world and of the vile tradeoffs you are willing to make to save your job. The cinema, the theater, and the psychoanalyst's couch are some of the instruments of catharsis that we can explore to understand its dynamic.

Chapter 12 (Escape from the Master Passions) sketches a map of the uncharted beyond. By a quick count of the books that have appeared in the last ten years bearing the word *beyond* in them, the beyond seems to be a popular topic of study. Nevertheless, demand for the beyond keeps growing: there is, perhaps, something missing from the accounts we are giving of ourselves and of the world. We chart the ways in which the beyond has been approached by modern thinkers and come back to central theme of the book—that of the captivity of the human mind to its own passions, of the sources and sequels of this captivity, and of its failed escape attempts. Given the inscrutability of the passions, we are interested to ask, What lies beyond the spirals of the passions, beyond anxiety, beyond the strange interplay of deception and self-deception that makes subjective reality a demential ride on a *montagnes russes?*

Master Passions

1

Prelude: Shadows of the Master Passions

Think back to a day when you had a performance review or expected to learn the outcome of a job promotion decision or a crucial test or exam. Try to remember your thoughts. At the end of that day, you will either have "made it" or "blown it." There are no two ways about it. There might have been many stories you told yourself to take your mind out of this either-or cycle. You might have envisioned how you would come home and share the good news with your family: how you would smile and modestly say, "I did OK," after first waiting for someone to ask. Perhaps you delved into the dream of the sunny tomorrow—of the day after you have learned of the positive outcome of the promotion, the spectacular performance on the exam, the tenure or partnership decision. You might have gone through your day leading up to the critical moment simply *assuming* that you have won—just as Blaise Pascal went through life choosing to believe that God exists.

On the other hand, perhaps you worked through the day developing a coherent story of why you failed—the conditions, the lack of a stopwatch, the cold in the classroom that kept you from concentrating—just to have it in your back pocket in case your performance fell apart. The obliteration of your own sense of meaning and self-worth—imminent in case of a "bad" decision that you cannot account for—is too much of a risk. It may be all right to stake your career on someone else's whim but not your *self*. Maybe you recounted the endless ways in which others (perhaps with a greater endowment than yours) have also failed at similar tasks in the past or the many ways in which others (perhaps with a lesser endowment than yours) have nevertheless "made it"—gotten tenure or received the accolade you now want. You might also have been working on alternatives, should your performance come apart: "No matter, I've always got . . . to fall back on." Now your family and loved ones appear as a quiet shelter from the perils of either-or. There is no either-or with them: they will not hold back their affection should you fail—or so you think.

"I've got other options," you might have told yourself, evading the lurking knowledge that these "other options" are not quite certain, not quite well worked out, not quite what you had wanted in the first place. Occasionally, a question could have popped up: "But have I really done all that I could do to achieve what I want?" Now a little trek through history may have begun, aimed at exculpating yourself from every possible shortcoming in your preparation, every smile from a superior that you did not return, every opportunity to study or to advance that you gave up in favor of a quiet moment with a friend. You might have felt the urge to turn against those claiming to have "supported" you—your spouse, family, and friends: "But for them I might have had this thing under wraps." "Could have, should have, would have" might have worked their magical ways on your mind, and soon enough you became the self-appointed "victim" of those who had previously been "loved ones." You saw yourself at the center of a feast where hideous "others" suck up your energy and leave you at the mercy of "the scum" making the decision.

You might have repeated to yourself that "this is just another day" and might have said it to others, as well, when asked. "Are you trying to convince me or yourself?" an insightful friend could have asked, had you met her on that day. You might have focused on the color of the leaves outside, the smell of the morning croissants at the café where on that day, as on many other days before, you got your coffee. The "everydayness" of this day might have soothed you and focused your mind on the here and now and away from the terrible bifurcation about to happen.

Master Passions and the Genesis of Master Narratives

What was your path? What strategy did your mind take to avoid the naked contemplation of the question mark? Part of the message of the book you are reading is that from the anxiety that is our most direct reaction to the unknown rise passions that guide not only our actions but also our thoughts. Unlike thirst, anger, or sadness, we are often oblivious to "having" them, making it possible for them to have us.

The way of ambition, for instance, might have taken you in positive directions—in building dreams on the assumption that you have already prevailed and in thinking of new ways to expand your causal powers—to prevail again in the future. Instead of feeling doubt and rumination, you may already be thinking about the next promotion, the next step toward fame, the next whatever it is that your desire creates.

The way of envy, on the other hand, rests on knocking down the achievements of others so that your own achievements take on a special or higher value. Envy can guide you to make all of your social comparisons downward—to see the incompetence of others, to see their successes as triggered by chance events and their failures as triggered by deep flaws in their characters and intellects.

Master passions cut across people: they generate and are generated by social phenomena such as corporate restructurings and takeovers, political revolutions, divorces and the ensuing custody battles. Think of the phenomena associated with leadership transitions. Baboons, as Albert O. Hirschman has pointed out, citing an anthropological example (Crook 1970, p. 7), manage group leadership transitions with such harmony, subtlety, and efficiency that they raise the possibility that, on the emotional scale, we are the backward ones:

Sub-adult males steal very young females from their mothers and attend them with every semblance of solicitous maternal care. The young female is rigorously controlled, and repeated retrieval trains her not to go away. . . . At this stage there is no sexual behavior, the female being yet two to three years from child bearing. . . . As these young interlopers mature and the overlord ages, the younger animal starts initiating group movements although the direction of eventual movement is dependent upon the older animal's choice. A highly complex relationship develops between the two animals which, by paying close attention to one another and by reciprocal "notification" cooperate in governing group movement. Old males retain command of group direction but gradually relinquish sexual control over their females to the younger male animal. . . . It seems that eventually old males resign entirely from their original reproduction units but retain great influence within the band as a whole, and young males refer to them continuously particularly before developing the direction of the march.

Contrast this textured dance of the would-be with the have-been leaders with the savage beheadings that accompanied the French Revolution: Georges Jacques Danton, Maximilien Robespierre, and other fiery, imaginative beings were cut down because they were held to run afoul of the rule of reason that they had helped to bring about. Contrast the elder baboons' gentle relinquishing of sexual authority to the coarse leadership transitions on corporate boards—where CEOs are sacked and sometimes arrive at work without knowing that they no longer have a job. Contrast the young males' soft and ingenious tango of the wills—negotiating leadership over the direction of the group—with the power grab that often taints the leadership transition in family businesses, creating resentment that festers for generations afterward and fuels grudge-driven power plays for decades thereafter. Contrast the growth of the young baboons into the leadership position—with gradual assumption of responsibilities and gradual acceptance by the rest of the group—with the great savagery that followed Joseph Stalin's rise to power: his purges, his mock trials, and his executions of thousands of people whose physical destruction served a purpose in his plans. Contrast the continuity of the baboons' social fabric with the great rift that is produced when a new political regime takes power—in the United States or abroad, now as before—and its leaders feel compelled to denounce their predecessors as instrumentally incompetent, morally evil, or both. Contrast the lack of vindictiveness of the elder baboons with the great showdowns in corporate boards and in academia, where revenge— though not openly pursued or acknowledged—is nevertheless what is most often feared and just as often aimed at by he or she who was displaced or denied tenure. It is perhaps time we tried to learn from the baboon.

Leadership transitions in human societies are accompanied by great stories, and master narratives that marshal all of human history to the defense of an ideology. The myth of the present as the apotheosis of the past— forcefully put forth by Georg Wilhelm Friedrich Hegel and Karl Marx as well as by dogmatic supporters of laissez-faire capitalism—is the perfect conceptual tool for clothing leadership transitions in the mask of legitimacy. This mask has many faces—according to the passions it aims to arouse. The ideologies of social progress and egalitarian utopias can appeal to the envious side of people—to their perceptions of inequality in endowments and opportunities, to the appalling working conditions of the man on the street, or to the inequality of opportunity for people of different race and sex than those of the dominant groups. The envious side can become an envious streak, as each social situation becomes an opportunity to assert one's social identity against threats from the "outside" or becomes an opportunity to redress some age-long injustice that has been shamelessly perpetrated against one's social or ethnic group by "them"—the powerful ones.

One can, on the other hand, sing the anthems of ambition—as does the Hegelian view of the Prussian state of 1807 as the apotheosis of a historical master-slave dialectic. So also do modernist conceptions of postindustrial society that equate overall social well-being with the material well-being of individuals, that trace well-being to scientific progress (to exculpate scientific progress from any accusation of enabling murders of historically unprecedented proportions), and that allow the perpetrators to abdicate personal responsibility by deferring causal agency to the laws of nature.

Such master narratives engulf the reader with hard facts that purport to establish their ahistorical and transcultural validity. Marx saw his materialist dialectic between the ever avid capitalist and the ever less autonomous worker as the driving engine for all societies and civilizations, independently of their location in time and space. He was ready to see relations of bondage based on material dependence within tribal societies and ancient civilizations as readily as he was able to see them among the workers and capitalists in nineteenth-century Europe. The modern evolutionary scientist sees Darwinian mechanisms operating to shape or determine all aspects of modern social behavior—even though a society that has grown up on an intellectual diet dominated by Darwinian theory may end up behaving in ways that are increasingly amenable to a Darwinian interpretation, thus shielding the Darwinian interpretation of social behavior from the tough empirical tests that scientific theories are heralded for withstanding. The arguments used to support master narratives and the actions that we use the narratives to justify become the levers by which they take over our own and others' minds. Often we do not behold these master narratives, but rather the master narratives behold us.

The Beholdenness of Reason

How is this takeover accomplished? Consider the play of emotions of a young man waiting in a line to catch a flight out of a snowy midwestern city so that he can see his wife on the East Coast of the United States. A snow storm is forecast, so this is the last flight he can catch for the next few days. His taxi driver took a wrong turn on the way to the airport, and the ensuing delay has left our man with only fifteen minutes to catch his plane. He is in a long line at the check-in counter, and when he points out to the clerk that he might miss his plane, he is told that others before him are also in danger of missing their flights. He is told all of this with a smile that tries to hide the ennui of a late night spent herding humans.

Suppose *you* are that person standing in line. Where does the mind turn? Perhaps to thoughts of revenge on the airline by a pledge to fly only with the competition henceforth? Perhaps to thoughts of wreaking destruction on the system of airlines, airports, and rules that keep people in lines (you can just see yourself smashing the nice clerk's face with your tennis racquet)? Perhaps to thoughts of *her* waiting at the other end, disappointed not to find you coming off the plane (and disappointed at *you* rather than *them*), of your mild panic of the abandonment of her reprimand ("you should have left earlier"), of a few days spent explaining what factors outside of your control caused you to miss the plane (to the point of disgusting yourself with your own claims of impotence)? "You used to think people were responsible for their actions," you might hear her snicker.

But then again, if you are lucky, you might stay positive (as football coaches say when they are down by a field goal but have the ball with five seconds remaining in the game), and your thoughts might turn avidly toward calculation—this many seconds per passenger, this assistance to speed up this person's check-in, this nudge to show her the red light at the end of the counter, this family of three that can be helped with their luggage so that they don't come back for it and hold up the line. Who said there was no hope for individual action that benefits several people?

There may be many other thoughts as well, but we have a loose categorization of thoughts according to their content: some are turned toward the past to what *should* have happened but did not, to what they *should* have done for you but did not, perhaps even to what your relationship *could* have been but was not. These thoughts can often lead down the path of anger, rage, and the will to annihilate or radically exchange what *is* with something that is not quite well defined. The other—no matter who he or she is—appears as a potential threat to your well-being, which is fragile at this point in time: those ahead of you in line are clear enemies (but for them you would be at the check-in counter), the airline reps are incompetents, and so forth. At its core, seen through this lens, society appears rotten and

•

ripe for destruction, perhaps by fire. You may derive pleasure from consummating these thoughts privately, but they do not further your case: the plane will still leave at the appointed hour without you.

However, you may also obsessively build up the future from the present by remaining awake for every minute thing you can do to speed the line of people. You might make each moment count without entertaining the possibility of losing in the end and not making the flight. When looking forward obsessively, there is just no time to consider this possibility. In either case, whether you are thinking enviously or ambitiously, your thoughts and actions are guided—though the guides are as well disguised as are the hard facts of the situation at hand. There is not a trace of the intentions that animated the discoverers of these facts.

The key to the hijacking of reason is the always-already-there feeling of the emotions that we are experiencing. Reason is beholden by passions, but the act of beholding is not apparent for our conscious awareness to behold. We cannot—for that reason—*explain* how passions ensnare us, as we currently have no language by which to describe something that the intellect has had so little time to witness. We can, however, *show it*—by the use of thought experiments and the elucidation of *mechanisms* by which ways of being (including ways of knowing and ways of seeing) are created from certain powerful emotions.

Passions as Escapes from Consciousness

A final thought experiment: Remember your own last look at a mirror—what you looked at, what you saw, what you told yourself when you saw what you saw. Was there a slight wink at a secret you share only with yourself? Were you concerned at the appearance of a new wrinkle? Were the thoughts cohesive and organized or only fleeting images that you have never seen since? Did you use this encounter with yourself to make plans for the day? Did you strike a pose—for yourself or for someone else? Did you feel like a stranger to yourself? Remember yourself as you watched.

Now, picture this: You are standing alone between two full-length mirrors. You are looking at yourself. You also see yourself looking at yourself, and so forth. Imagine there is a sudden peal of laughter in the background. A close friend is laughing at you, pointing out the blemishes on your body, your slight paunch, your fake smile. Pause and observe what your feelings and thoughts are.

Perhaps you register a desire to act, to move on and leave the mirror behind. The mirrored I will disappear, and your consciousness will assume a more familiar form. You might want to grow out your current life—to do stuff, build stuff, wreck stuff, and forget about the mirrors altogether. You might long to act—to do "no matter what," which may cure the unease that the mirrors might have brought on. You may want to build empires, start firms, buy stocks and bonds, compose a symphony, build a hospital for sick children, found a new science, establish a new theology. You may want to clean up the earth of industrial waste, discover a cure for genetic ills, better the material predicament of humankind.

You may find yourself through action, even in a situation where all action seems impossible or hopeless. You might live the plight of the prisoner in solitary confinement:

Only now that each drop of falling rain on top of the cell caused me to cringe to stifle the horrifying image did I understand the relevance of "solitary" in my sentence of solitary confinement. "Why do anything?" I hear my own voice saying from time to time. But not doing anything is also doing something. It is doing nothing. But you continue to exist, your body moves, your thoughts return—perhaps they can be stifled. "Mind, cease to think of the future," I command, but another drop falls on the roof, and the horrifying image returns. But look at how much freedom I have. I can move my leg up and down, to the left and the right. Ditto for the hands. I can move my leg up, down, left, right. And look: I can create infinite sequences out of these four simple movements. OK, now add the hands. What a symphony. And look, the music rises within me to accompany the dance of the body—body and mind dance together. And yes, I am the uncaused cause of all of this. I could have chosen to die. I can at any moment still: they left my shoe laces here. What careless guerrillas. I can choose to die any time. Each living moment is, then, an act of will. Let me have more of these moments. I cannot stretch my life's time, but I can wake up more often. Here, let me scout the darkness. How many shades of dark there are in the world, and the more frequently I tune in to them, the more I see. There is so much life in a single dark corner. The fucking drop again is going to scare me—no, not this time.

But acting requires a certain measure of unconsciousness—and you may want to make sense of the world, even if the sense-making activities you have undertaken are keeping you from acting. Yours might be the path of the myth and the narrative. You may want to change history through your writing (as Marx hoped to do) or to utter a word that will shatter the cosmos (Emil Cioran's ambition). You may want to craft, in language, an image of the world that will let you manipulate events, objects, and persons just as you manipulate words and propositions—by the use of the pliers of logical argument. You may want to find the one true theory that can lay the entire future of the cosmos before your eyes or *the* self-evidently true account of social history from times immemorial to times unforeseeable (a Hegelian and Marxian dream). You may want to prove that provable logical arguments can ground and span your seemingly infinite experience—that any proposition you can dream of is either provably true or provably false (David Hilbert's dream). Or you might want to subsume morality, aesthetics, epistemology, and all that is of the mind's domain into a single science (the ambition of many current evolutionary biologists crafting theories of society and culture). You might, in sum, be drawn to the project of subsuming the cosmos into the universe of your ideas and thereby gaining cognitive control not only over your experiences but over all possible experiences.

You might want to speak—to tell stories to the mirror and to the other-looking I who stands just behind you, looking at you looking at your self in the mirror. The other I may smile derisively or have a bored look on his or her face while watching you. We are all responsible for our faces after a certain age, as Albert Camus (1956) observed. You may feel that your face is in need of a justification, of a story that you can tell your laughing friend so that her laughter will stop ringing in your ears. No matter what that justification is, it will not be unassailable: there will still be some lingering suspicion that "you've got it all wrong."

Look carefully at the reflected I. If its image appears self-assured, have you ignored the possibility that you have built your life on chimeras and been led by the nose? If tired and worn-out, then are you ignoring the cornucopia of experiences—happy and sad—that life on earth has to offer? If ironic, are you not unduly arrogant to think that you know better than another—especially now that with the tools of empirical psychology you have discovered that we all think that we know better? If happy and hopeful, then where do you find the optimism to carry on when thousands of lies are told on our planet every second (some by yourself) and hundreds of children suffer ills inflicted by semiconscious abusive adults? You might want to try to make the ironic voice go away, but you can do so only by calling up another voice—the rationalizing voice. But that voice will be just as suspect as the original look. What is the story behind your face?

You may also detach yourself from the looking I. You could, for instance, break down the experience of looking at the mirror in a way that has nothing to do with the I—by noticing the small freckles on your nose, a slight blemish on your cheek, the weird strand of hair that has streaked down your forehead, the soft presence of the mirror, the white hairs around your temples as if these were characteristics of a foreign body. You might turn inward and notice the passage of time, how time loops around as you come back to the same perceptions—to the same thoughts and images. "I have been here before," you might think, as Dante Gabriel Rosetti wrote.

You may, of course, go down any one of these paths without knowing why you've done it. Your story may be that of a woman who sees blemishes of character in every one of her lover's friends while the coincidence of their relationship to her lover and her slavish dependence on his attention completely escapes her. You may, in other words, be self-deceived. Moreover, you may be self-deceived about not being self-deceived: you may believe yourself to always have been fully conscious—a "real" realist—or to have already become fully conscious. You might then be ripe soil for the flowering of the master passions.

You may, alas, go for neither word nor deed but dwell inward. You might go down what we currently call the way of madness. You might flee the mirror into the absurd, into apples that fall upward, into glarks that riphticlampick, into bugs nestled irreversibly in the cracks in the skin between your thumb and index finger, into little monkeys that turn your eyes and clean your ears on hearing your intentions whispered in *their* ears. You might think that your brother has stolen your heart and plot to slice open his ribcage to pluck it out and put it back where it belongs. You might long to slice off your wife's ears so as to avenge your mother's slicing of your ears. You may want to chew on the buttocks of a teenager who delivers your newspaper. You may want to see your own funeral or to pour your hot coffee onto your boss's lap in the middle of a meeting. You may come to forget that time exists and lose count of your days and nights, and you may experience the universe as a whorl whose center you seemingly are.

Whichever way you go—down the path of connected actions and stories or the path of unconnected actions and stories—you may do so in a way that is creative, that seeks to build, to extend, to grow the span of your me-ness and the intensity of your I-hood and the extent of your causal powers; to extend the span of your consciousness in the cosmos; to extend the understanding that your mind has of the workings of others' minds and plights. You may experience your will to freedom as a will to freedom *to* do various things—to create, to transform by the exercise of your ever increasing causal powers. Your flight from the mirror of consciousness may then take you to build corporate empires, to come up with new theories of everything that reduce experience to nothing but some mixture of entities that you fervently believe to be real, to build churches and dogmas, to raise cathedrals and corporate headquarters and civic centers and palaces, to try to invent new ways of turning lead into gold, and to bring more and more of the universe under the span of your personal control and understanding. It may also take you to the lands of manic states, of hyperactivity; of an energy that transcends the comprehension of your friends and colleagues; of psychotic states that bid you fly into skyscrapers; of images of yourself succeeding where Hitler and Napoleon failed, and of the magnates of American industry competing for an appointment to come and see you. Ambition can be lucid or mad, but it always seeks to increase the span of causal powers that the I exercises on the world.

You may rather seek to destroy, to ruin what has already been built around you; to denigrate, deny, and deflate; to deconstruct and trivialize; to put down and run down; to degrade; to joke and jest; to laugh snickeringly at another; to find him wanting and want him wanting; to blow up the constraints that weigh you down and that you have come to see in every object, person, and institution around you. You may want to construct arguments that show the uselessness of all arguments, write concertos that signal the end of the concerto genre, and put forth logical propositions that are not logically provable. You may want to throw over your wife and family for the fleeting glance of an unknown stranger just to assert your freedom to do so, to destroy your $100 million firm because your pasta was not tasty at dinner, to marry to defy convention, or to obey convention mockingly to make a mockery of obeisance. You will in this case experience your will to freedom as a will to freedom *from*—a freedom from others, from yourself, from society, all of which will become entities that must be destroyed.

Your flight from the mirror of consciousness may then take you down the path of negative criticism carried to an extreme for its own sake; of extreme skepticism—of doubt about the existence of all but yourself and eventually of doubt about your own reality; of questioning and relishing the pain of the destruction that your questions are wreaking; of visiting doom on the ideas of others; of looking down on your fellow man passionately. It might take you toward the no-man's land of the deep blue—the night of depression, wherein no one has the standing to speak, least of all your friends and loved ones and certainly not yourself because "why are you?" is the first and only question that any image that appears in the amphitheater of consciousness must answer and justify. It will take you toward the desert of malice, wherein all are guilty of something (the only problem is to figure out what they are guilty of), wherein all are lying (the only problem is to figure out their motives), and wherein all have achieved their ends by unfair means. Like ambition, envy can remain lucid or go mad, but its whispers in the amphitheater of consciousness have an undeniably bitter character all its own.

The Inner Work of the Master Passions

Ambition and envy are master passions because they grip the mind and harness the mind to their own ends completely. Unlike anger, ennui, or lust, each of which can be interpreted in different ways by the reasoning mind (anger can be turned into a will to create or a will to destroy, for instance), the master passions involve the I in its entire, conscious being. They presuppose and determine their own interpretations. They master the unruly, mysterious I completely and thus save it from rumination in front of the mirror of consciousness. There is no I left after ambition or envy has taken over. Consciousness is hijacked—all for the better, of course, since the mirror is unforgiving and will pop up wherever it smells unhijacked consciousness.

The anxious I experiences the master passions as states of the world out there, not states of the I. The envious sees reasons for envy everywhere. She sees envy in the envied other. She sees malice in the object of her malice.

She recruits morality to her self-righteously selfish ends and recruits reason to her destructive bent. She wallows in ill-will—just as Satan does in Goethe's *Faust:* "Destruction—aught with evil bent—that is my proper element." Did you really think that the luscious rhyme was coincidental and that the drip of the syllables into saliva was a mere accident of diction? No, Goethe meant for us to wallow in the destructive feeling—as he did, perhaps, when he wrote the play.

The ambitious sees opportunities for the extension of the I into the cosmos in every situation he is faced with. Each proximal end—once attained—becomes a means to another end that is just around the corner. Others' theories are objects of reduction, and one's own theories are the reducing means: "let me show you"—says the ambitious spirit—"why your results are just a special case of my theory." Conquest by subsumption is the creed of the ambitious intellectual. For the would-be conqueror, people are objects of seduction, and matter is the object of conquest. If it can be conquered or seduced, then it exists—thus ambition lights up the world.

Tomorrow is a beacon for the ambitious, just as yesterday is a beacon for the envious, for tomorrow is what is ultimately to be attained: conquest, alas, comes to us in time and through time. When we are ambitious, we look forward to making love, war, peace, and breakfast. We crave tomorrow, and we desire our futures; so our creation of the future is an act of desire. We see that action is at its core creation, and we give birth—at every moment—to our next state of being. The ambitious self is pregnant with its own future embodiments, screaming to be born.

Yesterday is the fixation of the envious because what could have been—but is not—is always at the center of his attention. What-could-have-been gives what-is its dark hues and makes what-will-be just retribution for the disappointment of being alive. When we envy, we look back on what could have been, on what we could have done, could have had, and so forth. We fixate on what he's got that we do not and on what she is that we are not. We think in terms of the not here, the not now. We live regretfully, as if the future is always already beyond our creative powers. We envy the I that might have been and unfailingly find it mirrored in the I that currently is.

Of course, by tomorrow today will be yesterday, and yesterday today was tomorrow. Ambition and envy interact. Having decided on a goal (the corner office), one might come to envy those who have it. In turn, this envy fuels the long sequence of inauthentic behaviors that will get one to the prize, the ever widening chain of intraorganizational manipulations that will eventually get one the desired position. One might be ambitious today to avoid becoming even more envious tomorrow.

Ambitious desire can also interact with the jealous guarding of an image or identity. Living up to an ideal (perhaps an ideal of righteousness or virtue or efficiency or sexual or professional prowess) can be a jealous urge—the urge to own that ideal by one's conformity to it. It becomes one's identity. But this identity often calls for the recognition of others, for the subduing of other wills to its causal powers. We want others to buy into the value of the ideal type that we have harnessed ourselves to. We want others to recognize that prowess at solving integral equations or at designing integrated circuits or at playing the guitar is *valuable* so that the value of the ideal type does not become diminished. Once accepted and entrenched in our own minds, identities and ideal types seek other subjects, to be molded in their own image. A jealous urge turns into an ambitious rage. The world is a playing ground for the passions.

We try to extricate in what follows the passions from the live consciousness that flees into them rather easily. Because we, too, are passionate, occasionally self-deceived, humans, we face a problem that has confronted observers from before the birth of science and will confront them long after its transformation or demise—how to describe the very phenomena that we think we ourselves may be in the midst of. Won't any claim to truthfulness be automatically impeached? Won't any claim to truthlikeness be a priori laughable? We realize, however, that we are in the privileged position of people writing to other people who may have faced the same problems, asked the same questions, fallen into the same late-night binges and addictions and suicidal thoughts, climbed the same ropes, pulled the same levers, felt the same lies on their flesh—as the characters that we investigate in what follows. Hence, we can appeal to our readers for insights about the validity of our insights. The thought experiments that follow are not moot. They will be carried out, in real time, with your own words and feelings.

The following essay is not a nihilist manifesto against the prevailing language of rationality in social accounts and theories and personal life stories. Even when our arguments invalidate or undermine certain claims and theories, our aim is not to destroy them or put their proponents to the shame of incoherence and hypocrisy. We do not want to cut into the intellectual flesh of modernity for the sake of the blood feast, while offering nothing in return or in exchange. Rather, we have written an essay whose aim it is to *understand* social phenomena *from within*. There is a great difference between *explanation* (as carried by the standard social sciences today) and *understanding* (as it is sometimes carried out by humanistic psychologists, philosophers, writers, artists, and interpreters of art). This difference can be exploited to increase understanding by heeding the explanatory power of theories and models, but it rarely is. Usually—as C. P. Snow (1963) has pointed out—the "two cultures" of humanistic understanding and scientific explanation live in splendid isolation from one another. Academics are frightened of each others' dialects; laymen are wary of academics; artists have turned to satire to cope with the widening circle of self-importance and distrust of the ever-less-willing-to-experiment bourgeois mindset; and poets have fallen on hard times. Much of the academic's fear is caused by the ever present danger of having one's theory reduced to another—leaving him or her without an identity, a narrative, a goal, a life story, and possibly without a means of livelihood.

However, the two cultures have much to learn from each other by building on René Descartes's subtle insight that an emotion is a sort of sense that detects a truth lying beyond the five senses. It is a sense that senses the predicament of the I, and it can, we trust, be awakened by exhortation and renewed experimentation with the self. Therefore, what you are about to read is an invitation to reflection—not an attempt at persuasion. We do not aim to achieve a synthesis of the two cultures. Such a synthesis may indeed not be possible with the expressive tools we have at our disposal. We rather want to open the gate to a realm in which explanation and understanding can coexist—not in splendid isolation but in dialogue.

2

An Orwellian Abduction: The Rationalization of the Passions

Pride, envy, and greed are the three sparks that set men's hearts afire.
—Dante Alighieri, *Inferno,* canto 6

Out of ferocity, avarice, and ambition, the three vices which lead all mankind astray, [society] makes national defense, commerce, and politics and thereby causes the strength, the wealth, and the wisdom of the republics; out of these three great vices which would certainly destroy man on earth, society thus causes civil happiness to emerge. This principle proves the existence of divine providence: through its intelligent laws the passions of men who are entirely occupied by the pursuit of their private utility are transformed into a civil order which permits men to live in human society.
—Giambattista Vico, *New Science*

Reason and desire often appear to be in a tension that can be resolved only through struggle. You would like, following your interest in keeping your family together, to be chaste and honest, but you lose yourself in a dialogue with a dear friend that turns into mutual penetration and then are faced with what you see as an unbearable tension between remaining authentic and remaining happily married. You would like to produce the best, most thoroughly researched article that you are capable of writing for your exam, but your thoughts gravitate enviously toward the kinds of arguments that others in your cohort are making and drive you to construct arguments that criticize or belittle theirs. You would like to follow through the logical consequences of your approach to criminal law for this particular case, but you bend your words at the last minute, thinking that too sharp an opinion might hurt your chances of being nominated to the U.S. Supreme Court some time in the future: "such a brilliant prospect" may echo in some chamber of your mind.

The Therapeutic Accounts That Modern Social Analysis Gives of the Passions

As selves fraught with passion but capable of reason, we have historically taken—as Albert O. Hirschman (1984) points out—two different approaches to the passions. The first is based on the impulse to condemn others' behavior, to find it unacceptable. This approach finds its modern-day expression in the work of some cognitive psychologists who find the reasoning of laymen fraught with biases and fallacies; they interpret choices that people make in laboratory settings according to a particular normative way of answering questions about uncertain predicaments. It calls for the active repression of passion by the exercise of reason—by the application of the rules of logic, for instance.

But the rules in question are not themselves established beyond doubt by philosophers and epistemologists. There is significant disagreement about which rules of reasoning are justified (because it has become clear that no rules of reasoning are provable by a process that uses them to guide reasoning) and about the value of justification. Moreover, as cognitive biases are portrayed as general laws of human cognition to which, by assumption, the scientists who discovered them are themselves exposed, and as the overcoming of these biases is essential in their functioning as scientists, the modern condemnationists are not internally coherent.

Now, argues Hirschman, a second strand appeared in the history of thinking about emotions. Some people—such as Giambattista Vico and Georg Wilhelm Friedrich Hegel—thought that they could discern a cosmic reason at play in the lives of men riding their passions into apparent chaos: "Hegel's . . . concept of the Cunning of Reason expresses the idea that men, following their passions, actually serve some higher world-historical purpose of which they are totally unaware" (Hirschman 1984, p. 12). The impulse to condemn thus was counteracted by the impulse to rationalize the actual as the rational and the rational as the real and thus to achieve a cosmic rationalism that claims to understand the aim and logic of human passions by referring to the collective destiny that individual actions driven by passions weave in order to create.

The critic and satyrist demurs. "How do you know?" he asks. "What makes you so certain that what you say is so and not otherwise? Until you can answer these questions, allow me to smile at your diatribes." The cosmic rationalist is dismayed: why is it that his insight has not revealed itself with the force of revelation to the critic, so that he sees that *it cannot be otherwise*—as Charles Taylor (1992) has put it? He can ground his vision of the absolute spirit only into action aimed at annihilating the minds that beg to differ—which is the essence of the great genocidal projects of history.

A third and very different approach to the passions emerged from the combination between Puritan dogma and individual rationalism, which took place most notably in Anglo-American countries over the past two hundred years. The Puritan often feels the need to hide the raw will to power, lust, and debauchery in a rationalizing discourse that exculpates him from his own nature. The "therapy" is based on the impulse to interpret behavior *as if* it sprang from an internal and coherent reasoning faculty and finds a powerful echo in the methods of neoclassical economists, who find a maximization-based explanation for every observed human action. The *as-if-ist*—or exculpationist—may be driven to action by passions that would horrify all of his friends and associates but explains his actions—even to himself—by appealing to interests that can be rationally traded off against each other and spoken about publicly. "It was an optimal, profit-maximizing move," says the CEO to his shareholders about the company he took over and broke up to avenge a years-old insult on the football field by a high school heartthrob turned nemesis.

Whither Interests? The Reconstruction of a Therapeutic Narrative

In his essay, Hirschman notes but does not seem to register the significance of the fact that the use of interests as principles that explain or justify a particular action first occurred in a treatise on state interests—by the Duke of Rohan in the seventeenth century) and recurred in the writings of people concerned with statecraft (such as Thomas Hobbes). "State interest" was the doctrine first introduced by Cardinal Richelieu to justify—on nonreligious grounds for the first time in history—France's involvement in territorial wars in Europe. The significance of these facts is this: as-if-ism sprang forth from diplomatic minds thinking through strategic situations because as an instrument of deception it is admirably well suited to its purposes of camouflaging intentions. A good lie is *plausible* in the same way in which a good camouflage is *congruent* with its environment. As-if-ism was selected as a Weltanschauung for building master narratives because of its powers to make social conflict disappear under the camouflage of reason and interest.

As-if-ism springs out of a false analogy—that of a group as an individual capable of expressing orderly, coherent preferences—an analogy that was not fully scrutinized until the writings of economists like Kenneth Arrow and Amartya Sen in the second half of the twentieth century. "There is no Pareto-optimal, complete, transitive social decision function that can be arrived at by majority voting, and we do not know any other way of constructing one," an educated person would have objected to the construction of the concept of state interest had he been around at the time of its first articulation. Nowadays, interest—and particularly self-interest—has perhaps become too much part of the self-concept of individuals for them to question its origins seriously.

How did this offspring of reason become so popular? Hirschman has an answer that is wrong in interesting ways: "The belief that interest could be considered a dominant motive of human behavior caused considerable intellectual excitement: at last a realistic basis for a viable social order has been discovered. But a world governed by interest offered not only an escape from excessively demanding models of states that 'have never been seen not have been known to exist'; it was perceived to have a number of specific assets of its own. The most general of these assets was predictability" (Hirschman 1984, p. 23). By invoking interests as explanatory variables, people could now hope to achieve greater interpersonal predictability—and perhaps greater predictability about their own lives.

But this answer seems to us to be incorrect. It is not *predictability* that a pattern of explanations of social phenomena based on reasons and interests has produced but rather the *illusion* of predictability in the guise of explanatory coverage. We infer predictive power from explanatory power and close our eyes to the difference. When we cannot predict, we retrodict and then persuade ourselves that we could have predicted if some (usually trivial) events had gone in a different direction.

Social and cognitive psychologists have minutely reconstructed the mechanisms by which modern minds persuade themselves of the orderliness and tameness of the world. They showed that people are by and large eager to *convince themselves* that they can predict and control their world. Hindsight biases pointed out by Scott A. Hawkins and Reid Hastie (1990) and by Baruch Fischhoff (1975) are strong ex post beliefs that one *almost predicted* or *could have predicted* a past event: its posteriorly reconstructed prior probability was found to be far greater than its true prior probability.

Psychologists have shown that people construct detailed deterministic models for random events—such as coin tosses—and persist in constructing new models as their predictions are disconfirmed by the data (Gilovich 1993). They also have shown that people's beliefs are chosen to maximize their subjective experience of control and predictability over a sequence of events (Langer 1975). These studies suggest that concepts that enhance the illusion of predictability and control will win out in the history of ideas over concepts that do not enhance it or rather that undermine its hold on people's minds.

The Unknown Unknown as the Unmoved Mover of Cognition

Anxiety often shows itself as fear of the unknown. The open acknowledgment of emotions such as envy and ambition as causes of human behavior arouses anxiety because it paints the picture of a world on the brink of madness, teeming with unknowns. What makes the emotional tantrum of a parent or a teacher so terrorizing? It is that a source of emotional shelter and physical protection—of predictable defense against the unpredictable oddities of the world—has now been destroyed. You never quite know what to expect again. What makes the experience of battery so frightening and world-shattering to the battered? It is at least in part the resulting loss of predictability and control—the fact that we are now dealing with someone who has lost control in the past and may do so again in the future.

Public language reflects these private terrors: we speak of "losing control" or of "losing it" to depict people who have freely given vent to their passions. We speak of mental "illness" and "madness" when describing people whose actions can no longer be understood by appealing to a view of humans as driven by interest and governed by reason. We speak of "going crazy" when we can no longer seem to keep our minds from ruminating on the departure of a lover. The organizing metaphor of this discourse is the terror that we feel in the face of the unknown. Speaking of people in terms of their interests is a therapeutic device: it helps hide the unknown just ahead of us. We are motivated to believe that other people are motivated by interests.

Speaking publicly of our private passions seems dangerous precisely because doing so raises the specter of violent conflict and unforeseeable actions. Suppose that two negotiators are disputing the salary raise that a major league shortstop should be paid next year. Each speaks of his client's *interest* in the matter—the team's interest in keeping the shortstop and affording his salary, and the shortstop's interest in getting as much money as possible. And each negotiator speaks as if his client's interest is also his or her own interest. Now suppose the shortstop's agent reveals that his client *really* wants to get the highest salary on the team and, additionally, wants to get a higher salary than another shortstop who has signed up with a different team. Now the team's agent also reveals that the team's interest is in keeping the player's salary in line with the other players' salaries so that he does not incite their envy. But, he agrees, that is just a façade: what is really going on is that the team's general manager, himself a former shortstop, is envious of the young fellow's compensation package already: increasing it further means alienating the coach. But this is a façade as well: the team's agent now admits, that he is motivated by getting the better of the player's agent (they both are famous for making masterful deals for their major league clients, and he is inclined to see these negotiations as a show-down). "Just as I had thought," says the shortstop's agent, agreeing that he, too, is motivated by jealousy of his own stature among players and envy of the other agent's gains.

Far-fetched? Careful observers of negotiation classes in business schools have noticed that quite often it is the fear of being left "one-down" or of coming out comparatively worse off than their negotiation partner that provides the strongest motivation for students engaged in mock negotiations as part of their class work. The negotiator's true utility function often has nothing to do with the maximization of gains but rather with the imposition of his or her will on the will of the other and with the salvaging of self-esteem. Being suckered is often the worst thing that can happen to a young would-be manager in a top business school. Getting the best of the other, on the other hand, is often a sign of prowess, intelligence, and charisma.

The negotiator's dilemma is not only—as has been surmised—the tension between creating and dividing wealth but rather the tension between the need to achieve a viable outcome and the need to impose oneself on the other, no matter what the consequences may be. This is not an interpersonal dilemma but an intrapersonal one. The language of efficiency often comes in only as an ex post rationalization of an outcome that satisfies the negotiator's need for recognition, for "special-hood," that fulfills the desire to subdue an opponent and to make the outcome of the negotiation no more than a direct outgrowth of will.

"... And the Ends Shall Be the Means": The Archaeology of Myth

Are people up to the deception tasks that the repression of the passions by the language of interests calls for? Many studies in experimental psychology (see Abelson 1986; Bargh and Chartrand 1999) suggest that, by and large, people's rational plans *follow* their behavior rather than lead it. Reason—construed as a body of propositions that we think justify our actions and a bunch of rules for combining together these propositions to arrive at actionable hypotheses—is generally used to *explain* actions that one has already taken rather than to motivate actions about to be taken. Rationality appears to be a façade that the decision maker uses to represent himself to himself and to others. "I am a rational person" is a pose that people strike for its intra- and interpersonal desirability.

It is perhaps no accident that the following two statements are true: (1) the social sciences that see people through the lens of interests all draw their empirical support from *explanations* rather than predictions, and (2) their predictive power is so poor that the most precise of these sciences—economics—has repeatedly been called "the dismal science." Prediction—not explanation—is the gold that the engineer and the physicist seek. Explanation—not prediction—is what the social scientist usually delivers, even as he attempts to clothe his studies in the respectable mantle of the natural sciences.

Modern conceptions of rationality and morality share many characteristics—most important a commitment to the regulation of expression and behavior by principles and a commitment to deliberation as a way of resolving conflicts among various principles. It is not surprising, therefore, that some social psychologists have also shown that morality follows desire just as rationality follows behavior: people judge fairness of a process not by objective or transcendental standards but rather by the outcomes of that process for themselves (see Loewenstein 1996). A casual inquiry into recent writings about popular science and psychological experiments shows that people regularly confound issues about ethics or morality ("what *should* I do?") with problems about the "true" description of the world. Norms of behavior (which supposedly we choose freely) are often justified by recourse to necessitarian arguments from evolutionary biology that often imply—via the reduction of consciousness to a biological phenomenon—that freedom of will is an illusion and therefore that moral deliberation is a hoax.

Killed someone recently? Take heart. The impulse to kill has evolved naturally by a sequence of inevitable steps: you are just one of those small rings in the evolutionary chain that takes us to the present. "It is the way of the world, and it is beyond my control," as the lascivious Valmont in Pierre Choderlos de Laclos's *Liaisons Dangereuses* might have said. Salivating over a playmate or a coworker? Think no more of it: all of us do, really. Some are just better at hiding it than others. After all, you've been married for four years now, and Helen Fisher (1992) has just enlightened us about the four-year itch that is our evolutionary heritage.

The specialized languages we have developed as a part of the human sciences seem to have been designed to obfuscate the relationship between thinking and feeling rather than to clarify it. They provide us with stories and pictures of ourselves as rational, maximizing, principled, truth-loving creatures that we can use to make marvelous retrospective sense of our behaviors. The gift of language is not merely that of an ability to represent the world in words for a purpose to be chosen freely. It is also a mythological one—of representing the self in words that together spin a narrative or story that establishes that purpose. Once a narrative is used to represent one's self to oneself, the freedom to create new ends and purposes to being has vanished: we live our own life narratives, through the roles we have preassigned ourselves in them.

For instance, are you a practicing economist? Well, then you are more likely to see people as motivated by narrowly construed self-interest than most people and probably less inclined to indulge in cooperative behavior—as the studies of Robert H. Frank, Thomas Gilovich, and Dennis T.

Regan have shown (1993). And this is not because you have selected yourself into the profession by virtue of your prior leanings (the authors of the study controlled for self-selection bias). Rather, you simply acquired an identity as part of your graduate studies—captured by the dominant economic picture that portrays resource-craving, self-maximizing individuals vying for scarce assets in a competitive environment. Are you an evolutionary biologist? Then you may be inclined to fashion your behaviors according to a story in which you are a bundle of genetic material, whose arch-purpose is to propagate further in time. A serial murderer? As some stories indicate, you may be inclined to fashion yourself as the continuation of another murderer's life work, wherein you will use techniques and choose subjects for your crimes that are similar to those chosen by a famous predecessor.

Narrative often smothers consciousness and—as Dan P. McAdams's work has shown (1993)—life stories and self-narratives are pervasive ways in which people relate to their experiences. They experience their lives as stories told from a particular standpoint—by a particular author, whose values and biases shape thoughts and actions. And if narratives are "theories of the self"—in that they generate the beliefs that guide our actions just as a theory generates hypotheses to be tested by actions—then they are subject to the same justificationist biases that haunt our approach to theories in general. We avoid or explain away "refuting evidence" and seek, instead, evidence that supports them or is at least logically independent from them (Nisbett and Ross 1981).

Prosecutors in murder cases sometimes try to show that the accused had both the motive and the means to commit the crime. If the works of the master passions are the crimes, then modern psychology shows that the means are at our disposal. Manipulating another involves taking advantage of her personal mythology and rationalizing proclivity to present an action in a familiar light, of her cognitive miserliness to foreclose on relevant alternative possibilities, and of her self-serving sense of morality to make her feel that her action sets her apart from others in the moral plane. Master manipulators have, at one time or another, used all of these frailties of judgment to achieve causal powers over others. It remains to be seen whether the motive can be fully established.

The Passions Dispassioned: The Modern Denial of the Passions in the Name of the Passions

No less of an abduction of the passions from the public realm has been carried out by those thinkers who have tried to provide explanatory "accounts" of the passions and the emotions. An account of an emotion can be a model, an image, or a metaphor. Folk psychology, for instance, provides a "hydraulic" model of the passions—as Ronald De Sousa calls it (1987)—whereby the passions are bottled up inside the rational, socialized self. The passions sometimes explode and produce sporadic bursts of irrational and potentially frightening behavior, such as massacres of fellow high school students, declarations of love or sexual attraction to a coworker, or public self-emasculations.

This view—one of the dominant ones in our public conversations today—is also perhaps the most self-defeating for it entails a passive rejection of the passions that may actually incite the aggressive releases it seeks to inhibit. The fear that one will end up alone and unwanted, bereft of money or the recognition of the other, builds up and has no means to express itself. It finds in the demonology of the other an easy escape mechanism: the others—our friends and coworkers—are the monsters who have locked up one's soul in the cage of self-doubts. Their actions appear to be aimed at ostracizing us—why else would they be smiling so coyly in our presence?—and the very thought of their existence is enraging.

Taking away their lives suddenly comes to seem both just and good; it seems, in any case, like it is the one satisfying way to express our sentiments. The lay psychologist is shocked: he looks for the "causes of violence" in brain scans and past records of violent behavior. He looks to the scientist to provide the right story to cover up the uncertainty that now looms at every corner. "Every man a walking time bomb": this is one conception of the cosmos the middle-class armchair philosopher or the civic-minded politician cannot tolerate without some therapy. The scientist is only too eager to provide this therapy in the form of theories, facts, and figures. Now the cover-up of the passions is complete, and peace is reestablished, at least until the next massacre in a garage or a high school campus.

Abductions of the passions do not have to be so coarse as a complete cover-up, of course. William James (1890), for example, posited that passions are cognitive reconstructions of ongoing physical phenomena: we are sad because we cry, and we are angry because we fight. Mental causation of physical events is, according to this view, an illusion. James does not eliminate mental events and consciousness from the ontology of existing objects, but he denies them the causal powers we intuitively feel that they have. But consider the following example:

A black curtain rises. On the stage, a young man is brutally beating a middle-aged woman. He is holding a knife by its blade and beating her with the knotted wooden handle. He hits her over her head and eyes, while holding her by her hair. A man's voice from the back announces that she is his mother. The fight goes on. The young man lets out a loud scream, picks up the blade by its handle, and thrusts it deeply inside the woman's throat. She falls. Now the voice announces that she had—together with her lover—murdered the young man's father. This explains the elated look on the young man's face. A movie clip of his father's murder is projected along the side wall. He lies naked in a hot tub. His wife comes toward him, dressed only in a thick black netting. She rips off the netting and throws it on her bathing husband, who gets tangled in its loops while struggling to escape it. A muscular man with an axe emerges from behind the door. He raises the axe and hits the bathing man on the head, splitting his skull, and once again, quickly, on the side of his neck. The projector goes dead. The voice comes on again and announces that the young man's mother—the woman on the stage—was not the same as the evil seductress in the movie clip of the bathing scene. That one had escaped. The young man on the stage was misled about the identity of the murderess. Another projector lights up the side wall. A large rock seems to talk in a voice that resembles your own mother's voice and tells the listener that the young man is fated to unjustly murder one of his parents. The projector goes off. Now the man's voice comes on again and announces this is not a play. The doors to the hall have been locked. The woman is a local millionairess. The young man really has killed her. Just to convince you, he . . .

As we play through a slightly modified version of the Oresteiad, you may find that your emotions change: they track the narrative, unlike what James's model say they should do—now outrage at the violence and the matricide, now righteous contentment at the son's revenge, now pain and confusion at the misunderstanding, and finally, fear for your own safety as a spectator. It is not *real* fear but mock fear—fear brought on by seeing a possible world whose instantiation is quite remote.

These emotions are remarkably responsive to the twists of the narrative, which produces changes in the image of what is *actually* going on before you. A matricide? Outrageous. A just reward? Heroic and tragic—futile and criminal, perhaps. A misunderstanding? Sad and absurd. If these events had occurred in your living room, before your eyes, you might have experienced just as many impulses to act—to save her from him (or him from her) or the young man from his fate. With every delay, though, your impulses might have changed: what was justified and right a moment ago now seems absurd in light of the new information. Your impulses would have been born and smothered by the words of the narrative.

Jean-Paul Sartre (1948) contributed a similar view of emotions to that of James, wherein an emotion is a substitute for a magical act that makes the object of the emotion go away. Fear of a lion, for instance, is a *substitute* for the—immediately impossible—magical behavior that makes the lion disappear. But how has the lion come to be *feared?* By what process have we become fearful of the objects that we now fear? What makes a part of reality the object of fear or lust?

Sartre makes the living I the willful source of her own passions, which in turn create the objects that they will latch on to. The I feels in love, betrayed, amused, even cold because she has *chosen* to feel in these ways. Robert Solomon (1993) goes even further: one feels guilty—he argues—because it serves a purpose in the greater project of making one feel good about oneself ("I am the kind of upright person who would feel guilty about this"). One then conveniently (and "willfully") forgets about this project because for the feeling of guilt to fulfill its purpose, it must *feel* authentic. One must deceive oneself about one's own true projects so that the means to attaining these projects do not lose their power to provide the desired outcomes.

The academic who has dedicated his life's work to interpretative field studies of organizational phenomena constructs an epistemological position ("constructivism") that is consistent with his actions and carefully guards it against criticisms that come from "realist" camp. The realist, similarly, constructs a methodological stance that justifies *his* life's work. He refuses to address the criticisms of scientific realism as a viable doctrine for learning about the world, even when they sprout among traditionally "realist" philosophers. Neither one can afford to believe that what underlies his epistemological commitment is the desire to justify a life's work, a sequence of behaviors that have solidified into a self. Each disparages the other's arguments, even before fully understanding them. "Fear and loathing" in organization studies—as John van Maanen has put it

(1995)—breaks out. Camps are formed. Carefully crafted invectives are prepared. The editorial review process becomes politicized: shooting down relativist arguments becomes a favorite occupation of the self-styled realists. The relativists congregate, make up their own conferences, exclude realists from attending them, and congratulate themselves for having achieved some measure of legitimacy, which they persuade themselves of by increasing the number of conferences, the number of dollars spent per conference, and so forth. Academic life becomes political life, and the life of the mind comes to mirror its passions.

Another easy answer to the question about the cognitive content of emotions comes from a biological perspective on the emotions stipulating that biological phenomena arising from evolutionary process *cause* consciousness of events in the same way that the physical properties of a table *cause* its material quality of "hardness to the touch" (Searle 1996). This constitutes a strange hijacking of *causation* as a relation between events so that it can pose as a possible relation between different properties of an object. Empirical psychology helps us give a counterexample to a beguiling view of emotions. Two psychologists (Singer and Schachter 1962) injected participants to their experiment with epinephrine (a hormonal substance known to cause palpitations and other sensations associated with anxiety and fear) and then placed the subjects in different social situations—some designed to elicit fear, others designed to elicit indignation or outrage. The participants reported experiencing the emotion that the social context indicated that they should or are most likely to feel.

This lability of the emotions may have some people running back to James's explanations, which they cannot do without denying the causal import of their own cognitive states on their feelings. The experimental subjects' propensity to act in particular ways correlated with the social setting and the cognitive events caused by the situation, not with the biological condition of the person. Although the result is not a conclusive refutation of the evolutionary interpretations of the emotions, it nevertheless indicates that the mapping between biological states and motivation is not a deterministic one.

Many thinkers in the Anglo-American tradition of philosophy and psychology have tried to maintain the separation between reason and passions to provide a greater analytical clarity and tractability of the passions

by means of reason. Their efforts, however, are doomed from the start because the separation of belief and desire, of feeling and thinking, is postulated rather than hypothesized. Thinking and feeling go their separate
ways in the tradition that has given us rational-choice theory and Bayesian
probability kinematics because we still lack a language for inquiring into
the emotional nature of the act of thinking. In contrast to this tradition, we
try to provide a means for *connecting* reason to the passions through the
faculty of *understanding* rather than through the faculty of *analysis* alone.
In the same way in which we understand the crying of a child who has just
fallen from a tree without necessarily being able to understand all of the
physical and biochemical laws making up the event we are witnessing, we
can understand many of the passions without being in the possession of a
complete analytical model of them.

Moreover, just as we cannot understand the crying of the child merely
by knowledge of the physical and biochemical laws that contribute to his
crying on this particular occasion, we cannot understand the passions
merely from knowledge of their physical, behavioral, and biological corre-
lates. We are wagering that the understanding to be gained by letting inner
experience speak will offset (through the insights it brings) the loss in analytical tractability that comes from letting the frightening subject speak for
herself. And who knows? We may be able to lay bare the true causes of the
fear of the Subject that has provided the hallmark of modernity.

To write this book, we wanted to react to the experience of being
trapped in the hermeneutic circles of various theories, dogmas, and ideologies, a common experience for modern academics. We wanted to come
closer to the authenticity of the novelist while preserving the traceability
and logical structure that might entice the philosopher or social scientist
into a dialogue on these topics. Analytical explanations allow one to do
logical audits of an argument. They create paths on which others can
"come along" and share the journey in the world of ideas. Such audit trails
are useful for communicative purposes, as they provide points of coordination in a dialogue that can become very complex and is in need of coor-
dinative principles. But, quite often, analytical explanation loses sight of
the communicative purpose of logical structure, in which case logical
structure can become an end in itself. This is a part of the tragedy of the
modern mind: seduced by its own creations, it has attempted to etch them

into the world before it becomes too apparent that their rendition of the world is frayed at the edges.

Hermeneutic explanation, on the other hand, risks "losing" the reader in the nuances and veils of the poetic undertaking of the writer. It is perhaps for this reason that the work of Edmund Husserl, Martin Heidegger, Henri Bergson, and Maurice Merleau-Ponty has not been fully internalized by the community of living philosophers and practicing social scientists. Perhaps also for this very same reason that the work of Georg Simmel and Michel Foucault has not produced schools of thought in mainstream sociology and that the work of Karl Weick has not been developed and amplified to its potential in the world of organization studies.

We have chosen to *live* the tension between the need for communicable structure and the need for insight. If a bridge between the two worlds exists, then it is a fragile bridge, one that must be constantly watched. To produce such an analysis we relinquished the idea of "law" in the explanation of behavior but—following Jon Elster's recent suggestion (1999)—we hung on to the idea of mechanism. We do not speak, then, of causes and effects but of possible worlds, accessible by various mechanisms. To unearth these mechanisms, we asked ourselves, What if it was the emotions—the impulses to act—that produced the narrative—the imagery and the logic—that in its turn amplified the original impulses? What if there were some passions that had us, as opposed to us having them? What would the world look like? How could we understand such a world? What would "understand" mean?

Why did we need to write about these subjects? Because the elaborate analyses of the passions to date have not documented the *work* of the passions. They have not *filmed* the passions at work in our conversations, thoughts, and actions but merely tried to get a conceptual grip on the passions, to provide reductive accounts of their causes and effects and essences. They have provided the *snapshots*. Passions appear in the philosophical, economic, psychological, sociological, and anthropological literatures as *objects* we can behold, as *things* that we have, as *events* that happen to us. We *have* passions, but we do not, in the classic accounts, *live* them. We want to show the *movie* and let the passions speak—insofar as this is possible—of themselves and for themselves.

To be sure, phenomena will never be able to speak for themselves for the simple reason that phenomena don't speak. But human passions are special phenomena because they often *reveal* themselves in language, through language and quite often *as* language, in the performative act of speaking in a certain tone or in the shadow of a certain intention. "In every language, what is said is never what is spoken," wrote Novalis. Words often do not reveal the objects they refer to, but they do, occasionally, reveal the speaking subject. By studying the language in which they reveal themselves, we can come close to hearing the passions themselves speaking, even though they are not speaking *for* themselves or *of* themselves but rather *as* themselves. They are not naturally *accountable* to our inquisitive faculties. They can only be *sought out* by a conscious effort.

The function of language is critical to our analysis, as language is one of the mirrors of being. It places the speaker as speaker in front of herself. If—as we have said—she *is* a passion, rather than *having* a passion, then the mirroring of the I in words is simultaneously a revelation of the I's passions in language. We will try to show that just as there are certain self-images that seduce us and shape our actions, there are passions that we can only with great difficulty escape—even as they are mirrored in words for all of us to see. But the fact that they do mirror themselves in words makes them accessible to the detective-minded.

The passions create what reality "feels like" for us. They are the ultimate fabricators of the world. The role that we propose for consciousness is to reconstruct the fabrication. Consciousness is reality's "private eye." It can watch when all the other senses are engulfed by the passions—provided that it itself has not also been engulfed; and it can, through *its* work, reveal the passions at work in fabricating the world we perceive. The mirrors that in the first chapter we proposed that we stand between stand for our observers, our admirers, our detractors, our friends, and our foes. The infinitely reproduced image in the mirror models our social penumbrae, roles, alter egos, poses—the echoes that our words make in the amphitheater of consciousness. We forced ourselves to stand and watch—in particular, to watch and experience our own temptations to move on and "do something else"—whenever these will come. We tried to focus on the ways in which we might want to escape the mirror. They are our escape paths: they take us away from the feeling that we are absurd, worthless, and devoid of meaning. The anxiety this feeling can bring on is the broth from which intentions, emotions, and passions arise. The more irrevocable the steps by which we flee the shadow of the absurd, the less likely will we be to find our way back. Hence, the most *useful* passions are the master passions—the passions that do not *let* us raise the question, "Why are you?"

We have aimed to write not a psychological treatise on the passions but rather a reconstruction of the passions at work. We do not therefore aim for completeness or for the greatest explanatory parsimony. Indeed, we will explain the value society places on these theoretical "qualities" by an excess of duly directed ambition. Rather, we try to explore various moments to which we have first-person access—by subjecting ourselves and the reader to thought experiments, by taking "trips" along literary paths, by playing out indelible scenarios from our own pasts. If we succeed in showing up the world as we perceive it as a "great escape" from the anxiety of the absurd, then that escape will no longer be available to us or to you because the appeal of that escape lies in its claim to "truthlikeness" or "validity." Once you come to suspect that the very idea of truthlikeness is a therapeutic ploy, a clever truncation of the process of thinking and obsessing, you will have to look the absurd in the eye—and remain in front of the mirror a while longer. This might lead to a dismantling and a radical new reconstruction of the amphitheater of consciousness that we have been constructing for the past fifty thousand years.

3

Anxiety: The Primeval Broth

. . . so Being and Eros lie naked in bed,
Unknown to the Future that prowls ahead.

If you could for an instant step outside of the trusting relationships you have built over the years—with your friends, family, and coworkers—you may be able to experience a feeling of either elation or dread, depending on the tradeoff that you make between your desire for autonomy and your desire for security. There is no a priori reason to assume that your current trust is not ill founded. Indeed, the inquisitive capacities of your mind are limited only by your will to believe in the relationships in which you have a stake: your spouse may, after all, very well be cheating on you while away on trips or pretending to work late. He or she would not admit it, of course, out of fear that you will leave the relationship. Many gossip and advice columns are filled with friendly suggestions for lustful and anguished husbands and wives who made love to someone else to keep it quiet and "never do it again." Or, quite possibly, he or she is thinking of another, secretly desiring another, perhaps even imagining sex with another while the two of you are together; and you would not know it (would you?). Inquiring about it will be useless: you will get a kind smile, protestations, an honest-sounding assurance perhaps. But what makes you think that fear cannot motivate the most perfect semblance of authenticity?

Consider your relationships at work. Perhaps promises (some of them implicit) from your superiors help you look forward to your advancement. They contribute to your sense of well-being, they help you "carry on," even when the days grow long and tiresome or boring. Your trust feels real to you. But is it well placed? Perhaps you have not noticed how the higher-ups are kind and generous to *all* or many of the others in the firm, even though they know very well that they cannot promote everyone. The superiors count on the self-deceptive proclivities of their protégés, of course. Psychologists regularly find that 90 percent of students in a classroom think they are above average. And if your superiors lie to at least *some* of your colleagues, what makes you think that they are not lying to you as well? Is it not clear that the more of *you* there are around, the safer *their* position is going to be in the future? They have something you all want; so long as there is a deep market for what they want, they hold all of the chips.

Consider also the world that makes up "everyday" for you. There are objects, events, and people. There are the furnishings of your livingroom. Some may be laden with memories and promises, such as the books that sit on your shelves and the sheets you cover yourself with at night. There is comfort in opening your mailbox everyday, comfort, perhaps, in having a bath or a shave. The comfort comes in part from the familiarity of the activity, the trust that you have placed in it as a source of fulfillment of and intention. The trust comes from the deeply intuitive nature of the objects that surround you: mailboxes and cookie jars, unlike "love" and "hope," do not usually disintegrate before your gaze.

Trust, however, is susceptible to sabotage. Letter bombs are getting smaller and easier to manufacture by the day. One can sneak in your mailbox at any time now. The fact that yesterday's bombs were large and cumbersome will not help you tomorrow, when the miniaturized package blows up in your hands and disfigures you. You need not try to soothe yourself by the thought that you do not have a high-profile job or a prominent role in the advancement of high technology. The new generation of bombers go for the "random" effect. They might have read the novels of Franz Kafka and seen the movies of David Cronenberg and understand that the absurd and the unpredictable, much more than the predictably evil, is what terrifies people. And these bombers may live for the terror, not just for the blood.

What about having a bath? What can turn *it* into an anguished experience? Surely guilt about self-indulgence can make its appearance at any time—and then you will see the pettiness of your savoring a bodily activity that many others cannot enjoy because they have no place in which to enjoy it. The objects that lend your life the comfortable feeling of everyday-ness can also perish in the next large fire. The timelessness of the trust that you have placed in them is misplaced: the end of your own life will separate you from them. Your relationship to them is temporary. Of each stage of your life, it is surely true that it, too, shall pass and with it, the objects and relationships that you now trust. And then?

Knowledge of the End and the End of Knowledge: The Hermeneutic of Anxiety

People, Martin Heidegger (1962) reminded us, are unique among the animals in their awareness that they are destined to end. They know that their being is a being-unto-death. Knowledge of our death pervades our life. We behold it with our bodies and our minds. It is a curious sort of knowledge. As Søren Kierkegaard (1963) saw, there is no concept of *subjective* death in our language, even though death is one of the great subjects of speculative thought.

Death remains nameless to us. It is perhaps the prototype for the nameless. We cannot fear it, for it is not a proper object, and fear needs an object. "Nobody," cries Polyphemus, when asked by the other cyclops for the name of the man who took out the light of his single eye—according to Homer's *Odyssey*. They laughed at him. "Nobody" cannot be sought out, feared, caught, and brought to fair punishment. "We need a name, otherwise we cannot take you seriously"—or so the cyclops tell him. We cannot master the nameless, and so we deny it exists at all.

Look at your hand. Can you imagine it as a collection of atoms? Can you then imagine the atoms as largely empty space? What is empty space? A substance? A fluid? It goes by many names, depending on which view of the universe you take. Albert Einstein saw it differently from Meister Eckhardt, who saw it differently from Isaac Newton. Categories that seem to ground the world for us dissolve—a hand into its tissues, its tissues into cells, cells into molecules, into atoms, into subatomic particles. And then?

We have come unto the nameless. All we had to do was to break up experience on ever finer space-time scales, by asking, Why? Whither? How? Where from? The scientific method of breaking down objects and phenomena into ever smaller subsystems for the purpose of analysis—for the purpose of getting a better grip on reality—turns out to be one of the quickest paths to the nameless. Infinities in the small are just as elusive as infinities in the large.

The nameless can show up at any time to undermine our most basic trust. Your lover can turn into a beast, fondling another's body while making jokes about the distribution of your own body fat. An object that stores a treasured memory can turn out to have been a fake. Your life can come to an unexpectedly immediate end in the fire following a car crash. Feel this fog for yourself. Do not just walk around in an airport, but try to feel the possible world in which a black-hooded man begins to unload an AK-47 rifle right beside you. It's only a matter of seconds before he notices you trying to weasel away. Do not just contentedly urinate in a public washroom, but feel the pipe bomb ticking within the plumbing. Do not just "Hello, dear" your way into your home, but listen for the other lover's secret departure. These are the lurking breaches of the covenant between humans and their world that we cannot accommodate in any given system of words because they challenge the premises on which our lives are built. No attempt to build new frameworks will salvage us from this ordeal of a permanently subvertible existence because no metaphors, no schemas, no models will render the eventual nameless—the one that is still there when all words have been exhausted—accessible to our eagerness to name.

It is *through* naming, however, that we feel that we have gained mastery over the nothing that looks on us from the future. The link between the nameless and the nothing is that the nameless makes possible the experience of the nothing in the present. We intuit our own biological ends and are trapped in a world view that is silent about entities that lie beyond matter. So dreadful is the idea of the nothing that we have had to give it an ontological status, as a therapeutic measure: indeed, such therapy may be the hidden purpose of the development of language in our world.

Language can heal. Saying that something is the case has a therapeutic, soothing quality. Think of a politician's "diagnosis" of a country's social problems. Don't his words often feel good? They feel good before they feel "right," but the implied causation is wrong: we usually find ways of making them "right" once they feel good. That is the hidden move in our ongoing game with the world: the valuation game, the one Friedrich Nietzsche rebelled against more than a century ago.

It is easy to experience the nameless afresh: just ask, Why?, How? Where from? Where to? of the objects, persons, and experiences that you encounter and that all bear "names." Then go ahead and doubt whatever answers come up. Doubt the claims of the sentences that are put forth as answers to your questions. Doubt the authenticity of those who provide them. Come up with stories that unveil their secret motives and desires. All it takes for the nameless to appear is for your trust to disappear. All it takes for your trust to disintegrate is your realization that trust is blind.

You will know that trust has disappeared when you feel that you simply cannot "go on." Then you might experience a sort of paralysis. To move competently, to "go on," you must trust in a model of the world—even an implicit one or one that is only dimly perceived. You implicitly trust "the laws of physics" to get you from one place to another. But now someone has convinced you that the support we have for these laws is inductive and that there is no logical basis for induction. Now you might no longer trust that the laws of physics won't change on you suddenly—since there was no reason why you should have believed it in the first. You might feel that you cannot just "go on" moving your legs and taking steps. Your *trust* in the laws of nature has been undermined, even though you may still believe that trusting in them is the best bet you have going.

By similar mechanisms, you might come to no longer *trust* that your current intimate relationship will continue: it may have ended a long time ago, and your intimate other may long have been dreaming of being with other people. You no longer trust that the objects that surround you have a material and sentimental essence that gives you the feeling of "abode" when you are around them. You no longer trust in the automatic continuity of life through the night about to follow and through the dreams—such as falling dreams—that sometimes seem to bring you so close to physical destruction.

The U.S. Central Intelligence Agency understands these ideas well. Listen: "A person's sense of identity depends upon a continuity in his surroundings, habits, appearance, relations with others, etc. Detention permits the questioner to cut through these links and throw the subject back upon his own unaided internal resources. Detention should be planned to enhance the subject's feelings of being cut off from anything known and reassuring." The text—meant to instruct Latin American security forces on how to extract information from prisoners (and obtained by the *Baltimore Sun* through a Freedom of Information Act request in 1983)—makes it clear from the very beginning that the breach of a man's trust in his world is the key to getting him (or her, presumably) to "regress" or to lose, progressively, his (or her, presumably) "capacity to carry out the highest creative activities, to deal with complex situations or to cope with stressful interpersonal relationships or repeated frustrations."

Surprise is the messenger of the nameless: "The manner and timing of the subject's arrest should be planned to achieve surprise and the maximum amount of mental discomfort. He should therefore be arrested when he least expects it and when his mental and physical endurance are at their lowest—ideally, in the early hours of the morning. When arrested at this time, most subjects experience intense feelings of shock, insecurity and psychological stress and have great difficulty adjusting to the situation."

The nameless lurks in the implicit—not the explicit: "The threat of coercion usually weakens or destroys resistance more effectively than coercion itself. For example, the threat to inflict pain can trigger fears more damaging than the immediate sensation of pain." Above all, the nameless lurks in the random: the CIA advises the "persistent manipulation of time, retarding and advancing clocks, serving meals at odd times, disrupting sleep schedules, disorientation regarding day and night, *un-patterned* questioning sessions, nonsensical questioning, ignoring half-hearted attempts to cooperate and rewarding non-cooperation" as noncoercive ways to induce regression to an undeveloped, rudimentary set of behaviors.

The CIA's experts have also caught on to the trick of placing a person in front of the mirror of consciousness, all alone, as a way of tapping into the elementary anxiety of being that—as experts in these matters—they recognize in most of their subjects: "Solitary confinement acts on most persons as a powerful stress. The symptoms most commonly produced by solitary confinement are superstition, intense love of any other living thing, perceiving inanimate objects as alive, hallucinations and delusions."

Loss of trust in life and the world can also bring us to the brink of freedom. We can become free of our own past and of human culture—the suppliers of names, models, myths, and metaphors, the great tranquilizers and the great therapies against the nameless. We can free ourselves from them because they no longer supply a home—a safe haven. But we may also dread this freedom. In fact, freedom may reveal itself to us as dread. Having access to many possible worlds means that "the one true world" that gives us security can turn out to be treacherous and false—and this gives us both the freedom to see how "it could be otherwise" and the visceral feeling of estrangement and generalized fear.

Anxiety as the Possibility of Freedom to Act, to Think, and to Doubt

Anxiety—Kierkegaard (1963) tells us—is the experience of the possibility of freedom. Freedom is an extravagant possibility. Imagine being able to *choose* or *create* the world that you live in by using your brain as equipment that you will put to use to achieve happiness. Imagine being able to turn your emotional dependencies on and off at will or being able to leave or to start any relationship at the call of your own reason. Imagine being able to feel passionate about *anyone* new or indifferent to *anyone* new according to your will, which you can change at any time without impacting on the authenticity of your sentiments. Imagine being able to not only flee the "reality of the senses" but to enact a "reality of the senses" of your choosing; to forge a new reality without either miracles or pretenses; to truly and authentically desire what you wish to desire rather than hide your desires in a web of rationalizations; to remain open to reasons even while experiencing passions; to give any name you choose to the nameless and thereby to create—at will—a new world for you and for countless others who will flee into it for fear of the nameless.

The possibility of freedom of which Kierkegaard warns us is as exhilarating as it is terrifying. We know it by its common names of angst, anxiety, fear, dread. This is a confused language, since fear is different from anxiety in that it has an object, but it contains a germ of authenticity: fear comes *of* anxiety. It is anxiety pinned onto an object, often unwittingly. To the "liberated," mother culture appears as a fraud—especially impudent and insincere in its absolute claims to truth and justice. It appears as a temporary shack in which we hide because we are afraid to face the fact that we are free to choose. Once we have left her womb, there is no return. The suspicion that we have returned to a fakery of reality will always be with us. All we need is one brief glimpse at the nameless for all names to become suspect, and all we need is to nurture the seed of doubt a little while longer than we are generally accustomed to doing for the names that set our minds in peace to begin to fray at the edges and reveal their make-believe character. Mother culture disintegrates in the face of repeated questioning, like all self-referential systems.

Some questions cannot, however, be dismissed. What do you know without doubt? The existence of some immediate object? But how do you know that you are not dreaming of this "immediate" existence? The steadfastness of a friend? How do you know he is not pursuing some other purely selfish interest in his relationship with you and faking his intimacy—maybe even faking it even for himself? How do you sustain the belief that the laws of nature will not change tomorrow? On what basis are you making the inference from past to future experience? Induction? How are you justifying your belief in induction? Not inductively, by any chance? If so, consider the fact that counterinduction can be counterinductively justified: and where does this leave these circular justifications?

Trust and doubt are antagonists. They cannot both hold sway in the mind at the same time. Decisive action springs from trust. It alone can rule the mind at the moment of an intentional action. Trust is qualitatively different from belief. It is a form of unconditional belief or a belief that is etched into our viscera. Trust is the basis of commitment; beliefs form the building blocks of deliberation. Where deliberation begins, trust ceases. To commit to an action, you must trust in your ability to bring about its intended consequences rather than simply believe that you *may* bring them about.

Something as "small" as turning a page cannot be accomplished without the *trust* that your hands will obey your will, that your anatomy will continue to obey the laws of physics, that the page will react predictably to the touch of your fingers. Any doubts as to these facts—and plenty can be raised—will undermine your trust and weaken your will. As a tool-wielding animal, man can turn the entire world—and his entire body along with it—into *equipment* (as Heidegger called it) but only through the exercise of *trust* and the temporary suspension of doubt and disbelief. Trust turns belief into commitment.

Trust cannot be a mere form of belief because belief is susceptible to questioning and to doubt, whereas trust is ultimately blind. You have an infinite number of opportunities to doubt the success of any intended action. The laws of physics may change in a way that will not allow you to use your hands any longer. There may be a drop of lethal poison on the page you are turning, which you will swallow the next time you moisten your fingers. Your thoughts about your thoughts about your thoughts may trigger a heart attack the very next moment, and your thoughts that this can occur may also trigger a heart attack, and so on.

Not thinking at all is not an option, as being entails some form of thinking. You know this, you know that you know it, and so forth, and there is no way to hide it from yourself, which you know as well. There is nowhere to go but forward through action, but forward is not an option, once you have lost your trust, because it entails the foresight and volition and purpose and planning that rely on the trust that you have just lost.

Anxiety can emerge from the discontinuities that come from reflecting on the mundane acts associated with practical experience. You really *can* choose at any point to stop brushing your teeth forever, to murder your pets, to strip naked in a the middle of a mall and sing the national anthem, or to kill your wife or husband with an axe during breakfast. Moreover, you can decide to do so without any reason for doing it. These are all possible worlds that emanate from daily activities. Recognizing that you are at any moment given to choose among these possible worlds is perhaps the defining moment of anxiety—the moment at which the possibility of being free reveals itself.

Culture defends us from the realization of our own freedom because it creates an environment of ontological security. We trust in our "names" and categories and ways of thinking just as we implicitly trust in our bodies and friends and family members. We have an umbilical relationship to culture that mirrors our relationship to our parents. Our way of facing the nameless is through a full-scale assault of language on nature. We create names for experiences and thus come to feel that we have mastered them.

Don't you feel better when your "condition" begets a "diagnosis"? And why? Supposing that your condition is "chronic," what does it gain you to know the proper scientific term for it? Nevertheless, there is a soothing

effect that naming has on the mind and body—a promise of physical mas-
terability, a cognitive mastery of the phenomenon that hides the nameless
that lurks from our directed awareness. Now language appears to us in the
capacity of a shelter from the nameless, built up over the years by theologians, scientists, and writers—most of whose great talents can be brought
under the umbrella of wordsmithing.

The Unmasterable Object and the Logic of Using Words

When a child picks up a modern scientific text, he is apt to be overwhelmed
by *words*—by their number and the lack of an intuitive link between their
meaning and lay language. Even psychology has coined new terms for
mental events that, theoretically, we should all have access to (otherwise
the scientists cannot claim universality for them, without which no science
can be done). In protecting these words from lay use (by making their
proper use dependent on correct definition) the psychologist insures himself against the charge that the nameless has not yet been mastered—that
his own ontology is incomplete, lacking, and full of holes through which
the nameless can flow at any time.

Thinghood implies—and induces—a sense of stability, of real being.
We call a collection of atoms that stick together a molecule, a bunch of
molecules that stick together a membrane, a set of organelles that stick together a cell, a set of people that interact an organization. We give these objects names because they seem to be stable over time: they deserve their
objecthood by virtue of their enduring presence. However, if we analyze,
say, the dynamics of the atoms in a molecule, we find that there are situations in which the behavior of the group of atoms becomes quite unpredictable or even theoretically impossible to predict over the long run, as is
the case with chaotic phenomena. Micro-level behavior negates the stability of the ensemble and thus the very thinghood of the macroscopic object,
which rests on our assumption that "it" is a stable entity.

This argument can call into account the very thinghood of that collection of atoms that we call a molecule. But *we* do not call it into account.
Neither do we commonly call into question the thinghood of organizations once we come to realize the complexity and indeterminacy of the interpersonal dynamics that make them up. We have a significant stake in

the maintenance of reified objects, even when our own analytical models challenge their objecthood and their ontological essence and reality.

The mind is a powerful creator of objects. Its sense-making project rebels against the modern scientific dismantling of classical ontology that emerges from the methodological commitment of the scientist to understanding by taking apart. Thus, on one level, logical atomism soothes us by making the world seem more intelligible; on the other hand, it rouses our anxiety by challenging our intuitions about inherited ontologies. A "thing" is not what it used to be three hundred years ago.

Think of the words in your own life, the mushrooming of code words in your profession, the words that encode your memories, the principles by which you guide your behavior, the principles by which you judge others. Most of these words—we predict—are likely to be nouns. This is not a coincidence. The assault of nouns on language is a symptom of the deep anxiety that we feel—our emotional means of dealing with the nameless because nouns denote things and things are the stuff of existence as we have come to think of it. Doors, chairs, and dogs; smiles, grimaces, and tears; fears, angers, and worries; life narratives, possible selves, and possible worlds: notice the pervasive *thinghood* of these nouns that refer to increasingly ethereal and elusive phenomena. The apparent advances of science on nature feel right—or true—because they are simultaneously and perhaps solely advances of language on the nameless and therefore therapies for the embattled I in the age of anxiety.

What grammar does and logic cements, poetry, satire, and parody can undo. Just when we thought that we have conquered the nameless by covering it in names to the extent that word and object seem indistinguishable, the poets come around to highlight the mysteries that we have tried to cover and then forget that we have covered. William Blake would have us look for the infinite in every perception. J. Krishnamurti admonishes that trying to grasp a moment in a word kills what we are trying to grasp. Poets create new worlds by putting together familiar words with familiar images in unfamiliar ways. Moments of silence become chasms. Empty rooms become occasions for terror and the breeding ground of demons from past experiences that we thought we exorcised long ago. The effect of the poetic moment is at once moving and unsettling because we see both *how* it could be otherwise and *that* it can be otherwise.

We are deprived—by the poets' games—of the immediate certainty of perception and of the comfortable link between word and object with which it seems that we were born because they were seemingly always already there. Many of the philosophies that we have set up serve the purpose of setting our minds at ease about the multiplicity of possible worlds. "*There is only one world,*" writes John Searle (1996, p. 1), so emphatically that we wonder whether he is trying to convince his readers or himself as well. When Immanuel Kant writes about the a priori categories that enable our minds to grasp the world—such as space, time, and causation—he gives us a safe ground on which to "walk" and "think." Now we can proceed forward in the unknown future secure in the knowledge that the world provides a safe haven from the nameless. The world, after all, is mindlike in its essence; or the mind is worldlike. In any case, we dare not fall, through the cracks of our mind, into the nameless.

When Hume (1974), on the other hand, shows up our belief in causation to lack the requisite logical support; when Einstein comes along and shows that our seemingly "deep" intuitions about space and time are not the only ones justified by empirical science; and when modern physicists argue persuasively that, contrary to "intuition," evidence for nonlocal phenomena can be observed in the quantum realm—we react with an enthusiasm that is suffused with anxiety, much like the reaction to a supposed eulogy of our work published by a comedian: we do not really know when the satire has begun and where it will stop. We welcome the new insights *as new laws,* even as we fear them as fundamental challenges to our all-too-eighteenth-century intuitions about how the world works. When cognitive psychologists and anthropologists come along and reveal just how culturally determined our "deepest intuitions" are, we cringe because the mapping of our "deepest intuitions" to the scientific "picture of the world" was the very basis for our ontological safety. Now there is no choice but to admit that reality goes by many names, just like the nameless.

Modern psychologists have provided interesting instances of the instinctive flight of the mind from ambiguity and incongruence and toward the "home" provided by a stable view of the world. When word and object part ways, anxiety rises and often turns into a fear that we identify with something or someone. Jerome S. Bruner and Leo Postman (1949), for example, asked people to identify playing cards displayed on a blank wall using a projector. Among the playing cards, they placed cards that had been manufactured to contravene the norms and usual principles of association used to identify such cards. There were, among their cards, sevens of red clubs and aces of black hearts. The participants reacted quickly—and erroneously—because they rushed to classify the cards according to the usual categories ("red hearts"). Even when given more time to identify the cards, they still identified the cards incorrectly but asserted that there might be something wrong with the cards. They looked uncomfortable. Solomon Asch (1955), another psychologist, showed his participants three different line segments displayed on a screen. He then gathered all of the "other participants" in the experiment in the same room and asked the "other participants" (really confederates paid to give the wrong answer) for their answers. Most of the actual participants experienced extreme discomfort with the task, and most decided to go along with the fake majority.

Participants in the cards experiment saw their security in the link between word and object threatened and reacted by denying the incongruence that was the root of the threat. Participants in the segments experiment saw their security in the link between the world and the other threatened and reacted by sullenly acquiescing in the will of the majority. "Home" may be a fake, but it is home nonetheless. Words provide such a home—but it is a home constantly endangered by the irony and sarcasm of the others and by the doubts that well up from within the self and that cloud one's "immediate" perceptions, showing that they are, after all, "mediate" and in particular mediated by the words of the other.

It did not cross the minds of any of the participants in these experiments (the confederates in their "illusion" and the participant in his "true" perception) that they could "all be right" —which is quite conceivable once we understand that they had different goals and different constraints to satisfy. To see this, we simply need to replace "truth" with "functional adequacy" of a statement, and the problem goes away. The many—which makes quite a natural appearance when we live in the worlds of will and intentions—disappears in the world of causes and effects, where "right" and "wrong" filter the set of possible worlds down to the one true world.

"We Have a Stake in Thinking Our Thoughts": The Foundations of an Unconflicted Life

We seem to have a stake in believing that there is a one true world. But thinking that we have such a stake is the most subversive thought the human mind has dreamed of because it reveals that the world of causes and laws is intentionally constructed, for a purpose that may be hidden and is often kept nameless in our interactions. Now anxiety is laid bare before itself because we can no longer convince ourselves that the objects of our fear are the *causes* of our fear. The realization that anxiety is the *objectless passion*—as Freud might have put it—is at the same time a realization that quite possibly desire itself cannot be what it seems: the attainment of its objects will never be the source of its quiescence.

The most familiar engagement of a person with her anxieties is the mysterious phenomenon of deciding. Decisions bring us face to face with anxiety: this is why they are considered such difficult moments. No longer are we at home among the familiar automatisms of brushing teeth, making coffee, or of making love in choreographed positions. We are no longer warmed over by the *absence of doubt* that blesses every instinctive scream, dart, shove, and gulp. We have entered the realm of the many and can smell the nameless lurking by the simple fact that there is no longer one true world to deal with, extending from negative to positive infinities of time. Rather, there are many worlds and many selves to consider and live through—one for each branch of the decision tree that sprouts before us.

Decisions are terrifying because within them the possible is too visible in the actual for us to ignore it. Think of the real decisions in your life— among different lovers, different potential spouses, different jobs, different homes. In all cases, what is at stake is the splitting of the thinking I along many possible worlds corresponding to the worlds one brings about through one's decisions. We have a bifurcation of the world that is also a bifurcation of the self, whom we had thought to provide continuity from past to future, from the known into the unknown, from the named to the nameless. We may doubt that this is a *true* bifurcation and may persist in seeking a "right" answer for our decision. Or we may take solace in fatalism or determinism and deny that there is ever any true choice to be made. But what about the decision to *accept* these theories as true? Or the decision to search for these therapeutic theories? We often sweep them under the rug and continue the search for pictures of the cosmos that will absolve us from deciding.

This search gives rise to the quest for the true and the right in the history of language. Both moral philosophy and natural philosophy spring from the attempt to master the point of decision, the moment of awareness that the self is not one but many, each following its own branch from the future into the present and past: for each different choice will commit us to a different interpretation of our past, aimed at placating the rising anxiety surrounding the break-up of the one true world that we had hoped would stretch as far into the future as we could see. Culture is a collective therapy aimed at placating individual anxiety.

Both moral and natural philosophers rely on the method of *justification*—of bringing forth reasons for taking one or another path of the decision fork. They do not seem to be aware that their strategy bids us seek reasons for each reason we put forth, *ad infinitum,* and therefore we cannot hope to converge to *an* answer, let alone to *the* answer. Infinity lurks again in the midst of our attempt to dissolve it or to hide it. The harder we try to hide infinity, the more salient it becomes: with each "Why?" appended to a stream of reasons that support each other, the possibility that the stream of "Why?'s" will not end looms larger and more potent. With every fresh reason given in an infinitely regressive stream, the persuasive force of the other reasons decreases. Again, cognitive psychologists have found support for this effect. Gregory R. Maio and James M. Olson (1998) have shown that the cognitive commitment of people they surveyed to a particular belief decreases when these people came to see that there would be an ultimate "Why?" about that belief that would have to go unanswered. Beliefs seem to obey the logic of dominoes.

We are left to decide, without recourse to an ultimate basis for deciding. The bottom line is that there is no bottom line. Choice marks the passage of time, whose arrow seems to stem from the irreversibility of our actions. But our anxiety about deciding does not stem from a secret wish to hold time still and thereby become timeless and immortal but from the unfulfilled wish to harmonize what is with what could have been. Decisions bring up the specter of the nameless, which in this case is the indeterminate—neither X nor not X, or both X and not-X, together.

Contradiction is infuriating. If it persists, it frightens us. If we are stuck in producing it, we come to be known to others as "mad." The indeterminate makes itself apparent whenever we try to arrive at a conclusive calculus of reasons for taking one path rather than another. Most decision problems, however, are *undecidable:* equally suspect and defeasible reasons can be put forth for taking one path rather than another. We celebrate Robert Frost's (1993) consciousness because (in "The Road Not Taken") he fully realizes that his life might have been different, and he refuses the "bottom-line" calculation, the therapeutic self-justification, the self-congratulatory "I did well":

Two roads diverged in a yellow wood
And sorry I could not travel both
And be one traveler, long I stood
And looked down one as far as I could
To where it bent in the undergrowth
Then took the other, as just as fair,
And having perhaps the better claim,
Because it was grassy and wanted wear;
Though as for that the passing there
Had worn them really about the same,
And both that morning equally lay
In leaves no step had trodden black.
Oh, I kept the first for another day!
Yet knowing how way leads on to way
I doubted if I should ever come back.
I shall be telling this with a sigh
Somewhere ages and ages hence:
Two roads diverged in a wood and I—
I took the one less traveled by,
And that has made all the difference.

There is an image in the poem, which, if we took in, might take *us* in. It is the image of reasons as therapy. Frost takes us behind the scene on which reasons play out their roles and shows them to serve a merely therapeutic function. They let us "go on."

We are ill. The illness we suffer from is awareness of the freedom to choose. Anxiety is precisely the sensation of the possibility of such a freedom. The language of principles, laws, causes, and reasons provides the perfect mask of this freedom. We look for the "right" move, the "right" path, and the right reason for choosing that path—not "a" right path but "the" right path. We seek to banish the road not taken from our memories and our flesh because walking around with the rift inside is debilitating. The shadow of the could-have-been is the seed of rumination, which we seek to avoid by the construction of well-connected stories. Occasionally, a Robert Frost, by a deft turn of language, uncovers these stories *as* stories, and then we look our own deepest desire in the eye.

What makes hard choices hard is that they split the self into as many different possible selves as there are viable options. The self that we aspire to is a coherent story spun by the I that selectively conjures up memories and experiences that seem to support the narrative. If I think of myself as a "physician" and of "physicians" as "security-loving dogmatists," then I might have a self-narrative that takes into account the many experiences of indoctrination throughout my medical school education, as well as the many temptations to choose a high-paying, low-stress subspecialty that I felt throughout my education.

Why does anxiety rise with decision time getting closer, once you realize that there is no "right" approach to making a decision? Most likely *because* you've realized there is no right approach. "No right approach" often means "no one true you"—no one true narrative that will provide the protective cocoon of the self. It is in the unity and truth of the self that we find relief from anxiety. The self is the subject's therapy against the anxiety caused by the nameless. Stories mask the nameless in the mind of the living I. Where the I loses its unity and validity, the nameless lurks. Then consciousness loses its grip on the I, which becomes a free-floating phenomenon that escapes the preestablished bounds of sense that had been spelled out by the mind. When you choose between places to work, you also choose between possible selves—or identities of the I. What makes the choice an anxious one is the realization of the multiplicity of selves where we had thought there is only one—the one true self. The fact that there *is* a narrative that goes along perfectly well with each one of the choices is what makes the choice a moment of *splitting* between possible selves.

The irreversibility of a choice makes the split between one's possible selves itself irrevocable. Instead of appeasing the mind, however, this feature of our world increases its turmoil. *What could have been* refuses to go away, even when *what will be* has been chosen. Our premonition of this lingering around of the "unwanted lover"—the rejected choice—makes choosing more difficult. The more difficult choice is, however, the greater will be the inferred value of the option that has been passed over. Foresight of the regret makes choosing harder still. And no matter which way you go, there will be something left to regret. Justification of a choice is the subject's attempt at therapy aimed at stopping the rumination from unfolding. Certainty is the master antidote for the ruminating mind. But once we recognize it as a mere antidote, most decision predicaments reveal themselves to be undecidable, as they pose the seemingly insoluble problem—how to decide without regret and in the absence of certainty that we have "done the right thing."

The solution that the mind provides is the denial that any choice at all is to be made, as the insightful studies of Leon Festinger (1957) have shown. There is a fork in the road—to leave or not to leave a relationship, for example. But there are many ways of denying the existence of the fork. One can persuade oneself that staying is "the only way" to behave that is consistent with one's identity (there is no choice). One can play up the advantages of leaving obsessively, to the point that the choice becomes equivalent to choosing between a large amount of money or a small amount of money (there is no choice). One can take up diving lessons and forget all about the choice (there is no choice). One can also persuade oneself that "no matter what one does, nothing will change" (there is no choice). One can deny that one's actions are irreversible: one may leave but persuade oneself that one will be "welcomed back," or one may stay and persuade oneself that one "can always find someone new." Choice must be "disappeared" at all costs, for it is the peeping hole through which we see that we are free—precisely the chasm that gets rumination going.

Culture as a Care-Giving Process: Therapeutic Departures from Freedom

There are many ways to mask the fact of the irreversibility of choice. Doing so, however, entails telling a different story about the world from the one currently told in most public circles. We might, like Nietzsche, spin a story about an infinite return of the mind along the same paths, with a twist: in the "twisted return" version, we actually explore *all* of the paths that we experienced as giving rise to real, anxiety-provoking decisions in our lives. If you experienced your commitment to get married, for instance, as the outcome of a true decision—a situation in which you could have gone "either way"—then in the "twisted return" picture of the world you will actually explore both possibilities, returning several times and each time exploring another possibility. We check current scientific knowledge and find that it could accommodate such a picture of the world. Now we've done away with irreversibility: we no longer believe in it. We are free to decide without the lingering anxiety that we will have incurred an irrevocable loss.

Persuading ourselves of such a story, however, is difficult because of the lack of support that it gets from the all-important others—our other great source of ontological security. We can understand the emotional plight of the great outcasts of the world, who held on to their beliefs in spite of generalized opprobrium and disbelief. Their opposition to their peers is the equivalent, in the domain of the emotions, of the young child's refusal of his mother's help and shelter when in danger. "No, thanks, mummy," the toddler miraculously speaks, "I'd rather learn how to kill serpents on my own." The visionary and the rebel "walk away" from the ontological security that the other's acquiescence in his way of seeing the world gives them. They choose to live inside the nameless for a while.

When it comes to mental bets on the "way the world is," the stakes are high, as few descriptions of the world do not have immediate implications for the situation of the I that tries to stem its own fall through time. All of us must place our bets, but many want to escape the risk and run to mother culture for help. The very idea of risk implies that there is a discontinuity between the past (neatly circumscribed by a single narrative) and the future (which presents several possibilities that we are aware of and several more that we are probably not aware of).

When we are aware of risk and of ambiguity, we stand, then, at a discontinuity. This is a point at which the narrative can change into one of a number of different narratives, and therefore many different narratives coexist. The narrated I—the self—is on a precipice because now there is no longer "one true self" but many, all competing for a share of "the truth." We must hedge our bets. The narrative does not provide us with a defense against the discontinuity but is, rather, the source or the cause of the discontinuity. Without a "continuous" narrative of the experiences of the living subject, there would be no narrated I and therefore no self as we currently conceive of it. At the same time, the narrative becomes the subject's "life buoy," sustaining him by covering up the possible worlds that each of his actions call into being.

What is the source of the narrative? The narrated I features a protagonist ("me") who has been set off from the natural world and from other people. Natural and cultural circumstances conspire to sharpen the definition of the subject of the narrative over time. "We become neither better nor worse with time, but more like ourselves," echoes an old saying. The story called a "self" can take shape—as psychoanalysts and sociologists tell us—in the early years of childhood, which supply both the means for narrating the I (language) and the model for narrating the I (the individualistic Western culture that makes the I the center of the self).

But why should I want to have a self? And what will I do with the self once I have it? Anxiety—the feel of the unknown—can motivate us to conquer or master or hide the nameless being of the living I by bringing it in the realm of familiarity and knownness through language. The familiar is part *of my self*—of the narrative that I have spun around my experiences. Thus, the self is an instrument by which the I seeks to master its anxiety. Stories soothe. Narratives calm the unquiet mind. Words, as Rudyard Kipling put it, are as potent as narcotics in changing the way the world is for us.

Inquiry and doubt can reveal the narrative to be a therapeutic ploy. The skeptic is, however, derided, the fallibilist is intentionally misunderstood, and the psycholinguist is unwelcome because they raise the terrifying specter that our narrative is suspect and possibly invalid. They raise the possibility that the most authentic experiences we have are "beyond words." But words are the tools we use to turn the future into the past smoothly. Socrates' "knowledge that he does not know" seems to many to be either a pose or a nonhuman state of mind because it casts in a dubious light the cherished emotional experience of knowing.

A Hermeneutic of "Knowing"

Now, after Socrates, it seems strange to talk about knowledge as something we "have" or possess, as a talisman that turns unknown into known. Rather, knowledge is better thought of as a state, a feeling, brought about by the act of turning a nonverbal experience into a verbal one. We know this feeling well: it is the comfort of hearing the trite "I love you" from a person who has in fact behaved lovingly all evening long, the feeling of "being able to exhale" when we arrive at a causal explanation for a previously unexplained phenomenon.

Just as the child tries behavior and persists along the paths where he received encouragement, the anxious tries narratives and proceeds along the path along which *he* is encouraged by others. Culture and society provide cradles for the seedling narratives of the many, as well as unconditional endorsements of the idea of the narrative. Without a narrative, you have no identity. Without identity, you are not a "real" person. "Know what you are about," a boy scout may be exhorted. "Trust yourself," yell self-help book authors. They mean "Trust your Self"—your narrative, your story. Trust to the point of ignoring anything that might disprove it. After all, this is what "believing in yourself" must mean for it to be tested by your resilience in difficult situations. And the "difficult situations" are the ones that jar your stories. Graduated as a high school valedictorian? Now that you are at Yale, you are but one of several thousand former valedictorians. *Numero uno* is no longer part of your image. Have never encountered a problem in logic you could not resolve? There are plenty around: you simply did not look hard enough. No longer can you tell yourself stories about the invincibility of your mind.

Escapes from the Nameless: Passions and Their Narratives

There are two—and perhaps many more—alternative paths on which the anxiety to establish the self takes us, depending on the support that we want to draw for our narratives from other people. The first path is based on entrenching our narrative by recruiting others to the same narrative. This path requires bending their wills so that they recognize the validity of our own life stories. It is the way of the ambitious. The second is entrenching our narrative by destroying or denigrating the narratives that others have built up. It is the way of the envious.

The path of ambition is to fight doubt by building up a narrative that is so deep and so convincing that doubting it is increasingly difficult. For this, one will want to become a master of the world, such that no voice can shake the "belief in oneself" that makes anxiety subside. There is desperation in ambition, but that desperation is rarely, if ever, exposed before the person who experiences it. The path of the envious is to revel in the destruction and diminution of all those who are facing the same predicament as the one he is facing or fighting the same battle. The deeper their debasement, the more horrible their plight, the greater the destruction of another's self, the greater the benefit one derives from this strategy. One will want to be the consummate critic, the human embodiment of the ethos of destruction. There is a desperation in envy that never quite sees the light of consciousness.

Ambition and envy *create* their own "realities" by lighting up our experiences in different ways. The ambitious and the envious live inside their narratives and subjugate their experiences to their evolving narratives. Ambition and envy are, in this sense, master passions. Once on one of their paths, we do not see that it could have been otherwise, for seeing it entails that our narrative may be invalid. The master passions are like rivers, whose tributaries are the observations that we recruit along life's way. These observations have as little chance of swaying our passions—of *changing our minds*—as the tributaries have of derailing the river from its bed. Our goal in what follows is to travel downstream along the master passions and see them at work in shaping "personality," "culture," and "history."

4

Ambition as Desire and the Will to Power

Philosophers have thus far only interpreted history. The point, however, is to change it.

—Karl Marx

O villanous! I have looked upon the world for four times seven years; and since I could distinguish between a benefit and an injury, I never found a man that knew how to love himself.

—Iago, in William Shakespeare, *Othello,* act 1

If ambition is desire, what is it desire *for?* What is its object? Consider not only what you currently want but also what you want it for. What does a promotion buy you? What about accolades on your next paper or project? Why do you want your next paper and manuscript to be read and understood by a vast number of people? What do you hope that recognition will bring you? Why do you cringe when thinking of your spouse in the arms of another? Why do you feel a vague malaise when you think that he or she may be secretly thinking of another? What do you feel when looking in a mirror? What does the mirror look like when you realize that you are too short to attract a certain person or too fat for the eyes of another?

Ambition is the desire for ever greater causal powers. Causal powers—literally, "powers to cause"—depend for their definition on the way we think about causation itself. Some philosophers, such as David Lewis (1986), analyze causation in counterfactual terms. Lewis would explain a sentence such as "B caused A" by the sentence "But for B's occurrence, A would not have occurred." This way of thinking about causation is deeply entrenched in the lay language that we use to assert our influence: "But for my hard work, where would you be now?" says the father to the son ("therefore, you owe me all you have," he sometimes implies). "But for us, you would go bankrupt," says the venture capitalist to the entrepreneur ("therefore, consider yourself lucky to get even 1 percent of the shares of the business," he sometimes implies). "But for our swift cost-cutting suggestions, the firm would have collapsed," says the newly hired CEO to his board ("therefore, you owe me the extravagant option package I am proposing," he implies). At the root of these assertions is a *wish*—not a fact and certainly not an incontrovertible fact. It is the wish to be recognized as causally potent. There is a way of presenting information that makes one's claims to causal powers irresistibly powerful: the ambitious are students of human credulity, and the powerful its current masters.

The counterfactual necessity that Lewis talks about is also at the root of social theories or the theories that we seek to impose on our observation—physical or biological. When Karl Marx (1981) speaks of a "historical trajectory" that will inevitably lead to the violent breakdown of capitalist society, he is saying that the world *cannot but* proceed toward such an end. When a psychoanalyst speaks of thoughts and dreams as wish fulfillments, she aims to show how a person's thoughts, actions, and mental states follow *necessarily* from early experiences and anxieties. When a modern economist explains a social fact (such as the relationship between profits and the number of competing firms in a market) starting from some laws of human behavior, he means to show how matters *could not be otherwise*, given what he knows about people and about markets. When a modern evolutionary biologist tries to explain behavior in terms of genetically inherited, ecologically beneficial or costly behaviors, she is trying to say that the current state of society is in some way a logically *necessary* outcome of past processes. Where contingency is invoked, it is done is a similarly necessitarian vein: the fact that an event is contingent is, itself, necessarily true.

Until credibly challenged by alternative explanations, such master theories are causally powerful: they cause people to act as if they were absolutely true or unconditionally applicable. Why do graduate students in economics *become* less cooperative as a result of their training in the axioms of microeconomic science—which posit that people act in ways that maximize their own interests? Because a graduate education in economics seems to provide answers not only to the question "How do social institutions work?" but also to the question "Who am I?" As metaphysical lenses on the self, theories are irresistible magnets for the mythological mind that only recently—on the time scales of conscious humanity—has begun acquiring the tools for awakening from the stupor of its own ideas.

Ambition Turns Ends into Means: The Inner Work of Ambition

The ambitious person is an unfolding spiral of self-assertions. He wishes to be recognized as the proponent of the theory that unified physics or as the author of the next intellectual revolution in economics. As soon as the tangible ends of immediate desire are met—the recognition of another person, the successful launch of a book, a victory in a political turf battle—they become the *means* to the next tangible end. Theories may or may not *represent* the world, but they certainly do *act* on the world, causing other minds to *fall into* the net of assertions and procedures for legitimizing these assertions that is cast by the scientist. As soon as the scientist's laboratory techniques have turned up a result that he has sought for the past ten years, that result becomes the means to achieving yet another result, which increases the scientist's causal powers over the object of his study and also over the people "in the field." Ends, once achieved, turn into means, and, with the passage of time, all achievable ends eventually become means for the ambitious mind.

What bewitches the body into action is often the feeling that "*this* achievement will finally bring contentment." The semblance of eventual satiation keeps us hooked on our desires and oblivious to the master passion that moves them. The graduate student would become exhausted if she had to contemplate all of the intellectual, interpersonal, and political travails that would take her to a tenured position. Hence she makes the assistant professorship seem like the end of a long and difficult road—a period, not a comma, in her career. Later on, even as a favorable tenure decision looms on the horizon, new political battles begin to entice the white-hot imagination of the politically mature academic; for now, there is much more to be won and that much more at stake in the game. There are professional feuds, chaired professorships, laboratory directorships, and so forth.

Ambition is self-fueling but also self-denying. We may want—out of ambition—to feel that we are ambitious and even to be known as ambitious in a general, unjudgmental way, even though we do not want ourselves or others to see any of our concrete and particular actions as motivated by ambition. We may portray them, rather, as self-effacing sacrifices that carry us *away* from our ambitious ends. The ambitious chief executive officer dons the image of self-sacrifice for the good of the organization, just as the self-promoting academic dons the garbs of self-effacement "for the good of the students."

Ambition is self-denying in a different sense as well: it is the desire that negates its own immediate ends on attaining them. If we say that we desire something because it embodies a value in itself, then as soon as we achieve the desired end, we see that ambition has gone on to hook desire onto another object. The achievement of a desired object leads to its subsequent devaluation. We see that our expectation of fulfillment was illusory and that unfulfilled desire takes hold of us again—this time for a different object. The young academic may realize that the acceptance of her article into the field's most prestigious journal has left her clamoring for even more professional recognition. She must also realize that her success was only a step in her quest for ever greater professional fame and power.

Fame is prized for its promise of causal power, which, in turn, begets even more fame. If people believe that a person has great causal powers, then they may heed his directions and exhortations, thus giving him causal powers that confirm their expectations. Just as celebrities are well known for their well-known-ness (Boorstin 1983), the powerful are powerful on account of their reputed power. Thus the powerful is famous, which he has become in virtue of being powerful: the power-fame spiral can begin with a rumor of power, which is the seedling of fame. Because ambition is seeded and fueled by the desire for ever greater causal powers, no degree of fame that one can attain is ever sufficient: for every level of attainable fame, there is yet another level that is yet more desirable.

Suppose you desire the recognition of a single other person. You may want him to show his recognition in his words and attitude toward you whenever you see one another. But why stop there? He could be devoting more of his time reading your words, thinking of how to please you, and aligning his actions with his expectations, of your intentions and desires.

But why stop there? He could also be thinking of ever new and imaginative ways to fulfill your expectations, to show that he is loyal, to prove that he lacks the autonomy that you suspect that he is hanging on to—perhaps to deliver a coup de grâce to your self-esteem when you least expect it. But why stop there? He could also be trying to police all of his thoughts toward congruence to your intentions and desires. Even when a single other person is involved, the desire for recognition can be insatiable. Why stop anywhere?

The Dialectic of Recognition and Subservience

If we see recognition by another as the provisional confirmation of our causal powers, then we will see that Hegel's dialectic of master and slave is at its heart a contest for the confirmation of causal powers and one of a great number of possible dialectics. The ultimate recognition from another is his unconditional commitment to one's own wishes, expressed or implied. Seeing one's intentions embodied in the actions of another is the shared goal that turns human affairs into an intimate contest for control.

A person—according to Hegel (1977)—is conscious of her own being but only tentatively and warily. She is *paranoid* about the nature of her being and seeks confirmation of her being in the submission of another consciousness to her own will. She seeks herself in another. Her counterpart proceeds likewise. "They recognize themselves as mutually recognizing one another," writes Hegel, adding that "each is indeed certain of its own self, but not of the other, and hence its own certainty of itself is still without truth." If the confirmation of being-for-oneself is the overarching goal of a person's self-conscious existence, then a struggle must ensue, for confirmation can come only from another who wishes for it with equal desperation: "they must enter into this struggle, for they must bring their certainty of themselves, the certainty of being-for-themselves, to the level of objective truth" (Hegel 1977, p. 33).

But why does Hegel insist on a life-and-death struggle between individuals for the confirmation of the self-consciousness of each? "It is solely by risking life that freedom is obtained; only thus is it tried and proved that the essential nature of self-consciousness is not bare existence, is not the merely immediate form in which it at first makes its appearance, is not its mere absorption into the expanse of life" (Hegel 1977, p. 35). Considered meaningful here, says Hegel, are not only the ultimate goal of the struggle—recognition—but also the process by which this struggle is carried out.

This is too strong a claim—as if in thinking instrumentally about achieving some ends we also think about the usefulness of thinking instrumentally, of thinking about thinking instrumentally, and so forth. Self-consciousness really is not infinitely deep at all times: reflection *can* be infinitely deep but in reality never is. It is far more plausible that the struggle for the assertion of causal powers—for recognition by seeing one's will embodied in another's actions—is *blind* or at best only dimly conscious and that the protagonists are pushed toward engaging in a life-and-death struggle by their ambition, which guides each small step and prevents them from looking at the interval they have traversed.

Seeing social interactions as the playing out of an intimate contest of the wills provides a completely different lens on organizational phenomena from those provided by master theories currently used, such as neoclassical economics ("individuals take actions that maximize the expected monetary values of the consequences"), institutional economics ("individuals take actions that minimize the uncertainty of their predicaments"), or evolutionary theory ("individuals take actions that maximize their inclusive fitness"). Of course, the master theorist may reply that we want causal powers to use them to maximize our wealth, to minimize our uncertainty, or to maximize our attractiveness to trophy sexual partners. Master theories, of course, are never quite refutable. What the power dialectic captures, however, better than its alternatives may be the raw feel of working "up a ladder," of telling strategic truths and half truths, of making midnight calls to board members to sack the CEO, of faking one's preferences to ingratiate oneself with the higher-ups, of getting the better of another in a negotiation no matter how much time and money have been lost in the process. Moreover, one can also argue that money, a secure social predicament, and the appearance of sexual success are themselves means to increasing one's own causal powers in the world. The consummate power player rides the intellectual fads of his time to the place where his will is unfettered and makes use of people's beliefs to safeguard his ascent. Profit maximization, like uncertainty minimization, can be useful in the form of justificatory accounts for one's actions. Culture is the camouflage of the master.

We go to work in hierarchies. Hierarchies are not only uncertainty-minimizing structures or profit-maximizing structures but also dominance structures. They not only shelter us from the capricious ups and downs of the markets but feed and cultivate our desire for power and recognition. Wills are asserted and subdued. The goal of the individual in the dominance hierarchy is to "get his way." Getting your way often means getting to the top of the hierarchy. The CEO is one of the modern prototypes of the master. He must answer to the board of directors, to be sure. But he controls their agenda and composition. He depends on his employees for information and expertise, to be sure. But he shapes their information-gathering strategies by asking the questions that they, in their information-gathering efforts, seek to answer. He designs their compensation packages, providing selective incentives to informants and "devil's advocates" who will—when called on—sabotage an opponent's claims.

The consummate yes-man—today's slave and perhaps tomorrow's master—fully understands the power of the one who asks. He never unasks the questions of the current master or rejects them as sloppy. Rather, he asks for clarifications. He asserts his will to power under the guise of his concern for clarity, all for the good of the organization. He disguises his power moves as profit-maximizing moves, as uncertainty-reducing moves, as moves motivated by his familial concerns and obligations. The master theories of modernity have provided the consummate players with terrific decoys. "It is not power that we seek," the theories help them say in different ways, suited for different contexts.

The intimate contest of the wills is played out on the organizational stage at every level. Each wants his will embodied in the actions of the other. Each wants to write out his power onto the body of the other. Each also wants to credibly deny his will to power. Asking someone to "have a seat" in your office seems like a cooperative move meant to induce comfort in the other. But it is no less a move in a power game: you have the standing to bid the other have a seat. Accepting the seat then appears to be an act of submission: the sitter acquiesces in the standing of the office holder to bid him have a seat. Each question represents a prompt of the attention of the other: it guides his attention to a particular subject. If he accepts the request to answer the question, he also accepts the causal powers of the questioner to guide his attention to that particular subject. Each answer given to a particular question represents an acquiescence of the questioner's causal powers. It is not a surprise that consummate observers of organizational power games have noticed that the key function of consultants is to give the executive team of the firm access to information that has been withheld by their employees. Information is the currency of the power game. Credible information is the foil. Accurate and actionable information is the gold standard. It is no wonder that words have lost their meanings in dominance hierarchies that span entire societies, such as the Soviet Union. In the evolution of a *langue du bois*—a wooden language—generalities and irrefutable statements are used to mask the information and intentions of the speaker. Words no longer refer, or depict, or represent. They no longer call out to the world. Assertion is no longer testable. Social structures provide not assurance but camouflage.

The dominance hierarchy often counterfeits its own currency. Each of its intimate, daily power struggles adds another set of defensive and dissimulative mechanisms to the repertoire of the dominance hierarchy gamesman, whose restraint becomes his own imagination. Without the mechanism of the market, without needing to persuade another with whom one is not in direct contest for authority of the benefits of mutual interaction, there is no institutional safeguard against the counterfeit of information. Deception has become an art. Death in Hegel's dialectic has been replaced by disgrace. Life-and-death struggles have been replaced by boardroom games. Only recognition—through the authority accrued to the "winners"—remains as the sought-after prize of the dominance hierarchy game.

Recent historical experiences would seem to refute Hegel's view about the fact that the life-and-death aspect of the struggle is essential to the protagonists: who would not avoid it if they had the means to do so? The mythology that placed the aristocrat and the knight at the center of social attention and admiration was replaced in the late twentieth century in part by the mythology of the entrepreneur—by a folklore that has the entrepreneur risking economic well-being, familial bliss, and stability to take the reins of his own destiny in his own hands. Suddenly it is possible to achieve apparent freedom without a lifetime of playing the dominance hierarchy games that one's parents have played repeatedly. Suddenly it is possible to command recognition without years of providing fake recognition to others, to "arrive" without "sucking up," to achieve self-determination without the need for massive deception and self-deception.

The attraction of "working for oneself" in modern times is not a negative reaction to seeing the product of one's labor "alienated from oneself"—as Marx thought. Rather, it is a statement about self-determination, about having causal powers over one's own actions. "I am the master of my fate, I am the captain of my soul," sings the poet, and we resonate inside, shaken by the elusive dream of self-determination, of causal powers at the behest of uncaused causes that begin and end in ourselves. The entrepreneur is mythical perhaps because he seems to us to be free: his will creates the rules by which others must play and the situations that others must adapt to, and his will to power keeps him interested in ever extending and enriching the reach and scope of his causal powers, until (he hopes) his will becomes embodied in the entire universe.

The Dialectic of Means and Ends and the Nature of Money

Money is the most fluid transformation of ends into means that human civilization has produced. As an end, money is often thought to be an object of desire, a prima facie motivator of activity. We answer "to make money" when asked why we engage in certain activities. But to desire money as an *end* is absurd: money has value only as a means to obtaining the objects, capabilities, and liberties that we desire. Once achieved, however, these capabilities are used to get *more of the same*. As Robert Heilbroner (1985) has pointed out, capitalism is distinguished from other forms of social organization by the self-perpetuating nature of capital: money is used for the purpose of getting more money. The causal powers embodied in the ownership of money are used to seek out greater causal powers, which can be achieved through the ownership of more money. The spiral of money, people, and money can obliterate all other expressions of the subject, as the "young millionaire" phenomenon has recently shown. Recently minted millionaires strive to become "repeat entrepreneurs."

Repeat entrepreneurs strive to become gurus and moguls. Gurus and moguls want to be remembered for their exploits, as the "giants" of American industry—the Carnegies and Rockefellers—are today.

"Money, the object of desire" having become "money, the means of securing the *true* objects of desire," once again becomes "money, the object of desire." There is an intimate relationship between this dialectic of means and ends and the search for ever greater causal powers. Just as every causal power desired becomes, once acquired, a means for the attainment of new causal powers, the money that we desire becomes, once we acquire it, a means for the attainment of more money. Money mirrors ambition into matter.

Scholars of organizations—and agency theorists in particular—have puzzled over the relative scarcity of compensation schemes in organizations that are based on sharp financial incentives for observable output. "Produce a $1 billion order for the firm," the pay-for-performance logic goes," and you will net $10 million for yourself." But that is not what most compensation packages in hierarchies look like. Instead, the chosen are promoted to higher ranks, bigger offices, higher levels of discretionary spending, more decision rights, more status and apparent responsibility.

"Irrational and inefficient," scoffs the economic theorist. He points this out to a few career bureaucrats. They smile condescendingly and ask to speak off the record. "What we want," they might say, "is power and the recognition that comes with it. Hierarchical rank gives us power—of the kind that we don't have at home (where our wives constantly berate us and threaten to leave and our children reproach us for all of our past choices) and didn't have at school (where we were told what to do) or at work when we joined the firm (when we had a boss or maybe even many bosses competing to give us orders). Now *we* get to say how it is. We get to stand in the spotlight of public attention. We get to command recognition by the implicit threat of demotion that hangs over each and every one of our conversations with our employees. What we want is *power now*, not power in some distant and uncertain future. That is what hierarchical status gives us. Money is useful, but is occasionally uncertain as a guarantor of power and recognition. It is often invisible. It provides freedom but not the promised recognition: there are too many millionaires out there, and recognition requires standing out among them. And there are only so many toys that we can buy for ourselves and our families before our attempt to buy recognition becomes visible and laughable. There is no more ridiculous sight than that of a person trying to buy respect. To the moneyed recognition seeker, the power games of the dominance hierarchy look increasingly appealing. Buying a place on the hierarchical ladder is suddenly possible: no wonder many entrepreneurs return to academia, where they tirelessly recount their exploits to wild-eyed students who want to replicate their lives. If you would like to gauge just how rational organizational life is, how well its phenomena reflect the underlying motives of the actors, read Hegel, not Adam Smith; *then* craft your verdicts about "irrationality" in the provisioning of organizational incentives."

Max Weber (1930) was the first to point out the uncanny link between the passion of the Puritanical Calvinist and the capitalist drive for worldly accomplishments. As Weber points out, at no time before the spread of Calvinist practices and beliefs in Europe and North America had the acquisition of goods and the diligent pursuit of wealth been considered an ethical imperative. Borrowing and lending money had gone on for many centuries before Calvin lived and worked, but money lenders were considered usurers, people who had fallen from grace into a lower spiritual state whose existence was to be merely tolerated. Now, for the first time, the pursuit of wealth was surrounded by the aura of tenets and dogmas reserved for only the highest ethical values:

Remember that credit is money. If a man lets his money lie in my hands after it is due, he gives me the interest, or so much as I can make of it during that time. . . . Remember that money is of the prolific, generating nature. Money can beget money, and its offspring can beget more, and so on. Five shillings turned in six, turned again it is seven and threepence, and so on, till it produces a hundred pounds. The more there is of it, the more it produces every turning, so that the profits rise quicker and quicker. He that kills a breeding sow, destroys all her offspring to the thousandth generation. He that murders a crown, destroys all it might have produced, even scores of pounds. (Benjamin Ferdinand, cited by Kurnberger 1855 in Weber 1930, p. 57)

Suddenly it is money—initially the object of possession—that is possessing. What mediates this possession of the possessor is the ambitious spirit of capitalism that has found a theological grounding in John Calvin's writings. For Calvin, the individual is not free to choose his destiny but can only discover it. He cannot influence what has been ordained for him but merely seek evidence for or against the fact of his ultimate salvation. Because, as Weber (1930, p. 57) writes, "the social activity of the Christian in the world is solely activity *in majorem gloriam Dei,*" success in worldly endeavors is a *sign* that singles out the elect, who are not saved because of their works but rather are successful in their works because they are the elect.

Calvin's thinking turns the night of self-doubt into a philosophy of action: "Who are you?" Calvin asks. "Wait, don't tell me," he continues. "You have many incentives to lie, even to yourself. Rather, show it, by your works." There is no purer example of ambitious endeavor and glorious myth arising from self-doubt in the history of the human psyche. No moment of one's life can go unspared because each moment is a moment when one could have searched to discover one's true value in the world. And surely enough, the capitalist preacher follows suit: "Remember that time is money. He that can earn ten shillings a day by his labour, and goes abroad, or sits idle, one half of that day, though he spends but sixpence during his diversion or idleness, ought not to reckon that the only expense; he has really spent, or rather thrown away, five shillings besides" (Kurnberger 1855, cited in Weber 1930, p. 59).

The Calvinist spirit of achievement may also be deeply etched into the psyche of the academic, who believes that one must have a spark of genius (which no amount of work will obtain) to succeed in the academic world *and* who works compulsively to get published and achieve tenure. His (observable) worldly achievement is a piece of evidence for his (unobservable) individual talent and endowments. Just as the spirit of worldly achievement burdens the individual with anxiety for each moment spent not earning money, so the ethic of the "production of knowledge" keeps the scholar employed possibly well beyond the point where his ideas are coherent and useful. "What should you be doing right now?" whispers Calvin's little voice in his ear on a sunny weekend morning, when his children are playing outside in the garden and calling to show him a new trick.

The Dialectic of Surplus and Impoverishment

Now we can also understand Marx's thinking about class conflict in a way that is consistent with Hegel's perspective, which Marx started from.

Hegel saw social history as an unfolding of the dialectic of master and slave—one risking his life in exchange for public recognition, the other forgoing recognition in exchange for certainty about the future. The capitalist master seeks to maximize the amount by which his revenues exceed his costs. No matter how much he already has, the master capitalist wants more: ambition is the desire for *more* of anything that can be desired because *more stuff* attests to *greater causal powers* by which that stuff was begotten.

Human labor appears as a cost to the capitalist, as a quantity that should be minimized. The laborer also seeks to maximize his excess positive cash flow, but he is driven to ever lower levels of income by advances in the technologies that lower the costs of production. Mass production is the form of organization of work in which human labor is maximally exchangeable for mechanized labor and therefore in which (in the Marxist metaphor) man is maximally exchangeable for machine.

Any effort by the laborer to escape his predicament through labor is self-defeating, since labor may, in the short run, net him more money. But it will also net the capitalist proportionately more profit, which he will use to buy machinery and perfect technologies that will further decrease the cost of labor. But the laborer cannot *buy* labor. Any other path is fraught with the danger of violent death or abject poverty. In the long run, the laborer's efforts are self-defeating, as his work helps finance its own devaluation. But the long run grows ever shorter, as firms compete on ever shorter time scales. So the laborer cannot hope to "get ahead" and somehow escape the devaluation of his labor by thrusting that devaluation on future generations.

The Dialectic of Desire and Fulfillment

A parallel dialectic governs the demand side of the economy—the dialectic of desire and fulfillment. Desiring an object, wanting to possess it, in part means wanting to achieve causal powers over that object or wanting the object to come under one's control. Desire of an object is desire for an increase of one's causal powers in such a way that they include the object in question. Because desire for an object is but a step along the way to achieving greater causal powers, consumption may not lead to fulfillment, as advertised. Rather, it can lead to more desire.

Acts of possession are addictive. But one may be addicted not to the object of possession but to the act of possessing. Suppose you would like to own a Porsche. You work long and hard, and one day you buy the car of your desire. You drive it, squeeze its throttle, caress its curves; you paint it, wash it, dry it lovingly. But every time you *consume* your Porsche, your Porsche *consumes you:* you reenact, in the act of consumption, the initial act of taking over the Porsche from Dr. Ferdinand Porsche's dealers. With each look at your Porsche, your desire for a fresh act of consumption grows: you end up craving another Porsche because each time you satisfy your desire by the attainment of an object, you stoke desire for the act of taking possession.

"Make it yours," the advertisements beguilingly call out, whether about a Macanudo, a moment on a pink beach in the Bermudas next to a shapely mate, or a pick-up truck. They promise the *fulfillment of having made something yours,* of the growth of your causal powers to subsume the thing itself. Consumption is not fulfilling but *addictive:* the consumer is consumed by the object that promises fulfillment by its consumption. The fulfillment that one is usually promised would—in the "standard view"—be the end of desire. The manufacturer cannot possibly want to produce *satiation* in the consuming subject; she rather wants the subject's desires to be set afire by the experience of consumption, which becomes itself consumptive.

Paradoxically, she can achieve the effect only by showing pictures of people *satiated* by consumption, people whose *consumptive* experiences have also satiated them. But with each immersion into the consumptive experience, the desire for further experiences grows in the consumer. Clearly, the advertisements are counterfeits of reality: their satiated people are satiated not because they consumed but in spite of the fact that they consumed. Consumption consumes. "There are two great tragedies in life," wrote George Bernard Shaw. "The first is not to get your heart's desire; the second is to get it." Thus, we have the dialectic of desire and fulfillment.

The Dialectic of Desire and Concealment

We also have a dialectic of desire and *concealment.* Rene Girard (1965, p. 23) observed that "force is only the crudest weapon available to consciousnesses drawn up against each other and consumed by their own nothingness. Deprive them of this force . . . and they will make others such as past centuries were not able to foresee." Girard offers as an example the "novelistic dialectic" that governs the revelation and concealment of desire: the lovers' high-stakes game of hide-and-seek behind words, poses, and actions. Each desires the other's desire more than he or she desires the other. Revealing one's desire entails capitulation and defeat: one has become the slave, whose will has succumbed to the causal powers of another; and just as an object does not incite us to action directed at conquest and seduction, the slave loses his interest for the master. The masterful concealment of desire keeps the other always on the verge of capitulation—wallowing in the dark abyss dug into the mind by the fear of abandonment and of irretrievable loss but too frightened of becoming irretrievably uninteresting to get out by revealing unconditional desire.

Consider the internal soliloquy of a young man who sees his fiancée brush her hair backward beguilingly before one of his male friends, her eyes digging deeply into the latter's eyeballs:

Oh, Lisa. And is this because of my earlier comment on the futility of marriage and of my invention of an optimal algorithm for testing the intentions of a prospective partner before making any commitments? Or have you figured out that I will attribute your gesture to a vindictive purpose, and—shielded from suspicion—are you taking this opportunity to reveal your lust for Roger? How worried I must look thinking these thoughts, while—look—you are bending over to pet his dog while (unwittingly?) revealing your panties to him. And look at how he feigns indifference and looks just past you. He understands the game. And you are torn (are you not, darling?) because now you have two indifferences to deal with—both equally stimulating. Ah, indifference, inspire me with your genius. Here, let me make another comment about marriage and liken it to a relationship between master and pet while stroking the dog to make it look as if I do not have any malicious intent and could be talking to the dog or even Roger. Good, that got your attention. Now if you show him more of your underwear, that means you really are acting unconsciously and vindictively. But no, you do not. You smile and look as if you have not even heard me and even manage to make it look perfectly accidental that Roger is now practically staring into your breasts, which somehow ended up under his nose. Now you withdraw with sullenness once you notice his animal grin, but is it withdrawal from him—no longer interesting because you have conquered—or rather withdrawal toward me, whom you have been tormenting mercilessly for the past hour? Ah, look. Now you are making faces again, stroking the dog as you would a lover's hair. How very clever. Now you have both of us piqued, wanting to think the caress is addressed to him but tormented by the fact that it may be addressed to the other.

And on we go. Torment is as limitless as the mind that creates it. We come not to a compromise, a denouement, or a fulcrum of desire but rather across a *dialectic* of desire and concealment.

Escalations: The Sadomasochist Dialectic

The sadomasochist dialectic is a sharpening of the dialectic of desire and concealment. The sadist assumes a dominant role that she asserts by asking for acts of submission from the masochist. The masochist enters the role by feigning *unwilling compliance* with the sadist's wishes. The masochist's reluctance is a crucial part of the scene that gets enacted: for without reluctance, without a *will that has to be overcome by the will of the sadist,* there can be no sadistic ecstasy. No sooner, however, does the sadistic moment arrive than the sadist is overcome by the desire to subdue again and to extract an even greater act of submission from the masochist. The sadist thought she was on the way to fulfillment, having mistaken the desire for *ever greater* causal powers for the mere desire for causal powers; instead, she is on the way to new desires, ever deeper, ever more beastly and unthinkable.

What about the masochist? When sadomasochism is a game, she can win by losing: for she knows that the sadist's ecstasy is itself *caused* by her act of submission, in which she has engaged voluntarily. The sadist appears then not as a master but rather as a slave: she is enslaved by the desire to enslave the masochist, who in turn stokes this desire by the alternate bequeathal and withdrawal of authority on and from the sadist. The more unspeakable the acts of submission become, the deeper the promise of ecstasy for the sadist but also the deeper the ecstasy of the masochist at the progressive enslavement of the enslaver.

Now it is the masochist's turn to become enslaved by her desire for enslavement, and she fantasizes over the next, deeper level of submission and beckons the sadist with a fleeting look. The more unheard of the sadist's demands become, the greater becomes the complicity between the two against the "culture" or "mores" whose bounds they have escaped. Thus, the ecstasy of the sadomasochist dialectic is not only ecstasy at the achievement of progressive causal powers over one another but also ecstasy at escaping the rules, bounds, and constraints of a cultural heritage that each carries around with her.

The sadomasochist dialectic gets played out—*sotto voce*—in the dialectic of recrimination, contrition, and resentment. The instability of modern marriages has often been attributed to the fact that women have suddenly found themselves with "other options" once they have entered the workforce. They can afford to walk away from difficult or unpleasant relationships and even to exchange current husbands for "better ones" in the so-called marketplace. So, at least, goes the economist's argument. But the argument fails to explain how two people who stood next to each other saying "I do" with apparent conviction when asked whether they want to spend the rest of their lives together, all of a sudden come to sign papers that would reestablish their relative identities as strangers relative to each other. How did they come to muster the requisite level of hatred and disgust for each other to carry through this process that turns a friend into a stranger? Possibly by a long spiral:

You left me alone on the eve of the birth of our child. You went off and pursued your writing and elevated conversations—what shams! And when you took me to my board examinations, you made off so quickly that I did not have time to remember to ask you for a watch. Little wonder that I failed. . . . I feel sometimes as if life with you goes nowhere, absolutely nowhere. You just keep me hanging on.

Contrition occasionally helps break these soliloquies:

You are quite right about the watch and about the hurry that I was in. I could not stand the look of that herd of people all trying to get into this profession to make a buck, all the while pretending. This is my problem. And I quite agree with you that I went off because I was getting tired of waiting for you to give birth. I just started feeling the itch for a conversation about my work. It is all selfish. But I see it, I see it. That is why there is hope.

And all is well, for a while. But contrition is a sword that cuts both ways:

Now you sleep peacefully in my arms, content to have brought me to say things I did not fully mean. But next time will be different. Next time I will quite possibly escape the cage of guilt.

And the cage of guilt tightens with every reproach, until bitterness overflows in one cathartic moment in which accuser and accused stand eye to eye and curse each other out: "I would do anything to keep you out of my sex organs," says one of Ingmar Bergman's characters in *Scenes from a Marriage* in a moment of rage. Once unthinkably brutal, divorce now looms like an escape.

The Dialectic of Seduction and Oppression

We have, also, at the beginning of a new century, a new dialectic driven by the angst over causal powers—the dialectic of seduction and oppression—of the layman by the scientist, expert, or theologian, whose ambition was most aptly expressed by Marx (1975, p. 34): "Philosophers thus far have only interpreted the world. The point, however, is to change it." Surely that is half-conscious uttering: for *whatever* we say and do changes the world in some way—though it does not change it *according to our will and foresight*. What Marx was after was a causal power that could be *purposefully* applied and that would produce the changes that one desired in the world. No sooner is the layman seduced by the theorist's ideas—usually offered as "liberators" of the layman from the dogmas of a prevailing system of government—than the theorist *becomes* the oppressor and recruits the layman's temporary enchantment to the project of establishing a new dogma or paradigm. Enchanted unto subjugation, the layman is once again an easy target for the next liberator. People need to be perpetually liberated from their liberators.

Marx—who turned the Hegelian master-slave dialectic into a story about the evolution of economic relations between people since times immemorial through times unforeseeable—was once asked by a journalist to say what he most hated in the world. Marx answered that he hated servility most of all. *Servility* is the abandonment of one's autonomy and the subjugation of one's actions to the intentions of another, whose own causal powers are therefore revealed and instantiated in the actions undertaken by a will no longer free to choose. In the realm of control and power, people are engaged in zero-sum games, and Marx empathized with the resentment of the vanquished.

Marx's own theory can be seen as a gigantic exposition of the workings of ambition, springing with great conviction from its master's own ambition to impose the structure of his own psyche on the history of the universe. Starting from the premises that religion is an opiate that the powerful give to the less powerful to increase their incumbent power and that all theories are at their heart ideologies—rationalizations of their authors' social and material interests—Marx is prepared to write down a master equation governing the unfolding of human history. Indeed, his philosophy was taught under the former communist regimes of eastern Europe as "scientific socialism"—an equation whose validating observations comprise all of known human history. He excuses himself from his own judgments of theories: the master equation is not (by his implication) a mere apology for its author's social position and interests; his righteousness is beyond doubt (to himself at least), and his logic is uncompromised by its wielder's wish-fulfillment projects. He exemplifies—by his own dogmatism—the opiate power of a theory.

Its predictive failures notwithstanding (Marx's theory predicted that world socialism would begin in the more industrially developed England rather than in the quasi-feudal Russia), the theory's explanatory accomplishments are beguiling. We are charmed into sympathy with the author's views by his ability to explain our immediate experience and resentments (the bending of our will to the requirements of an organization, a boss, or a spouse), the broader historical trends leading to the ouster of humans from fields and factories by machines, and the resulting increasing returns to private accumulations of capital. All are phenomena that we relate to, and they are immediately relevant to our personal ambitions. Because he succeeded in bringing a master passion to language, Marx created a *seductive* theory of society, whose recent fall into disrespect was accomplished by its conflation with the economic failures of the Eastern European dictatorships.

Another example of a theory as master narrative is provided by the intellectual history of neoclassical economics and its theoreticians. Milton Friedman, for example, seems to have had a competent understanding of how to build a church around a dogma: first, articulate a theory that assumes a little and explains a lot, does not contain a subversive element toward the prevalent self-concepts of those who have most influence in society, and gives strong answers to seemingly objective questions that can be asked of any theory, and then divert attention from the truthlikeness of the assumptions of the theory by coming with a meta-theoretical justification for the kind of theories that one's own theory represents.

Let us watch Friedman at work: "Positive economics is in principle independent of any particular ethical position or normative judgments. As Keynes said, it deals with 'what is,' not with 'what ought to be'" (Friedman 1953, p. 38). Notice here shades of Marx, who, by stating that all theory is really ideology, implicitly posits that his theory is objective and stands apart from the theories that he is criticizing, a view that Marx and Engels confirm explicitly elsewhere in their work: "The social structure and the State are continually evolving out of the life-process of definite individuals, but of individuals, not as they may appear in their own or other people's imagination, but as they really are, i.e., as they operate, produce materially, and hence as they work under definite material limits, presuppositions and conditions independent of their will" (Marx and Engels 1939, p. 37). We also hear a lugubrious echo in a letter from Joseph Stalin: "The Politburo has neither right nor left deviations. With comradely greetings. J Stalin" (Volkogonov 1991, p. 250).

Like Marx, Friedman is explicit about his claim to objectivity: economics deals with "what is." Like Marx, he contradicts himself—unknowingly—later on: "A theory is the way we perceive 'facts' and we cannot perceive 'facts' without a theory" (Friedman 1953, p. 39). But where do we stand on "what there is"? If fact is built on theory (that is, is theory-laden), then how are we ever supposed to know that facts are objective? Were not "facts" supposed to be the proving ground for "theory"? By now, his audience is probably willing to forgive inconsistency. In a world of cognitive misers, complex arguments often go unscrutinized.

Friedman (1953, p. 39) continues by advancing a relatively benign claim: "The ultimate goal of a positive science is the development of a 'theory' or 'hypothesis' that yields valid and meaningful (i.e., not 'truistic') predictions about phenomena not yet observed. . . . Viewed as a body of substantive hypotheses, theory is to be judged by its predictive power for the class of phenomena which it is intended to explain." You may not have even noticed the swift switcheroo that took place before your eyes, unless you were wide awake: Friedman has just placed prediction and explanation in the same boat: if a theory can explain, then it can predict, he seems to say. How many *predictions* of the occurrence of the 1989 revolutions in Eastern Europe are you aware of? None, most likely: otherwise we would not call them revolutions. How many accurate predictions of *any* social event are you aware of? On the other hand, we have a quickly rising number of *explanations* of those revolutions, all of which purport to show how matters could not but have taken the course that they eventually took.

Here is the subsequent move in this remarkable dramatic production: a theory, Friedman claims, should be judged not by the realism of its assumptions but rather by its predictive successes: "the relevant question to ask about the 'assumptions' of a theory is not whether they are descriptively 'realistic,' for they never are, but whether they are sufficiently good approximations for the purpose at hand. And this question can be answered only by seeing whether the theory works, which means whether it yields sufficiently accurate predictions" (p. 40).

Now comes the second play of the propagandist. Looking for "realistic assumptions" is a hoax, Friedman gives us to understand: "A completely realistic theory of the wheat market would have to include not only the conditions directly underlying the supply and demand for wheat, but also the kind of coins and credit instruments used to make exchanges; the personal characteristics of wheat traders such as the color of each trader's hair and eyes, his antecedents and education, the number of members in his family, their characteristics, antecedents, and education, etc." (p. 40). "It cannot happen in any other way but that which I propose," we are told. "To say otherwise would be to court endless rumination" (p. 41).

However, this argument is false. Here is why: a *realistic* theory of how wheat markets work does not make statements about the particular circumstances of time and place and person that inhere in that market (as Friedman suggests) but rather about the behaviors and proclivities of the people in the market that are *invariant* under as many different circumstances as possible. Thus, if people, no matter what circumstance they are in, fear death, then the fear of death is a *realistic* assumption to make about the causes of human behavior wherever a threat to a person's life becomes relevant—and its validity increases with the number of times in which we have tested this assumption and found that it holds up. Eschewing realism on the grounds that *complete realism is unattainable* is a useful ploy but no more: it is akin to saying that a commitment to justice is unwarranted because *cosmic justice* is unattainable or that a commitment to truth is unwarranted because *total* truthfulness is unattainable: they are surely less attainable the weaker our commitments to them are.

Theories as the Building Blocks of Institutions: Knowledge as a Form of Power

The use of ideas to increase one's causal powers is not limited to the interactions between individuals or between individual writers or thinkers and their audience. Michel Foucault (1972), for example, argued persuasively that the language in which people talk about biological disease, crime, and mental disease serves the commitment that dominant social classes have to institutions of social control such as the hospital, the prison, and the mental asylum. The prison and the police appear not as rational measures against or logical consequences of crime and criminality but as the generators of crime and criminality. To establish control over disruptions, social actors create the language in which we think of people who take goods without paying for them (thieves), transfer money from someone else's account into their own (con artists and fraud perpetrators), and inject themselves with substances that are controlled by the state or sell these substances for a profit to others (drug users and drug dealers). "Criminality" is a useful construction, a pragmatic use of language in the service of the will to power:

At the end of the eighteenth century people dreamed of a society without crime. And then the dream evaporated. Crime was too useful for them to dream of anything as crazy—or ultimately as dangerous—as a society without crime. No crime means no police. What makes the presence and control of the police tolerable for the population, if not fear of the criminal? This institution of the police, which is so recent and so oppressive, is only justified by that fear. If we accept this presence in our midst of these uniformed men, who have the exclusive right to carry arms, who demand our papers, who come and prowl on our doorsteps, how would any of this be possible if there were no criminals? And if there weren't articles every day in the newspapers telling us how numerous and dangerous our criminals are? (Foucault 1972, p. 73.)

Far from transforming thieves and murderers into honest people, Foucault (1981, p. 73) argues, the prison criminalizes them further because it involves them in a circle of delinquency, punishment, and disoriented exit into a world in which crime is the best solution to the problem of earning a living: "Prisons manufactured delinquents [who] turned out to be useful, and in the economic domain as much as the political. Criminals come in handy. For example, because of the profits that can be made out of the exploitation of sexual pleasure, we find the establishment in the nineteenth century of the great prostitution business, which was possible only thanks to the delinquents who served as the medium for the capitalization of everyday, paid-for sexual pleasure."

This could not be otherwise, for the prison system seemed designed to criminalize the prisoner's subsequent existence: "The moment someone went to prison a mechanism came into operation that stripped him of his civil status, and when he came out he could do nothing except become a criminal once again. He inevitably fell into the hands of a system which made him either a pimp, a policeman or an informer. Prison professionalized people. Instead of having nomadic bands of robbers—often of great ferocity—roaming about the countryside, as in the eighteenth century, one had this closed milieu of delinquency, thoroughly structured by the police" (Foucault 1981, p. 74).

The workings of the penal system thus produced—rather than being produced by—the seventeenth- and eighteenth-century thinking on crime and criminals. As a social institution vying for causal powers with other institutions (such as the church and the military), the penal-judiciary system needed to create a legitimate language for rationalizing its existence and expanding its causal powers further into people's minds and actions: "Knowledge and power are integrated with one another, and there is no point in dreaming of a time when knowledge will cease to depend on power. . . . It is not possible for power to be exercised without knowledge, it is impossible for knowledge not to engender power" (Foucault 1981, p. 75).

In economic science, it is language that confers the profession power over individual minds and bodies. Economic approaches posit that people are self-maximizing agents, meaning that they choose so as to maximize their personal gain from an interpersonal interaction. It is irrational, by this logic, to offer someone more than one cent when you are given $10 to divide between the two of you according to your discretion, when the only alternative to this agreement is that you will both lose the $10. It is also irrational for that person to decline your offer. Yet experiments time and again find people in the "driver's seat" offering more than the minimum amount—except if they are schooled in the axioms of microeconomics. It is as if the axioms of economic science lend the individual an image of himself and a lens through which he views the world that he is not fully conscious of. He simply projects this lens onto his predicaments and others' behavior to justify his own actions. It is the unconscious acceptance of mythology by the apprentice and the layman that gives theorists their causal powers over the world: Marx was the first of the master theorists to speculate this opportunity systematically—an ambition of which he did not make a secret.

The Intimate Struggle: The Self as a Battlefield

Foucault takes the idea of power struggle further—to the intrapersonal level, to the level of a struggle for power over one's own body. He finds it in the conflict between parents and children over the child's sexual desires and expressions in his discussion of the evolution of autoeroticism:

Children masturbate. Via the medium of families, though not at their initiative, a system of control of sexuality . . . is established over the bodies of children. But sexuality, though thus becoming an object of analysis and concern, surveillance and control, engenders at the same time an intensification of each individual's desire, for, in and over his body. The body thus became the issue of a conflict between parents and children, the child and the instances of control. The revolt of the sexual body is the reverse effect of this encroachment. What is the response on the side of power? An economic exploitation of eroticization, from sun-tan products to pornographic films. Responding precisely to the revolt of the body, we find a new mode of investment, which presents itself (in the form of) control by stimulation. "Get undressed—but be slim, good-looking, tanned!" For each move by one adversary, there is an answering one by another. (Foucault 1981, p. 83)

Looking at past issues of *Cosmopolitan, Seventeen, Esquire, GQ,* and *Vanity Fair,* it seems as if we are witnessing the Playboyification of American media: we have Cindy Crawford half-dressed, Cindy Crawford with ever smaller bikinis, Cindy Crawford with no brassiere, with pink, white, blue, black, red, and yellow panties of various cuts, Cindy Crawford nude, and so forth. The revolt of the body has found its expression in the lavishly photographed glorification of terse, tight, tanned flesh. But with each piece of clothing removed from a woman's body on the cover of the major magazines, sex and skin recede in importance from the oeuvre of the magazines as a whole. Skin has become commodified, and the indifference and everydayness of sexual encounters is suggested by the fake smiles of the models. The dialectic of desire and trivialization continues.

Frustrated Desires and the Knot of Organizational Politics

Intrapersonal dialectics are the *intimate contests for control*—as Tom Schelling (1984) puts it—of the body by various "selves" who want to assert themselves. We want to be "in control"—of ourselves, if of no one else—and the specter of "losing control" brings up the image of the madman, whose existence and authenticity of feeling we would rather sometimes deny or hide. And "being in control" is invariably asserted by wielding one's causal powers on people and objects that one comes into contact with. Let us look at that caldron of frustrated desire that inspired

Marx to write his anathemas against servility—the assembly line (based on a real case). Imagine it:

You are sweaty and tired, but you must keep on the plastic apron that scratches against your skin to dip metal plates into an acid bath before the next person down the assembly line can apply a coat of finish. Your breaks to go to the bathroom and your bodily needs such as stretching and walking about must all be synchronized to the great grid of people that keeps sending you a metal part every few minutes. Your freedom to think your thoughts is only apparent because you cannot absently dip the sheet into the acid bath without running the risk of burning yourself. And if it were only *your* burn! But it's not. There is your wife, who would no doubt scold you endlessly for being careless and "throwing away" your children's future because of your indolence. She already suspects you of it.

You are not even in control of your own flesh. You cannot think the phrase "Fuck it all" while holding the plate above the acid because the ensuing temptation to splash the plate or to kick the acid basin may prove impossible to resist. Your causal powers have been reduced to naught. You are but an effect waiting to be caused, that just happens to trigger other effects downstream. You are a mere link in a causal chain whose origins you do not see.

And so is your assembly-line mate—the one who is feeding you the plates. Can't he see that you are tired, that you would rather be elsewhere? Can't he see the infinite boredom of the flesh that colors gray your actions? He is feeding you the metal parts for dipping in the acid in the same way that you are feeding the next fellow down the line the metal parts for coating. There is no intention, only habit. There is no causation, only an automatic response to an external cause.

Now a bell rings, signaling the passage of another hour. Some workers get up and leave. You watch them and make a mental note of who they are. Later, when you will leave, you will punch them out on the old factory time piece so that they will also collect overtime pay along with you late workers. Presently you think no more of it; but later, a smile might light up at the thought of the deed. At last, intention! For the first time in your day, you are making something happen that falls outside of the mechanical rules of the factory floor. That punching out of the workers who left early is your doing. That cannot be denied. Sure, they will punch you out late in exchange on some other day, but this is merely a side benefit, one that you might enjoy, but not the cause of your breaking "the rules," just as return favors will not be what will motivate them to punch you out. This is purely a work of love, one that you all share and brings you together—the love of self-determination. In breaking the rules you are, at last and only for an instant, your own agent. Although you and the others could get jobs with higher hourly pay and better conditions elsewhere, you choose to stay with this arrangement because you feel validated as an agent on your own behalf by the little dance around the time piece. Moreover, the fact that you choose to stay in spite of having the option to work elsewhere for better pay further increases you feeling of autonomy. You are not, alas, an automaton, a sucker for cash, like so many in factory, line, and white-collar jobs around the world. No, you are free to choose to earn less in exchange for greater liberty, and that choice, once made, gives you a feeling of liberation.

Of course, the managers may be well aware of these thoughts of the worker. Even so, they choose not to do anything about it—no rules imposed from the top to stop the "cheating," no moralistic drivel about fairness and equity, no dismissal of the recalcitrants: "We know all about it, yet choose to do nothing," they reason. "We are powerful enough to do nothing, even though we know about it. This is the true test of our causal powers: mercy, or the free choice to do nothing even though we very well could do something and blow the little game up sky-high." The workers, in turn, may know the managers know all about it and do nothing, but they interpret it as a sign of their own causal powers: "Even though they know about it, they do not dare do anything. They know they cannot find skilled labor to replace us and work in these conditions. We have them at our mercy." The managers may also know the workers know the managers know about it and do nothing still. They will interpret this as a further sign of their causal powers: "The greatest power is that of which the subject of the powerful is unaware. These workers think they have us by the balls, when in fact . . ."

Consider the ivory tower of academia and the predicament of a tenured faculty member at a top-rated university. Presumably, we have gone from depths of servility in our previous example to heights of autonomy. But have we? The tenured professor has gained relative autonomy in his teaching and research activities. He is no longer feeling that he must return even the most despicably fake smile from a senior colleague to avoid jeopardizing his chances at a tenured position. "And for such a trifle as a smile," he might hear the voice of reason—perhaps his wife's or his mother's—ringing in his ears every time he would like to smash the fake smile with a steel bar.

Things are now different. No longer is he slavishly required to show up at all of the meaningless meetings that have given the word "boredom" a new meaning for him—all out of the fear that he will be thought slothful, ignorant, arrogant, or clueless by someone with decision rights over a piece of his fate. Now he is presumably free to experiment, to taste new intellectual fruit, to run real-time experiments on fellow faculty members and students and janitors to unravel the mysterious structures that hold groups and individual people together and write the theory of theories that he has dreamt about for a long time, to say his thoughts as they come to him, uncalculatively, without concern for the consequences that speaking his mind might have for his career.

And does he? Does he finally dare to smile when everyone else tries hard to show pity or remorse or sickly sweet concern for someone they feel nothing for? Or to raise the obvious objection that a piece of research is incoherent when everyone else basks in the Nobel credentials of the speaker? Perhaps, but only as an exception. The fight over causal powers that he must carry out for each to feel "in control" begins anew among the tenured few. "Sure, I got tenure on the basis of my hard work and quick wit," his story might go, "but can I make an impact on the rest of the school and the rest of the field?" Mere job security, he now sees, is for mere mortals—Hegel's slaves. What he desires is fame—causal powers over the minds of others.

How to accomplish it? The most immediate lever—the most visible sign of influence—is the appointment of junior faculty to tenured or almost-tenured positions. "Did you hear about what he pulled off?" he can hear his colleagues whisper about him among themselves, after he engineers the appointment of some smart but unruly young colleague to an important position from which tenure could be an easy target.

Alternatively, he might hear, "He's losing his ability to make things happen," after a no-tenure decision is passed on someone who did not ingratiate himself with the "others." Sure, there are always reasons and justifications that his colleagues will bring to mollify him: the rejected did not contribute to the group's research focus, he did not display the qualities of a team player, his ideas were over the edge. But, the tenured mentor quickly realizes, at the core of the appointment process there always was a test of his causal powers and of the causal powers of the more junior, newly tenured professors which they asserted by turning him down. In the world of power, there are no games in which everyone wins.

Doubt and Self-Doubt: The Intrapersonal Dialectic of Assertion and Subversion

We can see Joseph Stalin's bloody trek through history as the acting out of a painful intrapersonal dialectic—the dialectic of assertion and subversion. There was a fictitious self, an idealized vision whose name was "Stalin"—the man of steel, one of the greatest men of Russian history, and an infallible leader of the Soviet people—who was engaged in a life-and-death struggle for causal powers over the man's body with one Iosif

Dzugashvilli (Stalin's real name)—a small-time revolutionary and mediocre priest oppressed in his youth by his brutish father and intellectually frustrated later on by the lively intellects of Vladimir I. Lenin, Nicolai I. Bukharin, and Leon Trotsky.

The imaginary Stalin borrows with fervor from the giants of history—the "father of the people" epithet from the tsars for himself, the "enemies of the people" epithet from Robespierre. He passes himself off as an authority on arts, music, and all branches of science, coercing—according to Dmitri Volkogonov's (1991) biography—authors into sending him their manuscripts before publication, so that they may not incur his wrath for sending to print something that did not pass his scrutiny beforehand.

There is, however, always the suspicion that Iosif Dzugashvilli is still around, that "Stalin" comes to nothing. Trying to repress the suspicion is akin to trying to repress the thought of "white bears" by an act of the will. So Stalin "acts out the repression" and murders, systematically, all those in whom he hears the whisper: "Dzugashvilli, I know thee." And the number of his victims increases as he tries to repress his inner voices by murdering others. With each fresh murder, doubts spring up with doubled force, and they dance before his eyes, incarnated in new faces, whom he feels compelled to smash. Instead of realizing that it is the ghost of Dzugashvilli that he is trying to murder in his former friends and comrades, he instead sees the ghost of victims past at work in the deeds of victims future:

For Stalin, Trotsky had become the personification of universal evil. . . . Stalin saw "the hand of Trotsky" in every failure or disaster. In the political trials of 1937–38 one of the main charges was that of maintaining direct links with Trotsky, receiving his orders and instructions, and even meeting with him in Berlin or Oslo. [Trotsky had whispered, "Dzugashvilli, I know thee."] Being enormously envious and ambitious, he could not but feel his intellectual and moral inferiority every step of the way. . . . Only much later did I realize that he had been trying to establish some sort of familiar relations. But I was repelled by the very qualities that would strengthen him . . . namely, the narrowness of his interests, his pragmatism, his psychological coarseness and the special cynicism of the provincial who has been liberated from his prejudices by Marxism but who has not replaced them with a philosophical outlook that has been thoroughly thought out and mentally absorbed. (Volkogonov 1991, p. 157)

Like a whispering gallery of mirrors, Stalin's world would resonate with Trotsky's words, which, like whispers in a gallery, could not be silenced by the murder of the whisperers.

5
Envy and Jealousy: The Master Ratchets

Destruction—aught with Evil bent
That is my proper element.
—Mephistopheles in J. W. Goethe, *Faust*, part 1, scene 3

I never got more than the leavings of life, and when I couldn't even get those anymore, I started taking something from other people's lives.
—Convicted serial killer Stephen Nash, on his reason for stabbing to death eleven people

What we are asking is that the rich pay their fair share of taxes.
—U.S. President William Clinton

Someone will win the lottery—just not you.
—Billboard advertisement on I-93 entering Boston, 1999

Everyone's getting rich but me.
—*Newsweek* cover, July 5, 1999

When two people desire the same object and only one gets it, the other may feel a causally potent negative emotion that entreats him to sabotage or destruction. On the other hand, knowing that one has gotten something that another desires can engender a warm feeling (the happiness predicated on the misery of another that Dostoyevsky wrote about) that one may try to hide by feigning compassion. Finally, desiring something that another already has but that one could see himself as possibly having gotten can generate frustration and a desire to harm the endowed and lessen his enjoyment of his predicament. Covetous resentment, hypocritical compassion, and festering frustration are three faces of envy, the master ratchet of everyday emotions.

Subjunctives and Counterfactuals: Envy's Bait

If ambition is mobilized by answers to the question "What could I have or be?," envy makes its subject vibrate to the questions "What could I have had or been?" and "What if I had won rather than lost?" Max Scheler (in Schoeck 1969, p. 67) traces envy to the psychology of causation and control and sees it as a sensation of impotence—the frustration of causal might,

> which inhibits the striving after a possession that belongs to another. The tension between such striving and such impotence only leads to envy, however, when it is discharged into an act of hatred or vindictive behavior towards the owner of the possession; when, that is, owing to a delusion, the other with his possession is experienced as the cause of our painful failure to have the possession. . . . Genuine envy is no more possible without the particular experience of such impotence than it is without the causal delusion.

To envy, we must think it plausible that we could have had what the envied has but that we cannot get it. We see its possession by another as a sign of our impotence and therefore as a failure of our causal powers—the objects of our ambitious desires.

The Inner Work of Envy

Envy is the passion we long to hide—and that we are skilled at hiding from. Helmut Schoeck (1969), in his monograph entitled *Envy,* engages in a search-and-destroy mission targeted at well-known social and psychological phenomena: destruction by reduction to an envy-based mechanism. Ingeniously he traces the phenomenon of conformity to the subjective feeling of envy. He argues that Solomon Asch's experiments in the 1950s (showing that people asked to judge the relative length of a line segment will often defer to the opinion of a majority of experiment participants who—without the subject's knowledge—have been paid to give the wrong answer), as well as Stanley Milgram's experiments (replicating the findings in the United States, France, and Norway substituting relative tone duration for relative segment length) show a fear of "standing out" borne of the fear of becoming the object of envious feelings or envious retaliation. Milgram added a condition in his experiment wherein people did not have to state their opinions publicly: they could simply write them down on a secret ballot, which would not be revealed to the "others" who made up the coercive majority. He found, once again, a high rate of conformity—higher in the case of the Norwegians than of the French. One Norwegian subject explained, "I tried to put myself in a public situation, even though I was sitting at the booth in private"—lending support to the idea that an other-directed sentiment, such as envy, does not need a clear and present other for its embodiment.

Greek tragedy presented the misfortunes of mortals as the envy of the gods. In Aeschylus's play, Agamemnon arrives at home victorious from his campaign in Troy and walks on the red carpet that his wife Clytemnestra has laid out for him, while the chorus raises a soliloquy toward the Athenian sky, beckoning the glances of the gods:

Rare are those mortals who a friend arrayed
In fortune's smiles with eyes unenvying view:
The fateful poison rankling at the heart
A double smart inflicts; the sufferer mourns
His own peculiar woes—then at the sight
Of others more successful, sighs again.
I know mankind full well, nor need to learn
That empty as the shadow of a shade
Are many who with smiles my presence hail.
(Svendt Ranulf, in Schoeck 1969, p. 75)

Clytemnestra's beckoning—(according to Ranulf's interpretation of Aeschylus) is itself a temptation to the gods. Agamemnon, by accepting her honors and caresses, stands to draw their envious wrath. Half-conscious, he senses the danger and tells his wife,

Reserve such honors for the gods; frail man
Should tremble for himself when he delights
With stately mien to tread o'er gorgeous robes.
(p. 75)

but walks over the carpet anyway and does not excoriate Clytemnestra for her indecent remarks:

We shall never lack for purple carpets,
We have never learnt what it is to be poor.
(p. 76)

And do we not recognize Agamemnon's anxiety in ourselves? Think of a coveted promotion or contract or of a hoped-for letter of acceptance to an organization you long to belong to. Are you wary that talking of it confidently will jinx you? What is jinxing about jinxes is the belief that the expression of immodest confidence in your eventual success will *cause* your project to fail. Whatever causal powers you have (your little voices silently whisper), they themselves causally depend on the goodwill of the One who listens to every thought and word. Hence the obsessive fear of the jinx—which stretches not only to your own words but also to the words that you would allow others to utter in your presence.

Envy in Action: Resentment and the Drive to Destroy

Resentment drives the envious to action, for envy alone is not causally potent, as Immanuel Kant noted: "The impulse for envy is . . . inherent in the nature of man, and only its manifestation makes of it an abominable vice, a passion not only distressing and tormenting to the subject, but intent on the destruction of the happiness of others, and one that is opposed to man's duty towards himself and towards other people" (Kant 1985, p. 27).

But for resentment, envy would not be identified with malice, as it is in Milton's poem about cosmic passions, when Adam says to Eve:

. . . for thou know'st
What hath been warned us, what malicious foe,
Envying our happiness, and of his own
Despairing, seeks to work our woe and shame
By sly assault; and somewhere nigh at hand
Watches, no doubt, with greedy hope to find
His wish and best advantage, us asunder,
Hopeless to circumvent us joined, where each
To other speedy aid might lend at need:
Whether his first design be to withdraw
Our fealty from God, or to disturb
Conjugal love, than which perhaps no bliss
Enjoyed by us excites his envy more . . . .
(*Paradise Lost* 9.252–264)

His words are echoed by Satan himself:

Revenge, at first thought sweet,
Bitter ere long, back on itself recoils:
Let it; I reck not, so it light well aimed,
Since higher I fall short, on him who next
Provokes my envy, this new favourite
Of heav'n, this man of clay, son of despite,
Whom us the more to spite, his Maker raised
From dust: spite then with spite is best repaid.
(*Paradise Lost* 9.171–178)

Envy needs to be aroused to malice and spite for it to become causally potent; it needs a proximal stimulus. It frequently finds it because envy sees another's actions as envious, therefore potentially threatening, and therefore worthy objects of preemption or retaliation: "spite then with spite is best repaid." Satan sees *himself* in God and imputes his own motive to "his Maker." Once duly drugged by his own image, he interprets God's acts as themselves spiteful and thus rescues his own spiteful act as righteous, in the sense that it justly reciprocates spite: "spite then with spite is best repaid."

We might find resonances in daily emotional experience. How many of us can rescue a friend from a judgment that we have made about him? Have we judged him to be envious? Well, then whatever he does—even if an act of apparently unsolicited kindness—is secretly moved by his envy in our eyes. We think that he is acting either to try to dispel our idea of him (temporarily) or to publicize his lack of envy—to "do us one better." In this sense, then, envy is a master passion: for the envious sees his actions determined by the actions of people themselves moved by envy and does not fail to find the envy motive in everyone's actions. Amazed at the reliability of his own theory of human nature, he acts on it—having failed to look within himself as the source of the sentiment.

The Enemy Nearby: Envy and Proximity

Nothing begets plausibility like vividness, and vividness is a phenomenon of proximity. Schoeck (1969, p. 80)—who sees envy as a potent emotional kernel that accounts for many social phenomena—writes that "envy is above all a phenomenon of social proximity: American sociologists use the term 'invidious proximity' or, in other words, proximity that arouses envy. Envy is always between neighbors. The envious man thinks that if a neighbor breaks a leg, he will be able to walk better himself." Raymond Boudon (1981) notes that envy reaches its greatest levels in quasi-egalitarian societies, where people can "just see" themselves enjoying the same possession and status enjoyed by their neighbors but not by themselves ("I could have had it, but I won't"). Thus, physical proximity and proximity in relative standing both encourage envy among men and women.

You may envy the power of some corporate officer or the body of some model but not be moved to violent action or even to bitter thoughts by your envy. You may "put them out of your mind." But what if you had to take a bath after your bathtub was used by a person with a more beautiful body than yours and had to do so every day? You might imagine her body fitting lazily in the bathtub, her face pouting with simulated coquetry at the mirror on the wall. You might sense her excitement at examining her breasts in the mirror, tickled by the anticipation of yet another date with a handsome male who will lick her nipples. These thoughts come to you every day—perhaps several times in one day—and give you a feeling of malaise that spoils what used to be happy bedtimes.

And then, quite suddenly, you cannot take it anymore. One evening, you slash her face with the blade from an opened-up razor, and then horrified by your deed and honestly frightened by the consequences of her telling on you, you cut into her throat with a kitchen knife. Far-fetched? In 1959, a newspaper in Swannanoa, North Carolina, ran the headline "Co-ed Chopped in Envy May Be Disfigured" and went on to detail how Patricia Dennis, a student at Warren Wilson College, murdered Rose Watterson, her roommate, by striking her with a hatchet. The four hatchet blows fell between the young woman's eyes and her throat. Schoeck saw photographs of the two women that showed that Rose Watterson was prettier than Patricia Dennis, who appeared to be hostile and slightly overweight: "At the first hearing she stated her motive to have been jealousy and envy of her prettier room-mate" (Schoeck 1969, p. 82).

Envy and the Dynamics of the Growing Organization

Now suppose that you are the president of the fastest-growing company in your industry. The firm is staffed by technical wizards and hot-shot graduates from the nation's top business schools, and its atmosphere of excitement and internal competition is called "friendly" by some employees to pardon their slightly animalic behavior toward each another. Everyone seemingly wants to be part of the new firm—the firm that will make computers for the next millennium. "The thousand-year operating system," you think inwardly but do not dare scream it because of associations with the thousand-year reich that might cause public disapproval. In this atmosphere, you spot two young women—pretty, clever, ambitious. You've read Schoeck's book, and you smile inwardly: have they also spotted each other?

They have indeed. The upstart proposes a whole new way to approach manufacturing strategy for the entire firm. She is young and inexperienced, but she has seen where to strike. The expert oversees the manufacturing strategy of the firm. Her planning and execution have pinpoint precision. She is well-respected by her peers, bosses, friends, and colleagues. But the upstart is daring. She has convinced the firm's founder—an upstart himself—that the new strategy makes sense, and he is helping her put it forward. He calls himself a visionary but is, in your view, a showman who impersonates a real visionary with uncanny accuracy.

Still, "If one impersonates a visionary really well, does not one become a visionary?" you ask yourself, but that is your own envious little voice. You want to encourage the "cat fight" and carry out your own experiment. So you do not stomp on the upstart but encourage her. Her project has gathered steam and is speeding along. The expert must be green with envy. Of course, they see only one another and no one else; they are the only women on the floor. People in the firm are taking notice of the upstart's plans. And—what is this?—a committee is being set up to evaluate the different manufacturing strategies that the firm might take. You approve it yourself but feel that you have no choice: you have to see the denouement of this little episode. Now, the bomb: the expert gives an ultimatum to her boss. Either she heads the team that is doing the appraisal of different strategies, or she leaves. He acquiesces—after he calls you, that is. How could you say no? This was the perfect opportunity to find a way to keep both of these talented women with the firm. Of course, you take her recommendation. Of course, she feels good. Of course, you fire her from her position afterward and name the upstart to the position of worldwide director of manufacturing. Of course, you bring back the expert to a position of responsibility. This way, each can feel that she has won, without either admitting of her envy or feeling hurt in the process. Of course.

Jealousy: The Guardian of the Extended Self

If envy engenders resentment toward the one who has what you could have had, jealousy engenders resentment toward the one who might take away or diminish what you now have. "What could I lose—and how could I lose it?" asks the jealous self, and she does not tire of finding fresh objects of resentment. Everyone—and anyone—could be coveting what is now *yours,* and they are about to try to get it: that is the belief at the core of the raw feel of envy.

Imagine that you are at a party at a friend's house with your new fiancée. You secretly feel tickled that a woman with such lengthy and slender legs has chosen you as her mate—though you cannot consciously admit this to yourself. That evening, you notice that your friend—an athletic character with searching eyes—has asked her to dance to a slow and wistful tune. She smiles at him—beguilingly? Of course, how can you have overlooked it until now? You watch her watching him watching her and cannot but feel that her smile is there *in spite* of your presence: she is completely carried away with the dance. And look at how he responds to her undulations: he, too seems to have forgotten about you.

Over a drink, *en passant,* you remark on the way her body was taken up in the dance with the athletic male. "But I knew you were there, darling," she says ("Implying what exactly?" you ask yourself). Well, there are several possibilities. She may have been trying to make you jealous by signaling affection for the long-legged fellow, thus acting on her own jealous suspicions that you are interested in your friend's wife. Or ("How devious," you now think) she may be trying to hide her lust under the guise of her own jealousy, which she assumes that you are simple-minded enough to empathize with: she knows, after all, of your own jealousy, since you have just revealed it to her.

Later that evening, you try to point out to her the simple-minded nature of your friend and remind her of his smell, which you suspect that she dislikes: what does the smile she responds with mean? More agony: does she see through your (all too common) emotions and smiles derisively, or rather does she indeed agree, and is she simply amused at having made you more jealous? What if she has already figured out what you think she thinks you think? This hell will now go on forever! Will her eyes be seeing him while you are making love? And if you ask her outright, what will her answer mean? "Of course, not dear," she will say—and there goes the enigmatic smile again, driving you deeper and deeper into resentment of your now-former friend. You do not miss a turn to skewer him. "He has become so ugly!" you once come home saying, feeling very real and authentic inside. But no amount of skewering suffices: you have the vision of their bodies talking to each other in the language of a slow swinging song, and any response she gives you will be seen through that lens. "She is denying it!" you say to yourself if she agrees with your slurs. "Aha! She is defending him," you will think if she points out that you are being too harsh. Every action that you aim at extricating you from this jealous hell ends up digging you deeper into it. After a while, you come to bore her, and you envy the serenity with which she sometimes watches you struggle.

The Inner Work of Jealousy

Jealousy, like other emotions, can be the creator of cultural structures. The oft-cited incest taboo in many societies can be given a simple explanation in terms of jealousy: no family can survive the acting out of jealous resentment that would result from sexual relations between parents and their favorite children, between brothers and their favorite sisters, and so forth. And no society without a strong nuclear family unit has been known to survive over extended periods of time (Murdock 1960). How does it work? As always in the case of the emotions, a little introspection can take us a long way toward understanding the phenomena involved. Think of a current or potential lover, and think also of a mutual acquaintance that he or she could be attracted to. Observe your feelings as you play through images of a sexual liaison between the two of them: of jealousy, perhaps, of the loved one, of envy and perhaps resentment of the acquaintance that has now turned into a stranger or even an enemy. Now imagine that you had to live with *both* of them in the same house and watch the unfolding idyll every day. Your nights are no longer quiet—for you don't know whether your love is taking advantage of your deep sleep to slip away from your bed to visit his or her other lover. Sleepless jealousy quickly turns into resentment and anger, and you may find yourself plotting an accident by which the third person should meet his or her end.

Now imagine that your lover is a brother or sister and the third person is a cousin. Since you all share a large tent, you watch cautiously over your sibling's lustful gazes at your cousin. Indeed, all of your productive hours turn into a seamless web of brooding, watching, and obsessing over the two people who have ensnared your mind. You cannot go for a moment without images of them cuddling together under some sheepskin—and you spend your days trying to find the sign that will prove their guilt to you. Since you are not looking to prove their innocence, no news can ever be good news, although no news at all is also bad news. All this means to you is that you have not *yet* found them out: there is always tomorrow and one thousand more tomorrows after that. Your lover cannot stand the psychological torture you are putting him through and now does indeed turn to a cousin to whom he feels that he can talk freely. Now you interpret their dialogues as living proof for your suspicions and endlessly reproach him his infidelity; his own life, in turn, becomes centered around denying your wild allegations and bringing forth "proofs" of his innocence.

It is too late to let up, however: you think you perceive some desperate nuance in his denials and use this brilliant insight to construe each denial as a fresh proof of his guilt: why would he deny something unless he really did it? Envy has become the ruler of your days, and stilling your envy the primary concern of your relatives. But in your small agricultural community, the three of you figure heavily in the family's material fortunes: you are the youngest and strongest in the tent, and therefore the timely turnover of the earth and the tilling of the soil for the spring seeding depends almost entirely on your efforts. Nevertheless, the soil goes unbroken this spring, and now the family may have to give up some of the land in the fall to share in the harvest of the others in the village.

Envy, Jealousy, and the Logic of Initiation Rites

The resentment that comes from envy and jealousy can fuel the severe initiation rituals facing young tribesmen, new members of university-level fraternities and dormitories, intern and resident physicians in North America, and nontenured academics and graduate research assistants in universities around the world. "Why should you get away without going through what I had to go through?" asks the envious, who becomes, by his or her "correct" behavior, the strictest enforcer that a status quo can have. Envy can serve as the guarantor of the continuity of institutions.

Consider now how envy and jealousy could work hand in hand in a major teaching hospital to maximize revenues and minimize costs for the hospitals and the attending physicians who hold most of the executive power. Residency training periods for young physicians are physically difficult and promote a narrowly self-obsessed "when am I going to sleep?" attitude among them. These periods involve as many as three twenty-four-hour shifts in a single week, during which the intern or resident may be kept up continuously by demands from nurses who seek their assistance in caring for patients. Higher-year residents and fellows usually are allowed extended periods of sleep in special sleeping rooms in the hospital, and attending physicians stay at home and are usually spared the experience of asomnia by the residents' fear of waking them and incurring their wrath.

Envy and jealousy keep this machine going (and serve an overall profit-making goal of the senior physicians). Attending physicians enforce the requirements for twenty-four-hour shifts by strongly discouraging residents' attempts to escape the sleepless toil by invoking illness or personal circumstances. This role of guardianship is grounded in a sentiment best captured by a simple rhetorical question: "Why should they get it easier than we ever got it?"

Higher-year residents may frown on first-year residents' calls for help at night ("No one got up for us when we needed them. Why should we do it now?") because being third-year residents means they have gone through a difficult first year. Lessening the burden of the first-year residents therefore directly lessens the value of being a higher-year resident. Jealousy turns the evil eye on the usurper of one's hard-earned personal myth: the myth has to be guarded against the young usurpers.

Some nurses may be envious of the young residents' higher status and future financial perspectives and thus do not miss any opportunity to wake them up to request their assistance. Beginning residents envy each other's opportunities for sleep and professional achievements and jealously guard their own opportunities for rest and relaxation; thus they are reluctant to help one another by filling in for each other or sharing each other's duties.

The system as a whole could not have been more neatly designed for the maximum financial payoff to the hospital: most of the work is done by the lowest-paid physicians who can still be charged a physician's rate to insurance companies—precisely the first-year residents and interns that the network of envy singles out. Here the passions together conspire to produce an economically efficient—and proficient—entity, just as Vico had envisioned a few centuries ago.

Now, the tragedy arises: a young woman, admitted to a teaching hospital with a routine ear infection, dies while in the care of the staff. Her case is not one for which the attending physicians can fashion a quick and ready explanation in an unintelligible dialect. There is a simple reason for this: her father is a prominent lawyer. He knows all about the power of words to soothe minds into believing far-fetched explanations. He cannot have his daughter back, but he would like to understand the all-too-human causes of her death. He wants not revenge but insight. Ear infections are not considered to be fatal conditions. So what happened?

A jury examines the incidents surrounding his daughter's death and concludes that no one acted criminally. However, jury members fault the system of medical training for placing patients' lives in the hands of undertrained, overworked physicians. The criticism is met with silence for almost two years until papers begin to appear in academic journals, whose pages are the only means of systematic and inclusive communication for people who have academic pretensions. By now, emotions are somewhat more muted.

An attending physician then writes a scholarly mea culpa on behalf of his profession. He acknowledges that sleep deprivation may lead to slowness and poor performance in interns. But he is reluctant to suggest the obvious remedy—increasing the number of residents working at teaching hospitals. His own status as a survivor of the internship period will, after all, be threatened by the change. It is something that must be guarded. The stronger the emotion with which he guards it, however, the lesser the coherence of his arguments: he argues that nursing shortages are more responsible than sleeplessness for mistakes (but nurses don't make clinical decisions), that foreign medical graduates are incompetent (but foreign medical graduates did not care for the young woman), and that too few people graduate from American medical schools (but admission rates are kept among the lowest of any graduate schools by restrictive policies enforced by the American Medical Association). The greater the energy with which he guards his status, the greater its unresponsiveness to counter-arguments. But he knows that his flawed arguments take second place to money as the master persuaders, so he is a regular, contributing member of the American Medical Association (which is second only to the National Rifle Association in dollars spent lobbying the U.S. Congress), which has been set up to guard the status quo.

Envy's Master Narratives: *The Communist Manifesto*

Karl Marx and Friedrich Engels (1963) wrote *The Communist Manifesto* as if they intuitively understood the sway of envy on their readers' minds. It is—among many other things—a masterful appeal to envy: "The history of all hitherto existing society is the history of class struggles. Free man and slave, patrician and plebeian, lord and serf, guild master and journeyman, in a word, oppressor and oppressed, stood in constant opposition to one another, carried on an uninterrupted, now hidden, now open fight, a fight that each time ended either in a revolutionary reconstitution of society at large or in the common ruin of the contending classes" (p. 2).

Who are you? they ask. An employee? Then do you not see that your will has been subjected to the ambition of another person, who is reaping the benefits of your labor? A surgeon? Then do you not see that you are part of a system designed to line the pockets of health-care providers, that your actions are but instruments used for the benefit of their managers and share-holders? A teacher? Whose theories are you teaching? Would your paychecks keep on coming and would your tenure committee still vote for you if you decided to speak your mind and live out your will? So you go on living in an intellectually castrated state. Do you not see, common man, that in the domain of the will a zero-sum game is being played? Do you not see that others are always getting what you could have had, that you should have gotten what you could have had, and therefore that others are getting what *you* should have had? And how do you feel about it? Do you not feel as if someone else is making love with your wife?

It takes some doing to show that the causal powers of other people are something that *you* could have had. After all, what if you believe in the moral foundations of the world that you have come to know through the watchful eyes of your parents and teachers? Here is how Marx and Engels go about it: "Law, morality, religion are to (the proletarian) so many bourgeois prejudices, behind which lurk just as many bourgeois interests" (p. 354). In a separate piece, Engels echoes the same "unmasking" of bourgeois values: "Oppression by force was replaced by corruption; the sword, as the first social lever, by gold. The right of the first night was transferred from the feudal lords to the bourgeois manufacturers. Prostitution increased to an extent never heard of. Marriage itself remained, as before, the legally recognized form, the official cloak of prostitution, and, moreover, was supplemented by rich crops of adultery" (Engels 1963, p. 361). Why are "family values" not the same all around, whether or not you are a paid laborer? "The proletarian is without property; his relation to his wife and children has no longer anything in common with the bourgeois family relations; modern industrial labor . . . has stripped him of every trace of national character" (Marx and Engels 1963, p. 354).

Now that the moral foundations of the world have been shown up as shams, one more step is needed to show that you really could have what you currently do not: the ever present possibility of changing your condition through revolutionary action: "The proletarians cannot become masters of the productive forces of society, except by abolishing their own previous mode of appropriation, and thereby also every other mode of appropriation" (p. 355). And now, the appeal to willful destruction—the thunderbolt of envious resentment: the proletarians "have nothing of their own to secure and to fortify; their mission is to destroy all previous securities for, and insurances of, individual property" (p. 355). It is the "mission" of the envious in an excited state to destroy whatever makes the envied enviable. When you feel envious to the point of resentment, do you not wish for the diminishment of the envied?

It really is all right to live out your envious desires, say Marx and Engels. "History" itself is a guarantor of the righteousness of your actions:

Hitherto every form of society has been based, as we have already seen, on the antagonism of oppressing and oppressed classes. But in order to oppress a class certain conditions must be assured to it under which it can, at least, continue its slavish existence. The serf, in the period of serfdom, raised himself to membership in the commune, just as the petty bourgeois, under the yoke of feudal absolutism, managed to develop into the bourgeois. The modern laborer, on the contrary, instead of rising with the progress of industry, sinks deeper and deeper below the conditions of existence of his own class. He becomes a pauper, and pauperism develops more rapidly than population and wealth. And here it becomes evident that the bourgeoisie is unfit any longer to be the ruling class in society, and to impose its conditions of existence upon society as an over-riding law. It is unfit to rule because it is incompetent to assure an existence to its slave within his slavery, because it cannot help letting him sink into such a state that it has to feed him instead of being fed by him. Society can no longer live under this bourgeoisie: in other words, its existence is no longer compatible with society. . . . What the bourgeoisie, therefore, produces, above all, is its own grave diggers. Its fall and the victory of the proletariat are equally inevitable. (p. 355)

History, common man, they say, is on your side: dare to act out your feelings and you shall be rewarded, as those who understand the laws of history are.

Marx's passions move our souls—though we take his reasons to sway our minds. It takes *passion* to see the world communist revolution as the inevitable outcome of world history because we have to ignore the many societies—tribal societies, among others—that do not conform to his analysis. A sort of willful nonseeing can protect us from the damaging facts that refute the master theory. This will is fueled by the desire to not-know what does not immediately further our personal projects. Thus emotion rules the mind's eye because it has enslaved the mind's I.

Wielding the Manifesto: Narrative as an Instrument

In the hands of a master propagandist such as Lenin, the envious streaks of the *The Communist Manifesto* are put to efficient use. His practical problem was to take the envy and resentment that the well-to-do aroused when seen through a Marxian lens and turn them against the prevailing political government of Russia. To this end, he starts by diligently quoting Engels (1933, p. 75):

The state is therefore by no means a power imposed on society from the outside; just as little is it "the reality of the moral idea," the "image and reality of reason," as Hegel asserted. Rather, it is the product of society at a certain stage of development; it is the admission that this society has become entangled in an insoluble contradiction with itself, that it is cleft into irreconcilable antagonisms which it is powerless to dispel. But in order that these antagonisms, classes with conflicting economic interests, may not consume themselves and society in sterile struggle, a power apparently standing above society becomes necessary, whose purpose is to moderate the conflict and keep it within the bounds of "order"; and this power arising out of society, but placing itself above it, and increasingly separating itself from it, is the state.

Now Lenin gives the idea of the state a sinister penumbra: "According to Marx, the state is an organ of class domination, an organ of oppression of one class by another; its aim is the creation of 'order' which legalizes and perpetuates this oppression by moderating the collisions between the classes" (p. 383).

He aims at a shift of the worker's feelings toward the capitalist oppressors on the state as the organ of oppression. Indeed, he acknowledges that, in a classless society, a state has no longer a purpose and will therefore "wither away." But he introduces a critical new element: the state that is to wither away *is the proletarian state or semistate*—not the capitalist state, as Engels originally stated. Lenin dangles before the proletarian reader the prospect of an "avenging state," which he calls the dictatorship of the proletariat and which he believes is needed for the sudden transition from capitalism to communism to take place. Watch how he dwells on the repressiveness of the new proletarian state: "The state is a special repressive force. . . . It follows from this that the 'special repressive force' of the bourgeoisie for the suppression of the proletariat, of the millions of workers by a handful of the rich, must be replaced by a 'special repressive force' of the proletariat for the suppression of the bourgeoisie" (p. 392). By what miraculous and heretofore unseen syllogism does this follow? Something else is going on: Lenin creates the motivational state in a reader who feels for the "millions of workers [oppressed] by a handful of the rich" to believe that there really is a relation of logical entailment between Engels's analysis of the bourgeois state and his call for the formation of a dictatorship of the proletariat: And now we shove the crackers down *their* throats, he seems to be saying, like the cartoon character Iago in Walt Disney's *Aladdin:*

Again, during the transition from capitalism to communism, suppression is still necessary; but it is the suppression of the minority of exploiters by the majority of exploited. A special apparatus, special machinery for suppression is still necessary, but this is now a transitional state, no longer a state in the usual sense, for the suppression of the minority of exploiters, by the majority of the wage slaves of yesterday, is a matter comparatively so easy, simple and natural that it will cost far less bloodshed than the suppression of the risings of slaves, serfs and wage laborers, and will cost mankind far less. (p. 393)

What seems to be doing the work of convincing the reader in these sentences is a locution like "necessary," when in fact it is the prevalent imagery conjured up by "the wage slaves of yesterday" and "the suppression of the risings of slaves, serfs and wage laborers" that is getting the reader to see Lenin's "necessary" as his or her "necessary." Like the screenwriter of a film noir, Lenin takes the reader to an emotional place where he or she will experience the "right" feelings in conjunction with the "right" scene. Envious resentment is the silent director of the show that Lenin is putting on for us. His imagery arouses envy, which then creates the mindset to accept the logically suspect relations of entailment as persuasive. Lenin grasped that "knowing" means "really wanting to believe," and he makes use of this discovery by giving people a motive for wanting to believe his words: under the elixir of envious resentment, his logic can grasp the reader as impeccable.

The master narratives of envy strike the stringent chords of moral indignation and the search for fairness and justice, just as the master narratives of ambition strike the chords of efficacy, efficiency, and assertiveness. Silicon Valley lore in the late 1990s was full of tales of mindful and confident entrepreneurs who took on the Goliaths of their industries and "won." Moscow, Kiev, and Bucharest lore in the late 1990s was full of tales of "thieves" who made their riches by pillaging the hard-earned money of the man on the street who could not afford to pay his rent. This discrepancy is pointed out to the eastern culture-mongers: "Of course," they retort, snickeringly," the Western criminals are better able to disguise their lies and crimes. Besides, the Western press has always been duped." "Not so," reply the Westerners, outraged: "Western institutions are based on the ideals of truth and transparency. These ideals—embodied in everyday activities—have made it possible to create the abundance, wealth, and freedom of the Silicon Valley entrepreneurs." Each of these mutually dismissive accounts protects its own conclusions from refutation by external arguments. And, we are assured by philosophers and historians of science such as Thomas Kuhn and Pierre Duhem, we *can* always salvage our theories and stories from refutation, given sufficient will and ingenuity. The two worlds continue along separate spirals, downward through time.

Jealousy's Master Narratives: The Case of *Mein Kampf*

Adolf Hitler's writing, on the other hand, stokes one's *jealousy,* or the resentment of another who could (but does not) have what is currently yours. He is concerned with the genetic purity of the German nation—and he makes the German cultural heritage the object of jealous desire and therefore the reason for jealous resentment:

Any crossing between two beings of not quite the same high standard produces a medium between the standards of the parents. That means: the young one will probably be on a higher level than the racially lower parent, but not as high as the higher one. Consequently, it will succumb later on in the fight against the higher level. But such a mating contradicts Nature's will to breed life as a whole towards a higher level. The presumption for this does not lie in blending the superior with the inferior, but rather in a complete victory of the former. The stronger has to rule and he is not to amalgamate with the weaker one, that he may not sacrifice his own greatness. (Hitler 1963, p. 442)

Just in case you did not get the metaphor, Hitler gives an example that drives home the jealousy theme: "The fight for daily bread makes all those succumb who are weak, sickly and less determined, while the males' fight for the female gives the right of propagation, or the possibility of it, only to the most healthy" (p. 442). But, Hitler asserts, we are not talking about common emotions but rather about the will of nature itself: "the fight is always a means for the promotion of the species' health and force of resistance, and thus a cause for its development towards a higher level" (p. 442).

Now Hitler needs to create a palpable object for jealousy—one that inspires someone who feels "superior" with the requisite jealous resentment that drives him to take action against one of the "inferiors." What shall this object be?

Historical experience . . . shows with terrible clarity that with any mixing of the blood of the Aryan with lower races the result was the end of the culture-bearer. North America, the population of which consists for the greatest part of Germanic elements—which mix only very little with the lower, colored races—displays a humanity and a culture different from those of Central and Latin America, where chiefly the Romanic immigrants have sometimes mixed with the aborigines on a large scale. . . . The Germanic of the North American continent, who has remained pure and less intermixed, has become the master of that continent, he will remain so until he, too, falls victim to the shame of blood-mixing. (p. 443)

Now that we have an *object of jealousy,* we need a threatening subject to complete the triangle of envious desire: "The Jew forms the strongest contrast to the Aryan. Hardly in any people of the world is the instinct of self-preservation more strongly developed" (p. 452). And, writes Hitler with the usual emphasis on the "evident" of a good politician, the instinct for self-preservation gets in the way of building a territorially bounded nation, state which is the true cradle of any "culture": "For this reason, . . . , the Jewish people, with all its apparent intellectual qualities, is nevertheless without any true culture, especially without a culture of its own" (p. 454). Hitler has put the self-serving nature of the jealous subject to good use: it explains both why he does not have what the Aryans have—culture, which now becomes the object of jealousy—and also why he could want it and, envious of another's possession of it, sully it by "interracial mixing." The grip of Hitler's emotional and evocative imagery on the audience is far tighter than the logic of his propositional arguments. But why would anyone think that those of whom one is supposed to feel jealous might be envious—a key component for feeling jealous in the first place? Because the envy-jealousy complex has illuminated the world in a way that makes envy and jealousy seem like the engines of *everyone's* behavior.

Anarchy as a Moral Theory: The Hidden Passions of the Perpetual Revolutionary

If people can be caught in the web of passions that make their desires unresponsive to the attainments of their ends, then we can suspect revolutionaries of being motivated not by the deliverance of a society from an oppressive regime or patent injustice but rather by the desire to revolutionize *something.* The revolutionary moment is an emotional moment, with its own narratives, its own culture, its own ideology. The American countercultures of the 1960s and 1990s may have much more in common with other countercultures than with the ideas of peace and freedom that they seem to draw their life blood from. The will to revolt can be its own end.

Mixed metaphors of envy and jealousy color the rhetoric of anarchist writers like Pierre-Joseph Proudhon (1923, p. 51)—envy of the causal powers of those in authority and jealousy over one's own dwindling powers:

To be governed is to be watched over, inspected, spied on, directed, legislated, regimented, closed in, indoctrinated, preached at, controlled, assessed, evaluated, censored, commanded; all by creatures that have neither the right, nor wisdom, nor virtue. . . . To be governed means that at every move, operation or transaction one is noted, registered, entered in a census, taxed, stamped, priced, assessed, patented, licensed, authorized, recommended, admonished, prevented, reformed, set right, corrected. Government means to be subjected to tribute, trained, ransomed, exploited, monopolized, extorted, pressured, mystified, robbed; all in the name of public utility and the general good. Then, at the first sign of resistance or word of complaint, one is repressed, fined, despised, vexed, pursued, hustled, beaten up, garroted, imprisoned, shot, machine-gunned, judged, sentenced, deported, sacrificed, sold, betrayed, and to cap it all, ridiculed, mocked, outraged and dishonoured. That is government, that is its justice and its morality! . . . O human personality! How can it be that you have cowered in such subjection for sixty centuries?

Unless you are laughing at the vicious overflow of language, you may be able to see yourself subjected to the limitations and restrictions that government—and now the "free-market" institutions or "the large corporations"—place on your existence. This rhetoric is a lens through which we can see an entire day in our lives. How many actions are left in our days that we do not perform under the constraint of some technological rule or algorithm (toasting bread) or social norm (driving), that are not duly recorded and taxed (using a telephone or a modem, passing over a bridge), or that do not incur the likelihood of grave punishment if we misperform (running on assigned paths, riding a bicycle, paying our taxes, cowering to a policeman who barged his face into our lives for no apparent reason)? The Proudhonian lens casts these experiences in the grim light of a battle between man and an inhuman society that begets more causal powers with every act of compliance of the individual to its norms, at the expense of man's own autonomy. "To act is to fight," Proudhon writes accordingly.

Proudhon presses the reader down the staircase to a sort of madness. Forget about what he says, for a moment, and think of what he *does* by his writing: his written words *act out* a vengeful fantasy of envy of the causal powers of the "sinister other": "Let me find," he seems to say, "all of the instances of my life that are conceivably bound or governed by some law that originated outside of my will, and let me put large black circles around them." And, not surprisingly, he finds them everywhere in his private life. Let us follow Proudhon and carry out his search-and-destroy mission to the end. Why stop with the "obvious" laws of society and social order? Why not reach deeper into our psyche and, energized by indignation, find even in our minds and patterns of reasoning the effects of being brought up in a bourgeois household driven to imbecilic stupor by capitalist propaganda, of being educated by dogmatists who have replaced theological dogma by half-understood scientific dogma, of having to understand algorithms, catchwords, and modes of behavior necessary to get us entrance into various societies of intellectually frustrated sophists and pedants who want to cultivate an image of "knowingness"? But why stop here? Why not recognize that language itself—the living, breathing word—is itself an instrument of social control that shapes our intuitions and stamps our minds with prejudice? But why stop there? Why not agonize over the fact that our prelinguistic perception of the outside world is actually not so prelinguistic as we had originally thought—that the ways in which we learned how to read and write influence the patterns that our minds perceive and discern in the outside world—and set about trying to stamp out every influence of language on thought and of word on experience? But why stop there? Why not begrudge even the material reality of the world its causal powers on our minds and set about convincing ourselves and others that it really is the case that only *we* exist—that everything is only in our minds, that we have dreamed all of our experiences, and that our freedom truly is absolute. And when experience frustrates our projects because we cannot take off by flapping our arms, why not set about devising new anathemas and curses for our predicament—or for the predicament of the cosmos—and try to bring about its collapse by the utterance of a single word, as Emil Cioran once dreamed of doing?

What a "colossal activity for which there is no demand," as Alexander Herzen said of another anarchist, Mikhail Bakunin (1972, p. 13), who takes the Proudhonian project one step further to the stage of a spirit horrified by the history it has come to know as its own:

The entire history of ancient and modern states is merely a series of revolting crimes.... There is no horror, no cruelty, sacrilege or perjury, no imposture, no infamous transaction, no cynical robbery, no bold plunder or shabby betrayal that has not been or is not daily being perpetrated by the representatives of the states, under no other pretext than those elastic words, so convenient and so terrible: "for reason of state."

He tries to give anarchy a positive face: "see what you could have and envy what you could have—envy the future, for that will make you lust to destroy the present" (p. 15). Moreover,

We do not fear anarchy, we invoke it. For we are convinced that anarchy, meaning the unrestricted manifestation of the liberated life of the people, must spring from liberty, equality, the new social order and the force of the revolution itself against the reaction. There is no doubt that this new life—the popular revolution—will in good time organize itself, but it will create its revolutionary organization from the bottom up, from the circumference to the centre, in accordance with the principle of liberty. (p. 16)

And how are we to know that the "self-organization" of the revolution will not produce other emotional brigands like Bakunin, who will see the workings of Satan in its manifestations?

Bakunin directs our nascent resentment toward the present. He asks us to subordinate today's desires to tomorrow's ideals, but he forgets himself, he forgets his passion and vocation, which is not the construction of a new world order: "Let loose this mass anarchy in the countryside as well as in the cities, aggravate it until it swells like a furious avalanche destroying and devouring everything in its path" (p. 16). Perhaps his eyes were burning as he wrote these words, but they were not burning with a creative spark. Destruction is not a means to a better world; the image of a better world provides a justification for destruction—Bakunin's true calling. He is resentful because he is destructive. He is envious because he is resentful. Envy is the force that folds his destructive instinct back on itself and that denies his creative spirit its access to a constructive alternative world.

Transference of a Master Passion: Explaining Cultural Change

Lenin's metaphorical appeal to envy was echoed in the social events in which he took part. As Richard Pipes (1990) noted, economic activity under the capitalist regime was based on a striving for achieving the maximum return at the minimum cost. Money thus becomes the material mirror of the ends of ambition, as the desire for increasing causal powers found its dual in the desire for more money: having more money, indeed, caused one to have greater causal powers. What better target for envious resentment than the very ends of ambitious desire—not the destruction of this or that fortune, of this or that factory, but the destruction of money itself? The plan for the new communist economy favored by the left Bolsheviks featured the abolition of money.

Lenin agreed with the plan in principle. It harmonized with the view that the task of government was "the organization of accounting, control of large enterprises, the transformation of the whole of the state economic mechanism into a single huge machine, into an economic mechanism that will work in such a way as to enable hundreds of millions of people to be guided by a single plan" (p. 121). This was an eloquent testimony to the idea of making the envy of the masses work to fuel the ambition of one self—"a single plan," a single will, *my* will embodied in the living history of a new nation state of a hundred million people. The ambitious uses the envy of his subjects to smother the ambition of those around him.

Even as the project to abolish money as the medium of exchange failed ("the more the nationalized sector expanded, the larger loomed . . . 'its irremovable shadow,' the free sector," writes Pipes, p. 122), the Bolsheviks pursued the replacement of "trade by a planned and nationally organized distribution of products" (p. 122) as the 1919 party program announced: "The objective is the organization of the entire population in a single network of consumer communes which will be capable, most speedily, in a planned manner, economically and with the least expenditure of labor, of distributing all the necessary products, strictly centralizing the entire mechanism of distribution" (p. 122).

By 1920, the Bolshevik spiral of bureaucratic ambition had reached a critical momentum. The idea, it seems, was to turn the common man's envy of the wealth and liberty of his fellow citizen into a justification for the creation of new bureaucratic machines with unprecedented causal powers, reaching deeply into the citizen's private life and personal affairs:

While the production of industrial goods was turned over to the Supreme Economic Council, responsibility for the distribution of commodities was assigned to the Commissariat of Supply, another bureaucratic empire with an array of its own glavki and a network of distribution agencies. . . . A decree of March 16, 1919, ordered the creation in all cities and rural centers of "consumer communes" which all the inhabitants of a given area, without exception, had to join. The communes were supposed to provide food and other basic necessities upon presentation of ration cards. (p. 123)

Pipes notes that the economic centralization initiatives of war communism in Russia did not achieve their ends: a "shadow market" emerged to compete with the central network for the distribution of goods and services. What is remarkable, however, is not that they failed but rather that they succeeded at all. Think of what is involved in nationalizing assets or in administering nationalized assets. A competent and ambitious leader is but one of the necessary elements for building a successful bureaucratic program. The activities of committees are actually carried out by a multitude of functionaries, on whose activities the success of the entire program rests. If you motivate them with money alone, they will sell out to the highest bidder, in which case prized properties may go unprivatized. If you motivate them with the threat of losing their jobs if they do not perform adequately, they will devise better schemes for hiding their activities. But if they are already motivated by *envy* of the people whose assets are being privatized, then the work of incentive design has already been done. The envious is being paid to do something that he already wants to do and provided with a story that he can tell himself. This story makes his work appear "moral" or "rational" in a grander scheme than that of his own private world.

The Ethos of Socialism in Practice: Envy as a Layman's Way of Being

There was a fearful symmetry in the coming and going of communist societies: borne of envy and resentment, they were choked by envy and resentment and thus killed by their own spiritual parents. Envy works its magic in many ways: it can provoke resentful, half-conscious sabotage of another's property, "just so that he does not have it anymore"; it can hold the talented performer back from his or her initiative in a group out of fear of envious retribution from its members ("do not stick out, and all will be well"); it can lead one to think evil and wish evil on another, and these sentiments will lead to guileful action aimed at blackening the name of the envied; it can lead one to fear the "evil eye" of another—the look, curse, compliment, or utterance that can cause harm by its evil intent. Once unleashed, it propagates quickly: the boundless spiral of envy, which often explicitly incites destruction, itself perpetrates destruction as it unfolds.

Fear of envious retribution—of the evil eye and of its consequences—leads people to scale back their efforts and to rein in their ambitions. The energy to create is transformed into the energy to inveigh, to curse, and to destroy. Resentment festers; it takes energy to hide it. Society is impoverished by the envy of its citizens. Private enterprises borne of ambition and killed off by envy and fear of envy turn into large state cooperatives. Private offices turn into cubicles. Private homes shaded by happy, leafy old trees turn into large complexes of white-gray apartments, on whose balconies people gather to smoke and gossip about their neighbors' latest acquisitions.

Far from quelling envy, the ensuing equality stokes it: for now my neighbor is visible, and not only can I see what he has, but I can also just see myself having what he has and know that I cannot get it. I may envy his wife, his children, his job—all of which are now on display on his balcony—and turn bitter. As I deny—inwardly—the fact that I envy his life, his belongings, and his predicament, my resentment grows: for now he is the distal cause of my self-deception, as well as the proximal cause of my envy. And the doubt—the suspicion that my life and my being really does come to nothing—stokes my resentment as it itself grows. I cannot quell my doubt through action—through an act of creation—because I am afraid of the envy of another; perhaps I have even forgotten what it means to create. I criticize the work of others with zeal and eloquence—but put forth nothing in exchange: there is nothing to put forth, for envy is not a creator.

The envy-fear spiral engages us all: we live on the same block, and proximity is envy's stepmother. Our little economy—so efficiently organized for a world free of envy—grinds to a halt. New privations—of food, heat, and water—give rise to new spirals of envy and fear: "Why is he getting more than I am? Why is she not standing in the same lines? Why does he have so much free time?" Envy begets envy: "Why does he not envy me? Why does he not fear my envy?" Envy envies the absence of envy in another.

Of course, we often have many "good" reasons for inquiring about and expressing our outrage at the welfare of another. Justice demands equality of endowment, not only of opportunity. Overt consumption is vulgar. Apparent freedom from cares is inappropriate in a world where all are trying to show how much they are suffering. As Freud (1955, p. 12) writes:

What appears in society in the shape of Gemeingeist, esprit de corps, "group spirit," etc., does not belie its derivation from what was originally envy. No one must want to put himself forward, every one must be the same and have the same. Social justice means that we deny ourselves many things so that others may have to do without them as well, or, what is the same thing, may not be able to ask for them. This demand for equality is the root of social conscience and the sense of duty.

If we follow the history of the envious society to its logical end, we will end in Fyodor Dostoyevsky's underground, wherein there is no privacy for the individual: all acts are public acts, for now envy has become attached to the right to privacy itself. Consciousness of self has now become consciousness of the other who watches the self. Each watches the other and therefore watches the other watch her, watches him watching her watching him, and so forth. Action grinds to a halt, and people live out their lives through the eyes of others: they are—even to themselves—the images that they see in others' eyes, images that they guard jealously every waking hour.

If the geographic expanse of the society is too large for people to lose their physical privacy, television fills the gap and makes psychological privacy impossible to achieve. Now the private has become public by means of the public becoming private. No longer are sexual relations open to the fantasy or the imagination of the individual. Desire is desire for the prowess of the TV hero and heroin: it is envious desire. The prototypically successful man and woman have entered the bedroom of the envious and are watching him from his TV screen.

6

Want, Will, Wish, Would: The Predicaments of Desire

There are two great tragedies in life: one is not to get your heart's desire; the other is to get it.
—George Bernard Shaw

The quenching of thirst is not a typical image of satisfying a desire or of satiating a want. We rather think of thirst as a *need,* even though we can *do without* satisfying the need when it presents itself. It is true that we cannot go on *forever* without water, but even if very thirsty, we can go without water for *just a little while longer.* What we do not know is just how many such *little whiles* it will take before we lose consciousness. Hence we drink water *out of anxiety,* not out of thirst—out of the fear that thirst will get the better of us and the anxiety caused by contemplating the unknown that follows. Anxiety turns desires into needs.

We might realize that responding too quickly or too anxiously to "take care of our need" might make the experience of desiring a liquid more intense: the greater care we take of ourselves, the more care our selves require. Few of our desires can be quenched in the same way—by what looks a priori to be the attainment of their objects. The desire for the recognition of another person, for example, might take the form of the desire for one of his smiles, the desire for a physical surrender to your caresses, or the desire for a look of understanding even after we interrupt her concentration with a question. But the fulfillment of these desires always leaves us desiring more—not necessarily because we doubt the authenticity of the other but because we doubt ourselves in a way that cannot be "quenched" with a smile: self-doubt is always already at the core of the desire for recognition. With each fulfillment of the proximal desire—for the smile or the caress or the look—we also stoke the doubt that lies hidden, for why else would we have desired recognition in the first place?

The Dramaturgical Nature of Desire

In spite of what experience could teach us, we continue to experience ambitious desire always as fulfillable—perhaps inexpensively so. Our thirst for recognition always looks as if it is about to be quenched, only to loom larger with every new instantiation. But both contentment *and* resentment breed desire. The resentment caused by unfulfilled desire (think of being sexually rejected by a spouse when feeling amorous—the hot experience of what we call "frustration") can also be a fuel for greater desire.

Frustration in fact *is* a form of desire—to the extent that we think of desire as a state of being that is escaped through a sort of fulfillment and of fulfillment as the escape from the resentful state. When frustrated, we experience desire as resentment, which, in conjunction with the awareness that fulfillment would soothe the resentment, generates even greater desire. Frustration and the promise of fulfillment are equally the fuels of desire.

So is, for that matter, the fear of regret. The thought of what one *could have done,* of what one *could have been* is the seed of a rumination that we desperately want to escape sometimes. "I would have liked a larger bathroom," a young wife might tell her husband *after* finishing the move into their new home. "I would have liked to become a psychologist," you might tell yourself after finishing medical school. "Wouldn't it have been a great day for hiking?" you ask your children after you are halfway to the beach. "Would have, could have, should have" are the thought-shapes of envious desire—desire for what could have been but cannot be.

The Cognitive Knots of Envious Desire

On its face, such desire seems incoherent because it is a desire whose fulfillment is known to be impossible, usually leading the desirer to contemplate her "luckless" life. It *is* possible that some people are simply unfortunate—that their *would-have, should-have* desires are recognitions of desires they really did have but could not fulfill and are simply late in bringing them to awareness. It is usually more plausible that envious desire is not originated in a thinking I and therefore that no sense should be sought in it beyond its being. In this interpretation, envious desire *is* the kernel from which the thoughts and actions of the thinking I are originated. Envious desire is, in this case, a primitive kernel of experience, perception, and volition; it is a world builder and a world maker for the envious desirer.

Envious desire finds its objects *out there:* it illuminates the world with the bluish light of regret and misgiving. The *envying* is racked by regret in part because the envier never stops to ponder the impossibility of the "could have been" that is the object of her desire. She sees each bit of reality as the sad penumbra of what could have been on what never was. She is always already regretful, resentful, and guilty. She has come to see herself as a concatenation of "could have been's."

Here, a second illogicality intervenes—the regretful I's fear of regret—and it turns the envious I into the jealous I. Unaware that she has construed her life as a sequence of "could have done's" and her predicaments by a nexus of "could have had's," the envious desirer is actually jealous of her being. She treasures her current endowment and is fearful that action will lead her to *lose* something that she will later regret having foregone. Because she does not realize that she *always does regret* the past, she sees her own actions as the causes of her regrets—as "foolish decisions" that have left her "worse off" than she was before. She does not want to give up—by her actions—what she believes she has, and she sees the chance of losing out in most of the actions she takes.

Her approach to decisions is guided by the impulse to preserve an extended self. Her relationship to her objects is one of *jealous possession*—as is her relationship to her beliefs. She guards her possessions from theft and insures them against loss. Her relationship with ideas mirrors her relationship with objects. Chief among these ideas is her self-concept—a concept, an image, a myth, a narrative, an idea that she *has* of herself. Hanging on to this idea—shielding it from disagreement, from refutation, from diminution, or from modification from experience or from the words of others—turns into a modus vivendi for her.

Jealous desire can be self-defeating. It is the desire for *what already is the case*—for what we already possess, for what we already are, for what would already qualify as the fulfillment of any other kind of desire. We experience jealous desire as the fear of losing something or "someone." How odd that we do not realize that jealous desire turns the way we think of people into the way we think of material objects that we *possess*. As with people and objects, so it is with self-concepts and self-identities. Since self-images are populated with objects and social positions and professional degrees, we experience jealous desire as the fear of losing some particular endowment—material, interpersonal, or psychological.

Jealous desire can covet the present just past and abhor the future about to come. It shuns reinterpretations and new approaches to the past or to problems of value and meaning because it is at its core a commitment to one particular image—the image it guards. It shuns new ways of cutting up perception into objects and concepts insofar as images are not merely passive perceptions. It discourages reflection about ends, insofar as ends and values are already embedded in the image that it guards: judgments of worth are already embedded in the image of what is. To be persuasive, jealous desire must be persuaded. To be convincing, it must be convinced. Just like a movie is unattractive if the actors regularly peek from behind their masks and remind us of the farcicality of the situation, so jealous desire loses its grip on our minds if it is shown up as a director or stage manager rather than the real thing.

A Hermeneutic of Jealous and Envious Desire: The Myth of Narcissus

Think of Narcissus leaning above his pond, where he has been lured by the curse of the nymph whose love he did not return. His desire has all of the elements of the absurd—of the desire for the impossible—that belong to envious and jealous desire. On one hand, it is a desire for the image in the pond—always as it *just has been* because the image always changes. With each passing glance, Narcissus begrudges time what it has just swallowed. "I would have liked to keep that smile forever," he might whisper at the passage of an expression from energetic spontaneity into grimace and falsehood. The desire for what just passed is the mortal's constant revolt against temporality. It stands as an eternal anathema against time.

The envious desirer says, "If only I could . . . ," and his wishes are aimed at "trading places with . . . "—something that can be accomplished only by rolling back time. If you go back far enough in time, you can always come up with a plausible interchange between two events that would have turned up the desired outcome in the actual world—a word spoken slightly differently, a stray bullet abated from its target, two atoms trading places for a nanosecond. This is the link between anxiety and envious desire: the envious desirer *opposes* by his desire the flow of time, which, in his anxious moments, he perceives as rendering life and world devoid of sense, value, and meaning.

Narcissus cannot bring himself to leave the image in the pond. Even if he tells himself that he is being absurd—that self-love makes its object ugly— nevertheless he cannot look elsewhere. He cannot say, "The image depends causally on my presence, and therefore it is a sign of my powers to end its existence," and says, rather, "I depend on the image." There is no Narcissus without the image of Narcissus in the pond. "There is no me without him," the betrayed young lover tells herself to justify not leaving the relationship. "There is no me without the image of myself lecturing," the academic tells himself to justify yet another compromise. It is by comparison to an image or to an other—the precondition of all envious desire—that modern individuals often constitute their "selves."

Narcissus guards his image. He resents the wind that ripples the water, the leaves that fall into the pond and taint the image, the imperfections in the songs of the nightingales that accompany this scene of silent adoration that has repeated itself so many times before and since. And he succeeds, for his mind "clears" the image of the impurities that the passage of time colors it with. The mind has the power to abstract the invariant from the concrete with uncanny accuracy, and Narcissus makes the error of assuming that purity can be found only in the timeless.

But there is one force that Narcissus's will is powerless against—the passage of time. Narcissus is unconscious of the temporality of the image, of the fact that his image will end, will pass into memory, along with his own being. He does not perceive the change in what he wants to see as forever unchangeable. Each present is seen through the lens of a thousand pasts that endured through time. Beholding the image in its timeless essence is also a way to deny the temporality of each present moment; for the image, unlike the seeing I of the beholder, has come to stand outside of time. This is the link between jealous desire and anxiety: jealous desire is the will to deny the temporality of each passing moment, and awareness of that temporality causes anxiety because only timelessness has come to be identified with sense, meaning, and value, whereas temporality calls forth images of ephemerality, naught, and dust.

Compare narcissistic desire with the desire of the consummate bureaucrat who sees himself as the vehicle of propagation of an institution forward through time. His instinct for preserving the status quo is passionate: it is not inertia or apathy; it is the bureaucrat's desire for permanence that keeps organizations running, often past the point when they are desirable or effective. He may not be able answer the question "Why?" more than three times in a row about anything about his life—the rules at work, the habits he cultivates, his dinner menu, or his reading habits. He may not be able to justify any of the myriad standard procedures he has put in place at work with respect to the goals of the organization. But he stands by them ferociously. He will defer to rules wherever there are rules to defer to, he will turn down personal appeals wherever rules can be found for doing so, and he will exercise his veto rights over any initiative that entails meaningful change.

His power is a negative power: it is a power that is most readily manifested through saying no and clothing no in the garments of locally legitimate explanations. No maintains the status quo and enforces the image of the bureaucrat as the guardian of this status quo. It is a power that he exercises by deferring to rules and principles that apparently do not depend on him. The bureaucrat absolutely denies that he has any choice in the application of the rules. "These are the rules" is the reason he gives for his actions—even to himself. The rules rule the bureaucrat's world. Principles are the ultimate arbiters of morality, not the minds that create and use these principles to make decisions. The lure of Narcissus's pond—the lure of atemporality—is the glue of the rule-based organization.

What Narcissus Would Not Have Understood

Contrast the past-directed desires of Narcissus with the forward-looking desires of Napoleon, or Hitler, or Alexander the Great—who "wept because there were no worlds left to conquer." Their desires are directed at the future—at bringing about a future state of the world that they have willfully created. It is the desire to create time—the time to come. Living through time—rather than against time or in spite of time—is how ambitious desire lives. For such a desire there are no accomplishments or end points of an effort or an exertion, except as mechanisms of pacing the self

along. There is no comparison and no taking stock of various achievements. There is no gauging or benchmarking of the outcomes against the
outcomes achieved by others. There are no contests whose aim is to establish the superiority of the desirer—although contests may be *instrumentally* useful in pushing the desirer to higher levels of exertion. The purely
ambitious desirer lives out his desire: there is no need to bring the object of
his desire to language for objects are never ends in themselves. They are
simply *means* to keep a desire not yet conscious of itself accelerating down
the loops of time.

No such desire is keeping Narcissus by his pond. He can only *let happen*
what is already happening without his help. But it is a begrudging letting
happen that animates him, a letting go in spite of oneself. The image creates him—his locked-in mood—just as he creates his image in the pond.
This image is of one who does not want to leave his image. And since he already *is* or strives to achieve his image, he always *becomes* what he already
is: he is always already *there* as a self-perpetuating image.

A Hermeneutic of Ambitious Desire: The Myth of Sisyphus

Sisyphus, according to the Homeric myth, has been sentenced by the gods
to push a boulder up a mountain. At the top of the mountain, the boulder
slips and rolls down to the bottom, where Sisyphus begins his work anew.
This sequence is repeated in eternity: Sisyphus knows it, the gods know it,
each knows the other knows it, and so on. This is significant because if
Sisyphus thought the gods thought he thought there *would* be an end to his
ordeal, but actually *he* knew that he had fallen into eternity, then he might
desire to push the rock up the mountain to *deny* the gods the satisfaction of
watching him *try* to stop or to effect some end to the process (like destroying himself or the rock). On the other hand, if Sisyphus thought he *could*
actually stop pushing the rock, then his desire to keep pushing the rock up
the mountain would guard an image of himself as a stoic victim of the de-
bauched tenants of Mount Olympus.

But neither of these conditions is true of Sisyphus. He knows that he
cannot *but* continue. His is ambitious desire in its purest form because
the end point—the point of taking stock or of reveling in the accomplish-
ment of the goal—has been expunged from his world line. Sisyphus does

not—as Albert Camus (1960) has claimed —enjoy a moment of contemplation at the top of the mountain, and his trek down the mountain is not carefree and pleasant without the burden of the rock. In fact, the rock is no burden at all. The exertion and fatigue that we think torture him on his way up the mountain are only projections of our own experiences wherein exertion and fatigue are aversive conditions. But in our case, these are aversive conditions because they forewarn the body of imminent destruction, or they are aversive *in order* to forewarn the body of imminent destruction. Current pain saves us from future destruction by providing the warning signals that bid us go to a healer, change our ways of living, or stop whatever it is that we are doing that may be causing the pain.

Whichever way you look at it, the destruction of the body—present or future—factors into the aversiveness of the exertion and therefore in the *fact* that exertion for us is a form of torture. But Sisyphus already *is* in eternity: his corporeality does not have its own ending written in its physical essence as does ours. Therefore, for him exertion is not torture, and the stroll down the mountain cannot be *relief* from torture. For all we know, the toil up the mountain may leave him free to contemplate, the stroll down the mountain may be a bore, and he may experience disappointment at the top because the descent is less conducive to thought than is the ascent.

For Sisyphus, there is no problem of ends as there is for us. The proximal end of his task has already been determined. There is no problem of means either—for he cannot *but* do what he has been fated to do, *in the way in which he has been fated to do it*. In fact, there is for him no means-ends distinction to begin with. It is by no means clear whether he is pushing the boulder to place it on the top of the mountain or whether placing the boulder on top of the mountain has the function of getting him to push the boulder. The gods are more powerful than the garden-variety human tyrants we find throughout history. They do not tell him, "Push the rock up the hill, or else we'll give you something harder to do." Indeed, they cannot do so: doing so would be an acknowledgment that they do possess not the power of *determination* but merely that of coercion. Sisyphus, for his part, cannot do what he wills, but he can will what he does. As he does so, *he makes his own causal powers infinite* and stamps his will on the boundless space-time cone in which the gods have locked up his afterlife.

Seen through the prism of Sisyphean desire, the predicament of the perpetual entrepreneur is at once intelligible. The entrepreneur *enterprises*.
He creates companies, groups, teams, technologies, industries, and even
societies. Modern American society can be understood as the partial creation of industrialist entrepreneurs like Andrew Carnegie, John D. Rocke-
feller, E. I. Du Pont, Bill Gates, Lawrence Ellison, John Chambers, and
Craig McCaw, who created the infrastructures for transportation, financ-
ing, computing, and telecommunication that underlie the modern American organization. It is a mistake to try to understand the plight of the
perpetual entrepreneur through the lens of greed, the desire for accumula-
tion, or the deliberate ordering of a life according to challenging yet tangible goals. Very few entrepreneurs retire after they have achieved a
particular level of wealth. Most toil on, creating new social structures. The
reward for the entrepreneur is in the act of creation. The *process* of creation motivates them as much as the product of creation motivates the rest
of humankind—just as for Sisyphus the ecstasy of the now—of the freedom to decide to keep pushing his rock uphill—makes his alleged torture a
delight.

Sisyphus is the antithesis of Narcissus in the realm of desire. He desires
ambitiously. He desires the life that he has been given for its own sake—
for each instant that makes it up rather than as a means to something else.
There is no light at the end of the tunnel, nor is one desired. With each passing moment his causal powers increase, not because he has increased his
span of control over the world but rather because he has willed what has
just happened to him. Narcissus, on the other hand, sees the passage of
time as either a constant menace to his image, against which he must fight,
or as the kernel of melancholy and regret that stokes his desire for the image in the first place.

Desires as Kernels and Levers of the Passions

To the extent that desires are as causally potent as they are short-lived, we
might say that they are the levers by which the passions guide our actions.
The actions they motivate will later become the collection of stories, theories, and myths that together make up the narrated I, the self. Because master passions depend for their inner life on the narratives that we can

generate, the footprints of the master passions should be visible on the bits of affect—the desires—through which the passions act on the world. Thus, it is useful to talk of ambitious, jealous, and envious desires that propel these greater, more encompassing passions forward through time.

We can recognize the forms of jealous desire embodied in the wish for a new home or an apartment, in the pleasure with which we pick out new mahogany furniture for a new office, in the looks with which we seek to impress a new partner into giving us an exclusive smile. Mahogany desires are image desires. Image desires are jealous desires. Models with tanned, taut bodies display the clothes that we desire to wear ourselves—a desire for the image of the body we *cannot* have transferred to the clothing that we *can* have. With each new acquisition, however, our desire is renewed. The deception involved in the desire is quietly uncovered. Possession reveals itself with each act of consumption as an illusion—the illusion of *eventual contentment.*

Each new bikini worn in pursuit of an image begets a desire for the next model of the bikini, not necessarily because the model herself has changed bikinis (she almost always does) but because the possession of the bikini— wearing it in front of a stranger, a lover, or a mirror—has only intensified the consumer's desire. She does not want and never wanted the bikini but, rather, wanted the bikini image, which is precisely what she cannot have because to truly *possess* an image is to behold it *timelessly* or outside of time. Even when we reach the pinnacle of contentment of a pose that we have always wanted to strike, we are foiled by its own passage into memory. We misidentify the resulting frustration with a desire for another model. We confuse the desire for the timeless with the desire for the object. The timeless image is what we want to become, to be one with. But this is precisely what the physical predicament of the self does not allow. Therefore, to consume the image in a time-bound world is to experience the desire for consuming it anew. Acquisition is not satiation but resembles it from afar. It holds the promise of satiation that it cannot deliver.

There is also a way to desire a bikini enviously. It is a desire for what would have been had the desirer and the model traded historical places. By owning and wearing the bikini, the wearer appropriates part of the fate of the model—part of the model's identity. Envious desire is the desire for the *would have been and the could have been* that often come to pose in her mind as the *should have been*. Envious desire can spring forth from the counterfactual "What if I had been *her*?" which begets the much more virulent "Why her and not me?" It is desire for the impossible that is so near. The nearer *it* is, the greater the desire. Your neighbor's home and garden may be far more desirable than the gardens behind Buckingham Palace. A colleague's office may be desired more intensely than the corner office of the boss.

Ambitious desire, by contrast, recognizes the bikini as a stage along life's way toward another end. The bikini is a means to something—to bathe in the sea or to impress someone for some ulterior purpose. The ends to which wearing the bikini is a means are themselves means. Indeed, only the finitude of deliberation constrains the ambitious mind to partition history into means and ends to begin with. Otherwise, all of history would be laid out as an inexorable continuum in which the notion of distinct cause and distinct effect loses its meaning.

It is easy—because of this artificial partitioning of history into means and ends—to confuse ambitious desire with jealous or envious desire. The ambitious desirer may speak of ends, just like her jealous and envious counterparts. She may exhibit wishes for winning a contest, for impressing another person, or for bridging the gap between herself and the front runner in a race, but these wishes are for end points that are but stages and steps: they are *instrumentally* useful for the pursuit of other goals that themselves will turn out to be but stages and steps.

For someone who desires jealously and enviously, ambitious desire seems like nihilism because it recognizes no final stage of the hierarchy of desire, no final good that one must strive for. The jealous may pursue the ideal principle, or the ideal instantiation of the ideal principle, and so forth. For her, the image is inextricably intertwined with reality, and she sees the image in every bit of reality, wherein she pursues the image with every action. "You have destroyed my beloved image of you," says one jealous desirer to a friend, as if the latter had just intentionally shattered a porcelain vase painted with the image in question.

Jealous desire permeates moral and practical reasoning like a living spirit. It makes us see timeless principles embodied in the activities of scientists and moral philosophers, physicians and theologians, professors and judges, politicians and parents. It makes us see family values in a household where people have long ago ceased to listen to each other or professionalism in a hospital where physicians have long ceased to care about anything more than getting sleep and avoiding malpractice claims. Jealous desire saves us from ourselves by collapsing the world into an image.

For the envious, the final good will be the feeling of defeating another, of getting ahead, or of winning the contest with another: "It is well enough to win," the envious may say to himself, "but the victory is that much sweeter if everyone else loses." The world always already reveals itself to him to be worthy of envy. He turns a dire eye on the values, thoughts, words, beliefs, actions, and predicaments of others and is always on the lookout for the put-down phrase. Of course, the *reasons* for the put-down always seem to the jealous to be objective: "not working well with others," he might say of a brash young psychologist applying for a position; "a poor judge of people," he might say of a young economist passed over for a promotion in the bank. Therein lies the self-deception implicit in any form of desire that has been placed in the service of the passions: we must hide from ourselves the fact that the desire itself lights up the world in a way that makes its objects seem enviable.

7

A Self against Itself: An Aesthetic of Rage

The only initiation is to nothingness and to the mockery of being alive.
—Emil Cioran

L'enfer—c'est les autres.
—Jean-Paul Sartre, *No Exit*

Rage, rage against the dying of the light.
—Dylan Thomas, "Do Not Go Gentle into That Good Night"

When we turn bitter, we may experience both a desire in its original form and the impossibility or futility of attaining that desire. The two feelings go hand in hand: we can no longer surrender our selves to the pleasure of desiring what has just become impossible without experiencing the bolus of a curse forming inside our intestines. Let us say you wanted to be loved by a particular person and had dreams of spending many happy moments in his arms. He, however, greets your revelation with irony and asks you if you are quite sure it is not yourself that you love in him. His smile tells you that he already knows the answer. You might experience disgust at his smug knowingness that grows out of the pain at the realization that he does not want you and hence at the impossibility of attaining your desire. Both feelings are juxtaposed onto the original desire that comes up and makes you live through your ordeal over and over again.

The Inner Work of Rage

Rage can come like a flash when we live our frustrations over and over again. Intellect and emotion are caught in a dance in which each reinforces the other. Being cut off by a driver on the freeway at rush hour is a paradigm example of the interplay between frustration and rage. You are frustrated to begin with because opposite your desire to *get there* more quickly has arisen the overpowering force of circumstance—the traffic jam. You might ask yourself, "What are these fucking people all doing on the road at this hour?"—a question you might fully understand to be ridiculous, since it is the end of the work day, and "these fucking people" are doing the same thing you are doing. There is the radio and even a book on the back seat that you can read—since only minimal attention needs to be paid to the road in these modern times where financial liabilities stem from any unpredictability in the design of the highway system. But these may strike you as only digressions from the main show that is the traffic jam and its implications for how you view life—which appears in its real, bleak form.

You are keenly aware of the fact that your desire to get home more quickly is continually opposed by the events on the road, events you come to see as the doings of a slothful, decadent, imbecilic population of drivers. There is no longer a middle ground between you and the other, who sits behind the wheel of the automobile in front of you. Fantasizing about James Bond-like gadgets by which you can destroy his car and get ahead, however, can keep your mind occupied for only so long: you soon become aware of the impotence of your own thoughts to cause any actual change in the traffic ahead of you.

So your thoughts meander to your relationship with your boss, which you now find disgusting: How could you ever have told him you thought highly of his half-baked ideas? What depth of fear and mendacity did you have to reach before dignifying his ideas with praise? The grim light of revelation falls on your marriage as well: your well-fed children strike you as repugnantly lazy, and their mother might emerge—cowlike in your imagination—as the warm cushion for their petulant rituals. Plans for leaving your life come up, blossomlike, and you even manage an acid smile as you remember Sartre's, "L'enfer—c'est les autres" and realize that "les autres" might not be only the idiotic drivers ahead but precisely those whom you had thought to be an extension of yourself.

Suddenly, the incident!—the jerk cuts you off. As you watch yourself losing it, you realize that you do not want to bring your actions under what some people call control. It is precisely the loss of control that you cherish—the bile-colored stream of words that you bellow through the open window, the incessant honking that you are doing "for punitive purposes," the pounding of the roof top of your own car with your fists, the sudden fits of acceleration and deceleration against the nonperson ahead of you. All of these actions, engaged in perhaps half-consciously, look to the slightly amused observer behind you as if they are helping you let out some of the steam that you have built up.

But you may feel differently because you realize that with every sign of outrage you give a fresh admission that you are impotent—that you are caged and really cannot do anything of consequence, either here or elsewhere. You might now realize that your entire life is a traffic jam. You are trapped in a car, a marriage, a family, a job. You have been trapped in a situation for a long time. Society should be put on trial for entrapment, found guilty, and condemned to hang! But no hangman is up to the task, and no judge is up to the calling. There is only you: small, petulant, hopelessly lost in the cauldron of petty emotions. Who would ever trust you as a judge? You reek of subjectivity.

Rather than bringing catharsis and a sense of fulfillment, your acting out might only amplify your rage. It is a mistake to think that rage is a gateway to fulfillment—that beyond the obscenities and the violence you will find peace. Indeed, the common wisdom that speaks of letting off steam points in this mistaken direction: it points you along the path of deeds that you wait for to deliver you from your own thoughts and feelings. The moron ahead of you becomes indistinguishable from your boss. Your boss blends into your wife's image.

The number of people you cannot stand anymore! You might give a lot for them just to go away. They are, after all, the causes of your suffering. Rage is nothing but the recognition of the inevitability of suffering. At one point, after much cursing, you might feel tired, you might even begin to laugh. But it will be an uneasy laughter, for nothing has been resolved. Your car is still behind the car of the person that cut you off, and you now have the realization that your life is a traffic jam to live with. You will have to greet your wife tonight after thinking of her as a cow, and you will have to smile at your boss tomorrow after thinking him an idiot. Not even a chance at authenticity has been left for you in this world! Nothing has been resolved. There has been no catharsis—only a postponement and perhaps an initiation "to nothingness and to the mockery of being alive," as Emil Cioran (1972, p. 74) put it.

The traffic jam is not a necessary and sufficient condition for rage in our example. With a different wife, with a different boss, with different children—who knows? Perhaps you could have tuned in to the harp and flute concerto on the radio and gazed far into the summer fields instead of staring at the car in front of you. The traffic jam is just a facilitator: it has made proximal the impotence that you already are feeling in your life. You cannot escape the rage by escaping the traffic jam. You have just been served notice that you are trapped: the traffic jam is the notice, the alerting sign, not the entrapment, properly speaking. No matter how things play out with you and your car on the road, there will remain the rage. You can escape it only through fatigue or exhaustion.

The Opiate of the Enraged: "Lucidity" as Self-Deception

The enraged of the past century—such as Friedrich Nietzsche and Emil Cioran—started out (or so they say) in search of meaning, God, and certainty. When they found none in themselves, they despaired of anyone else's chances of finding them and, enraged, turned their desperation into a morality play about lucidity: "To be fooled, to live and die duped is certainly what men do," writes Cioran in *A Short History of Decay* (Cioran 1972, p. 83). And Nietzsche admonishes in *Beyond Good and Evil* that

> the falseness of a judgment is not for us any objection to it. The question is to what extent it is life-promoting, life-preserving, species-preserving, perhaps even species-cultivating. And we are fundamentally inclined to claim that the falsest judgments are the most indispensable to us; that without accepting the fiction of logic, without measuring reality against the purely invented world of the unconditional and the self-identical, without a constant falsification of the world by means of numbers, man could not live. . . . To recognize untruth as a condition of life— that certainly means resisting accustomed value feelings in a dangerous way; and a philosophy that risks this would by that token alone place itself beyond good and evil. (Nietzsche 1909–1913, p. 283)

Nietzsche includes the mental faculties and cognitive categories that Kant had made the a priori of understanding part and parcel of the necessary lies that we must live. Time, space, and causation are just such fictions, and the belief that they are necessarily authentic or true in a way that does not appeal to experience is a useful lie—a lie that we all engage in more or less unwittingly. We may not, then, be liars, properly speaking, but we certainly are lied to: we are duped.

This incipient obsession with self-deception and the haunting disgust with the necessary nature of self-deception will sprout and grow barbarously, and it will be echoed in howls by Cioran (1972, p. 36) sixty-three years later: "History: a factory of ideals . . . lunatic mythology, frenzy of hordes and of solitaries . . . refusal to look reality in the face, mortal thirst for fictions. All the feelings milk their absolute from the misery of the glands. Nobility is only in the negation of existence, in a smile that surveys annihilated landscapes. Once I had a self; now, I am an object." Having sought ultimate certainty and found none, Cioran argues, modern men and women are left to climb along the dead ends of the mind, all the while trying to persuade themselves that the mind offers bona fide paths to salvation.

The duped shares with the cuckold and the idiot a certain loss in dignity—one that cuts deeply into the heart of the social creature. This painful spill on the *amour propre* is the feeling that both Nietzsche and Cioran feel churning their insides and also the one they try to save themselves from through their words: "To be fooled, to live and die duped, is certainly what men do. But, there exists a dignity which keeps us from disappearing into God and which transforms all our moments into prayers we shall never offer. . . . The ideally lucid, hence ideally normal, man should have no recourse beyond the nothing that is in him" (Cioran 1972, p. 39).

But this arrogance of the thinker itself appears disgusting and worthy of contempt in Cioran. His rage feeds on itself because the end point of each one of his bouts of rage is a trigger for the next bout. He collapses in curses that seek not to communicate but merely to express an inner suffering: "The spectacle of man—what an emetic! Love—a duel of salivas" (Cioran 1972, p. 71). And we—and perhaps he himself in other moments—are right to suspect him according to Nietzsche's teaching: "Whoever despises himself still respects himself as one who despises" (Nietzsche 1909–1913, p. 285).

Rage as a Form of Entrapment

Rage is an emotion in which we are sometimes trapped by the very thoughts we think up to escape it. It is a passion that can be brought on by the words and thoughts we think to escape it. Just like the arrhythmic heart can lapse into dangerous arrhythmias when we think of the arrhythmia and its dangers, the raging and enraging thought can be brought on by thinking about the rage that it has caused. Trying to forget *him* or *her,* the very center of your life until she decided to elope with someone else? Trying to not feel the rage at being betrayed by the close friend that she or he eloped with? These attempts—far from having the therapeutic function we hope for—have an amplificatory function: we can become enraged about the fact that we are enraged.

Rage, once acknowledged, is already a failure of personal control. Consciousness of rage is an admission of a lacuna in our causal powers—perhaps the most painful lacuna of all because it is the admission of a failure of self-command. The self can no longer be commanded by the self to calm down, to think, to reason, to feel empathy with those who are witnessing the outburst. Thus, rage is the self-devouring master passion, for it is directed at itself. There is no light at the end of the tunnel for the enraged, for if there were, the rage would already be over: the tunnel would already be gone.

Awakened from a bout of rage, we may feel as if we have come back from the deep sleep of the alcoholic. If there is a meaning in our experiences, then that meaning escapes us. Witness Cioran (1972, p. 51) again: "The moments follow each other; nothing lends them the illusion of a content or the appearance of a meaning; they pass; their course is not ours; we contemplate that passage, prisoners of a stupid perception. The heart's void confronting time's: two mirrors, reflecting each other's absence, one and the same image of nullity" The self that stood between the mirrors has lost itself in rage.

It may be a mistake, however, to identify rage too closely with the will to destroy and annihilate. Although it most often makes its appearance in the criminal's coup de grâce, in the madman's squeals, and in the philosopher's animated anathemas, rage can also appear as a constructive urge, as in the rage for perfection or the rage for excellence. The tennis player's obsessive drills, the pianist's hours of practicing the same piece late into the night (in spite of inner howls that unmask the ennui of repeating the same passage until the life has been sucked out of it), the academic's seemingly endless journeys into the world of logical arguments and empirical "facts" are all actions driven by passions driven to a pitch. This drivenness is called *rage*.

Rage is an acceleration imparted to one's journey along the spiral of a passion. It is a speeding up of consciousness along the spiral of self-destruction. We should henceforth amply and conscientiously study the life work of the accomplished sociopaths, torturers, and master criminals to discover the entrapment of the mind by rage because in the grip of rage people can overcome empathy and fear of consequences in order to maim and kill. Rage focuses one inward and shuts off contact with those who just might become victims. It only appears to be directed outward—at the moronic drivers, the annoying spouse, the donkey of a boss. For this most intimate of passions also works to shut off the feeling subject from openness to the world and to keep its thoughts and feelings focused on a single, predictable trajectory.

8

"The Truth Is Always Incredible": Deception and Self-Deception

If [Stavrogin] believes, then he does not believe that he believes; and if does not believe, then he does not believe that he does not believe.

—Fyodor Dostoyevsky, *The Demons*

Two vice presidents of a large American corporation are staring each other down in front of the company's executive team. At issue is the allocation of $100 million, which is to be split between their divisions. The projects that are being considered make it impossible for the money to be evenly divided, as each wants to fund an $80 million project within her own division. Each of them wants the lion's share of the money because she knows that the larger project will enhance her standing in a company in which having control of more money is what power is understood to be. Can this be said in so many words? Imagine:

—I want more power. That's the reason behind all of this charade. There are, to be sure, reasons I could give for why I want the money, but the energy with which I pursue those reasons does not come from the reasons themselves. It cannot. The reasons are just there, to bring up or not bring up as I please.

—So do I. And I feel the same way about my reasons as you do about yours. Only one of us can get it.

—Obviously, arithmetic dictates it.

—Not arithmetic but rather your unwillingness to lobby for more money.

—What about your unwillingness to lobby for more funds?

—Our interests are directly in conflict.

—It seems that my interests dictate that you be destroyed.

—Mine dictate likewise.

In the interest of interpersonal stability, the discussion cannot go down this path. Open conflict—and particularly open and irreconcilable conflict—is to be avoided in organizational settings, to such an extent that the avoidance of the recognition of conflict becomes the motivator for a large number of organizational activities. A little voice of "reason" intercedes in the discussion of our example, and the discussion concentrates on the reasons for and against various proposals. The organization—including the combatants—is united in believing that the resource-allocation problem can be solved by rational argumentation.

Reason as a Therapeutic Agent: A Caricature of the Western Psyche

But can it? Rational argumentation proceeds when one side makes an argument and the other side refutes or confirms it via some evidential or normative statements. If one VP, for example, thinks that the project that she is seeking investment for will have a return on investment of 100 percent in one year, she will present an argument for why she thinks this is the case. And the people in attendance will shake their heads knowingly and opine on the claims that the young lady is making: her argument may be true in view of X or false in view of Y. But does the fact that the wise believe X or Y settle the issue? Not at all: for the woman of action can in turn challenge the validity of X or Y and therefore rescue her own argument from refutation, in precisely the same way in which a Newtonian physicist can rescue his theory about the motion of a newly discovered small planet from apparent "refutation" by observation statements (Lakatos 1970, p. 85):

A physicist of the pre-Einsteinian era takes Newton's mechanics and his law of gravitation N, the accepted initial conditions I and calculates, with their help, the path of a newly discovered small planet, p. But the planet deviates from the calculated path. Does our Newtonian physicist consider that the deviation was forbidden by Newton's theory, and therefore that, once established, it refutes the theory N? No. He suggests that there must be a hitherto unknown planet p" which perturbs the path of p. He calculates the mass, orbit, etc. of this hypothetical planet and then asks an experimental astronomer to test his hypothesis. The planet p" is so small that even the biggest available telescopes cannot observe it: the experimental astronomer applies for a research grant to build yet a bigger one. In three years' time the new telescope is ready. Were the unknown planet p" to be discovered, it would be hailed as a new victory of Newtonian science. But it is not. Does our scientist abandon Newton's theory and his idea of the perturbing planet? No.

He suggests that a cloud of cosmic dust hides the planet from us. He calculates the location and properties of this cloud and asks for a research grant to send up a satellite to test his calculations. Were the satellite's instruments (possibly new ones, based on little-tested theory) to record the existence of the conjectural cloud, the result would be hailed as an outstanding victory for Newtonian science. But the cloud is not found. Does the scientist abandon Newton's theory, together with the idea of the perturbing planet and the idea of the cloud which hides it? No. He suggests that there is some magnetic field in that region of the universe which disturbed the instruments of the satellite. A new satellite is sent up. Were the magnetic field to be found, Newtonians would celebrate a sensational victory. But it is not. Is this regarded as a refutation of Newtonian science? No. Either yet another ingenious auxiliary hypothesis is proposed, or . . . , the whole story is buried in the dusty volumes of periodicals and never mentioned again.

When will the Newtonian concede that his theory of celestial dynamics has been superseded by Einstein's theory? There is no law of logic requiring him to do so at any point. He can just keep writing grant applications requesting funds to send up more satellites on increasingly improbable missions. Suggestions from philosophers of science that simplicity be one of the virtues of a theory will seem ad hoc to him. They seem contrived to justify what they perceive the history of science to show. Why should the simplest theory be the best of all true theories? Won't a more complex theory make us more mindful of possibilities? Won't it increase our understanding of the world? Isn't it especially because of the simple-minded obsession with simplicity that we have been lurking in Newtonian darkness for so long? Newton's theory, after all, has always seemed to us to be very simple. The Newtonian, then, can keep spinning out new initial conditions and salutary assumptions to rescue every new version of his theory that seems to be refuted by evidence. There is no crucial experiment that establishes one theory and refutes another, although, in retrospect, it helps to find an event that one can point to, as it preserves the semblance of integrity that the scientist tries to project.

Identity as a Narcotic

What keeps the Newtonian going after his theory has been disproved? What keeps Albert Einstein going before there is any semblance of evidence for his new theory? We do not know but can guess: the theory has become part of their identity. Whatever setback the theory suffers now has become their setback as well. Whatever slight of evidence or logic is imputed to the theory is also an imputation to their persons. The will to assert and argue is not implied by the fact that the argument is assertible. What is needed is a motivational account for why we assert—sometimes passionately—that which can be asserted.

This motivational account is supplied by the will to overcome suspicions about the value of the self in a universal scheme of values. Assertion is an implicit attempt at persuasion—of oneself or another. Why else would you assert? Imagine making statements to a wall. No one is listening to what you are saying. There is no mind that is swayed by your words or that can, in principle, be swayed by your words. Your words are causally impotent. What gave them causal potency to begin with was the possibility that they would sway another mind or excite a response from another person— the possibility that they could *persuade*. But now it's only you and the wall—white, tall, silent. Would you still talk?

Perhaps—though maybe you might not voice your words. It is not necessary to voice them because there *is* someone listening and capable of conscious apprehension of your unvoiced words, and that is yourself. The possibility that you can persuade yourself of your own ideas can move you to put these ideas into words. You bring thoughts to language because language allows you to have a relationship with yourself. It allows you-in-the-past to signal to you-in-the-future. If these signals are—by some standard—coherent, then the system of signs that you produce confers an identity on you. You are identical to yourself: your identity persists through time. Saying and asserting are forms of persuasion—not only by yourself of yourself of the substance of the assertion but also by yourself of yourself of your own identity.

Words as Tools: Assertion and Persuasion as Acts of Taking Control and Possession

Assertion can be a form of control. By saying or asserting, we can seize control not only over the nameless perception but also over the elusive identity of the speaking subject. You are, perhaps, familiar with the staff meeting in which someone puts forth a proposal and is then unresponsive to counterarguments. His defense of his own arguments is all the more energetic the more valid the counterarguments are. He prefers his arguments to any alternatives because they are *his* arguments. It is the "mineness" of an argument that makes the argument attractive because it confirms the identity of the one whose argument it is. Abandoning the argument feels like keeling over. It feels like defeat. We cannot, under the seductive power of our own words, "let our ideas die in our stead," as Karl Popper (1979) suggested we do.

Persuasion of another often requires deception. If you do not take the substance of an assertion seriously and if its purpose is laid bare before your mind, then you will not be able to make the assertion with the required conviction. You will seem a sham to yourself, and your project will seem like a hoax. There is some deception in any attempt at persuading yourself of some fact or belief.

Why, in spite of this, do we get such pleasure out of persuasion? Why are we satisfied to persuade another? Often it is because persuasion is an extension of our causal powers—the causal powers of our thoughts and rhetorical devices. We have taken one more step toward the denial of our own nothingness: for "nothing" cannot have causal powers; it cannot persuade. The idea of nothing may be quite potent, but that is because the *idea* of nothing is yet something.

But is the intent laid bare in the act of persuasion? How can it, without undoing the effect? Suppose you chuckled with glee once someone admitted she was mistaken and came around to your view. She might gasp when realizing that all you were after was an assertion of your own wit and prowess. She realizes at once that her mind is nothing but a trophy for you, and your ideas lose their grip on her mind. She frees herself from you. But how did you get her to take in your beliefs in the first place? By showing them to be as objective as possible—that is, as independent from your personal will and personal aims as possible. *You would not believe them were they not true:* this is the path you want her mind to follow. Later, once you bring her mind under your control, she will believe that the fact that *you* hold a particular belief makes it true. Judgments about causation are themselves causally potent: she first believes that the objective truth of a particular belief causes you to hold that belief, but inadvertently she then slips into believing that your holding a particular belief causes it to be true.

The Professional as Stage Director: The Dynamic of Persuasion

You go to your doctor, complaining of some pains in your neck. She gives you a diagnosis that you do not quite believe and a course of treatment you cannot relate to, as the terms are unintelligible. There is a tension that you have to resolve between your intuitions about your own condition and the physician's diagnosis and prescription for a course of treatment. But there are more beliefs that enter into the picture, some of which you may not be immediately aware that you hold. The physician—you think—speaks with the authority of science: she would not be a physician if she did not speak with the authority of science. The authority of science, you also believe, is based on the fact that all of its practitioners follow the same precepts of investigation and that their beliefs are disciplined by the same logic. You also may believe that this logic guarantees convergence of their beliefs to truth or maximal truthlikeness. If this were not the case, then how could science be so "successful"? Therefore, you believe that a necessary condition for a scientist to hold a belief is that the belief be true, or more truthlike than alternative beliefs, which means that a scientist's holding of a belief is a sharp, reliable, and credible signal that the belief is true— so reliable, in fact, that there is negligible difference between believing that the scientist's opinion is a signal for the truth of what she opines and believing that the scientist's opinion is a *cause* of the belief being true.

This chain of reasoning is carefully cultivated and preserved by the medium and the decor of your interaction with the physician. He is a master choreographer. First, you almost always wait for him, even if there are no other patients in the waiting room—just as the ancient Greeks had to wait for the oracles to speak. A usually bespectacled secretary—almost always a woman (reinforcement of a particular cultural metaphor that goes hand in hand with "authority")—hands you forms to fill out, brochures to read, charts to go through and check.

Finally, the oracle itself appears draped in white, introduces himself as "Dr. X," and then proceeds immediately to call you by your first name. Physicians do not have doctorates and do not have to pass the scrutiny for mastery of a field and originality of research that other researchers must pass to receive doctorates. Nevertheless, physicians are *most* likely to introduce themselves as "Dr. Such-and-so." Most holders of doctorates—

except those who feel that "Ph.D." is a required appendage to their last name on a book cover—introduce themselves by first and last names only. The "Dr. X" routine immediately creates the semblance of intellectual ascendancy that will help him slowly gain authority over your body and mind.

Ahh, his office! The walls are draped with diplomas, all framed, from various institutions. Most of the inscriptions, however, are in Latin, a language that has not been taught as part of mainstream curricula in U.S. colleges for fifty years. So you have little chance of understanding what they say. Some diplomas have on them familiar Latin inscriptions: "Veritas" ("Truth," that is), reads one from the Harvard Medical School. But how did the framers mean this inscription to be read? As an assertion that nothing but truth comes out of Harvard? This sounds a little presumptuous—if not preposterous. Perhaps it was meant that the institution as a whole is dedicated to the pursuit of truth? Then how does producing unintelligible diplomas for people who will wear white coats and display them on walls serve this purpose? In any case, the intent of the framers is not decipherable from the diploma. And unless you pause to think a bit, you are again likely to be taken in by the calligraphy and the crimson coloring of the diploma.

Now we come to the actual interview. "What hurts?" But you might get the feeling that he is not really listening. Perhaps he has formed the diagnosis already? His writing of notes on his paper pad does not seem to be in synchrony with your answers. Perhaps he is composing a commentary on your answers? Not clear. You suspect he is earnestly trying to concentrate on what you are saying, but he cannot: his gaze keeps slipping past your eyes.

The exam preparation: "Undress, put on this robe, and I will come to see you," he says. But why "undress"? You complained of neck pains. Perhaps there is a reason, but he does not mention it. Then again, perhaps there is a motive, and he *cannot* mention it. Take some time to appreciate the intricacy of the choreography. You are at a disadvantage, slightly shivering under the little gown, feeling vulnerable among all of the white paraphernalia. The exam room is white and cold—in the interest of sterility, of course. You did not really think there was no justification for this.

Now the exam: what you said earlier during the interview does not seem connected with his maneuvers rights now—and he does seem as though he is listening *for* something in particular. If he does not find it, he moves on. Then, "I'll see you in my office when you are dressed." The diagnosis is couched in inexplicable language—Latin terms mispronounced in English. Perhaps you wonder if he knows what they mean? Ask him, and he will use more mispronounced Latin terms to explain it. Now ask him again: What has, in his opinion, caused the condition? What is the physiological mechanism? Ask him to stop and explain every term you do not understand—and watch him get impatient. Is it because he cannot figure out what billing number to use to recover the costs of the time foregone for your interrogation, or is it, rather, that he feels the stage props are about to be shown up?

You feel the full weight of his displeasure: he wants to close off and prescribe some medication. "But wait," you say. "I still don't understand what you are telling me." You go on with your questions—"What does this mean? How do you know this? What is your opinion based on"—and you discover (maybe elatedly) that the white lab coat and the diplomas on the wall are props in a carefully staged play, in which you are one of the movable pieces. At a not too deep level his explanations will break down in the face of simple questions ("Why? What does this mean? How? How do you know?"), either by becoming internally incoherent or by leading to some sentence that tries to be convincing without any grounds but fails because its groundlessness is obvious ("I'm as sure of this as I am of anything").

Incorrigible Beliefs: The Savant's Toolkit

It seems that to recover control over our minds from our savants, we must first save ourselves from our beliefs about the knowingness of the savants. But can we save our minds from our beliefs? Consider the following story about incorrigible suspicions (Oksenberg Rorty 1988, p. 12):

Jonah, a newswriter, resents Esther, his editor, whom he thinks domineering, even tyrannical. But as bosses go, Esther is exceptionally careful to consult with the staff, often following consensus even when it conflicts with her judgment. His colleagues try to convince Jonah that Esther's assignments are not demeaning, her requests not arbitrary. Jonah comes to believe he was mistaken in thinking her actions dictatorial; he retreats to remarking that she derives secret pleasure from the demands that circumstances require.

What will convince this man? Suppose he sees Esther weep alone in the cafeteria after having to give him an order that he was obviously sullen about. Then he reasons that she is posing. He states this much to a friend over a beer. The friend points out that she was alone: who could she be posing *for*? Jonah then reasons that she is posing for herself: she wants to believe that she is not the kind of person who could give orders that go against the wishes of her employees. Now the friend points out that there is no way for her behavior to disprove this hypothesis: perhaps Jonah is engaging in some self-deception of his own. To this Jonah retorts that he knows that he is an unusually objective person—and gives an example.

Identity as the Choreographer of Interpersonal Situations

Consider the plight of the corporate hero who saves his employers' shareholders repeatedly from fraud and shame by exposing the crooks and the incompetent managers that he happens to work for: "I mean, I am always ready to submit my letter of resignation after such a discovery," he explains afterwards. "I would not dream of benefiting from the downfall of my superior even if he has done something that I would personally let him go for," he adds forthrightly. "It's always difficult to figure out if budgeting slips reflect genuine errors or willful distortions meant to benefit a specific person. Of course, you can never say for sure. But when things keep happening, when there is a pattern in these slips, you begin to wonder. Don't you agree?"

It is pointed out to him that the slips are a series of shortfalls and windfalls that wash out to zero over a one-year period: "Hey, errors are errors. They happened to average out to zero this year. But next year they may not. Like I said, it's the basic intent that counts—the basic quality of the people you are dealing with. If the person is a perpetrator, they should not be allowed to get away with intentional distortions in the budget, even if on the whole, the firm did not lose any money this time."

He is reminded that in his last job he discovered a similar pattern of wrongdoings that led to the firing of his boss for just cause. "That was a different situation," he interjects. "There, the case of embezzlement was much more clear-cut. It was much easier to make. A clear paper trail pointed to the wrongdoer, and the procedures by which the money was transferred among the different accounts was clearly afoul of the by-laws of the bank. And don't tell me that these by-laws had never been respected in the past. By-laws are by-laws. An officer should be bound by them, and his actions should reflect his commitment."

But why is it always his immediate boss that ends up being the crook? Does not the pattern strike him as meaningful? "And you know what?" he asks with a laugh, "even when I was young, I always uncovered the money my mom was stashing away in the kitchen cabinets and reported on it to my dad. It did not matter to me that I would be punished and would have a hell of a time with her alone in the house afterward. Sure, she was using it to buy clothes while he would have used it for pot. But it was *his* money. She had not earned it. She was just a housewife who ordered me about. She was my boss, but he was her boss. What'd the world come to without a higher-up to guard us against our guardians?" Alas, we remind him that the boss's boss may himself be a crook but that we do not have anyone to report his crookedness to. "I see where you're going with this," his eyes finally show some understanding, "but you're wrong. You're trying to say I keep going from place to place framing my immediate superiors so I can look good to their bosses, whom I have intentionally cast in the 'good guy' role. You're wrong. It's not all in my mind. My father really did punish my mother for her thievery and eventually drove her out when he suspected that she was unfaithful. Left her out on the street. Just like that. In time, he managed to find someone else. Sure, he had been seeing her for a while—this other woman, I mean—even while he was still coming home to my mother. But what is a man without a mistress? Know what I mean?" We do, Jack.

Beliefs as Possessions: What Does It Mean to *Have* a Belief?

It sometimes seems as if beliefs are like possessions, as Bob Abelson wrote (1986), but occasionally it also seems that *we* are the possessions and the beliefs are the possessors. We defend our beliefs against refutation in the same way in which we defend our possessions against theft and damage. But here is where the analogy ends. For our possessions usually serve some instrumental *purpose* and lose their value as possessions once they cease to serve that purpose.

This purpose may be purely symbolic—such as the assertion of our causal powers over the object or person that constitutes the possession. But once the possessing of the possession ceases to symbolize our powers and control, the possession itself loses its value. Don Juan loses his appetite for the young women that he has sexually conquered very shortly after the seduction takes place. This slackening of the will to possess could also occur when the possessing of the possession is defiled in our minds by someone else having possessed it previously. Once again, sexual possession "for the first time" feels different than other kinds of possession. Male and female virgins alike can have a mystique and purity that sexually experienced humans may lack.

Beliefs are different. They are fickle, nimble, clever, and selfish. They behave more like possessors than like possessions because it is easy enough to dismiss or part ways with a possession (the symbolic "throwing out" is also a physical and irreversible adieu)—afterwards, "out of sight, out of mind." If it turns out that "absence makes the heart grow fonder," then that is just too bad: for the possession is irretrievably lost. Not so with beliefs.

Try *not* to think of a green earthworm for the next thirty seconds. Now tap your hand on the table every time you have thought of a green earthworm. How many times did you count? Most people cannot *not think* of a particular object. They cannot, similarly, part ways with a belief that they hold by an act of volition similar to the one that precedes throwing out an old book we no longer want around.

Gripped by a belief, we can become enslaved by it: our minds work in ways that help the idea become entrenched. We seek out evidence that confirms the belief, as many experiments in cognitive psychology show. We perceive predicaments and even ourselves in terms of the objects and metaphors that support our beliefs (like a frame supports a canvas or a building). The vernacular attests to our ambivalence about who possesses whom: we say "holding a belief" or "having a belief," but then we also say "being possessed by a belief" or "gripped by a belief" or "under the impression." Language speaks through us and attests to our anxieties: from subjects using beliefs as tools we become objects being used by beliefs that amplify their hold on our minds.

A Thorn in the Side of Modern Man: Sartre's Suspicion of "Bad Faith"

Philosophers of self-deception—like Jean-Paul Sartre (1956)—have posited "bad faith" as the root of self-deception. Bad faith is a state of being in which we purposefully hide from ourselves something we sense, or know to be true—some fact or some belief that does not sit well with how we currently feel. "If I were to believe X, I would feel bad (ill, mad)," the fear-driven self is supposed to reason, were his inner-directed therapy explicitly articulated.

With Sartre, bad faith already implies some degree of consciousness: some conscious decision is involved in my choosing to think that my hair flows sensuously off my scalp and to repress the scant evidence relating to an incipient bald patch on the back of my head. According to the bad-faith account of self-deception, I am at some point in time deciding not to bring up the evidence in question, or I am putting a lot of energy into stressing the image of smoothly flowing hair to drown out the evidence of the bald patch.

The self-deceived, in Sartre's version, is just like a criminal who talks nervously and profusely for fear that his silence will be interpreted by the commissioner as an implicit admission of guilt. He talks a lot, much of what he says is true, and yet he communicates nothing of relevance to the investigation. But this account does not square well with the experience we have of self-deception: I may think of the smoothly flowing hair, and it may not occur to me to think of the bald patch. The image of the hair flowing smoothly *takes me over*. There is no deceiver and deceived here; there is simply a mind that has been taken over by an image.

Whatever negation there is of the bald-patch evidence, it is only a negation from an observer's perspective—an observer who has seen that I have seen the bald patch and sees now that it has completely vanished from my mind. But here, truth herself may be stunned to find out that I am not negating the evidence of the bald patch but rather negating that the evidence of the bald patch negates or in any way affects the image of the sensuously flowing hair (which can also flow, though more sparsely, out of the fringes of a bald patch). Of course, this is not always the case: the image of the smoothly flowing hair brings to mind other images and associations—

poses of wit and languor that would vanish if, instead, the image of the bald patch were to come up. Thus, the fact that I only rarely see the bald patch is critical to my being able to entertain these pleasurable images of myself.

Smallness-of-the-Mind: The Inner Work of Self-Deception

Surely this is self-deception? It is, but not in the sense of *bad faith*: for there is no deceiver that consciously does the deceiving. Rather, it is a deployment of the mind in a single direction, for a single purpose, to the music of a single image. It is self-deception as *small-mindedness.* Small minds cannot grasp "complicated thoughts" because thoughts trigger in them immediate emotional responses—strong dispositions to take action. Complicated thoughts, however, cause complicated feelings that are not immediately actionable. Unactionable but powerful feelings are confusing and anxiety-provoking: at once we know *that* we should act but not *how* we should act.

Suppose that, out of amorous jealousy, we have just killed. But we killed cleverly: we used our previous legal education well. Rejected by the sought-after lover, we feel unsure of what to do. We consult the Pythia if a citizen of ancient Greece, a priest in 1640s Paris, a psychoanalyst in 1930s New York, a psychopharmacologist in 1990s Toronto. Instead of answers, we get intricate and futile-sounding questions such as "What is a number, that a man may know it and a man, that he may know a number?" and so forth, each according to his own bent and phrased in his own dialect. Even the psychopharmacologist (though perhaps less literate than his predecessors) declines to supply a prescription and talks instead about the shaky epistemological foundations of clinical science.

All are trying to indicate the same thing—that the answer that we are looking after may, after all, be a question. But without an answer that fits our model of what an answer is, our anxiety grows: society looks united in its quest to expose us and deny us our happiness forever hence. The crime appears, after all, to have been justified. Once one crime is justified, other crimes are as well: words have such a fine way of covering an endless range of possible events. We might smile at seeing—many years later—our distorted portrait on a television series about serial killers.

"Logical Fit" and Personal Entrapment: The Dynamic of Persuasion Revisited

Suppose we want to get someone to act according to our will. To do so, we may have to persuade her that her actions will not in fact have been caused by our will. That may be fatal to the project because she would recognize in our intention the diminishment of her own consciousness and will. We can, for instance, persuade her that she *wants* to take the action in question for her own benefit (because she is the kind of person who *should take that action,* for instance). We might want to persuade her that her action will instantiate a universal principle—rationality itself or some moral value, not merely the will of our minds—which means that she must be made to see that the principle is true or good and that its truth or goodness, not our will, is the cause of her belief in it. To do so convincingly, it helps to be convinced of the principle ourselves. Thus, just when we think that we have subjugated her will to our will, we discover that our will has been subjugated to the belief that gave us our powers to begin with. To be convincing, it is best to be convinced. Nothing convinces like conviction.

The convictions of another can be the ultimate anchors of our own beliefs. Do you realize the extent to which your actions rest on a web of belief spun by people who have at one time or another communicated with each other? As you press on a switch intending to turn on a light, you believe that your actions will have the effect of lighting your room or desk. Why do you believe this? Because of your knowledge of the physics of the electronics hidden behind the switch? Most likely, you believe that the action will have the intended effect because of your past experience with light switches. In so thinking, you are no more rational than the chicken who believed, one fatal Sunday morning, that the farmer was coming—as he always had—to feed her rather than to chop off her head.

Suppose, however, that this is the first light switch that you have ever seen, though you have seen other devices like it in the past. Someone tells you how it is supposed to work. How do you decide whether to believe him? You may look at how he is dressed, within the context of the interaction. Does he look knowledgeable? Does he sound competent? Does he have any apparent motive to lie to you? Is there a bomb connected to the switch that he wants you to set off, and does he have a reason to want you to set it off? Is he himself *convinced* of his own explanation? Do his facial expressions agree with his verbal expressions, or is there a strange lack of congruence between the two? Does he look past you as he speaks?

Suppose your examination of the speaker has gone very well. Do you now turn to an examination of the spoken? Do you begin to study the laws of physics that govern the transmission of an electrical signal through a conductor? Now that you understand these, should you not also study the processes by which knowledge of these laws was arrived at? If they are inductive, then again you are no better off in your reasoning than Russell's chicken. If they are deductive, then they must rest on some assumptions. And how do you know these assumptions are true? By what process were they arrived at? By one that stresses criticism and realism? What about the claim that observations are theory-laden? How does this argument impact the validity of your newly acquired beliefs? By a process that stresses fallibilism and purports to take scientific knowledge toward greater levels of truthlikeness or verisimilitude over time? But what about arguments that show that the only uncontroversial measure of verisimilitude that we know of is invalid (Miller 1994)? Where does this leave you? And how do you get around the argument of a radical skeptic that—starting from the premise that you can be justified in believing in immediate perceptions only if you are antecedently justified in believing that you are not dreaming—concludes that you are not justified in believing in the reality of any perception?

Action in the Face of Doubt: The Kinematics of Belief

Reasonable doubts, it seems, abound. Yet action requires the recruitment of *all* of the fibers in a muscle. There is no analogue in action of the less than full commitment that we experience relative to the beliefs that cause the action. Muscles cannot be ambivalent. At the instant of action we are committed and find it difficult or impossible to act if in fact we are not committed. Yet we may be unable to justify our commitment, even to ourselves. It seems that we have overestimated the power of reason. It may be persuasion, rather than reason, that takes us to commitment and therefore to action, and persuasion—as Wittgenstein wrote—starts where reasons have stopped. Because we know how difficult conviction is to produce internally through conscious reasoning, we are easily taken in by the conviction of another. That is, it is both an easy way out of the skeptic's harrowing line of questions and a way of justifying our own cognitive commitments.

To convince yourself of this argument, do the following thought experiment. Take a belief about the external world—some cause-and-effect relationship—and try to strengthen your conviction of it by considering arguments for believing it to be true that involve what others have said or that are congruent with a credible source (some famous scientist, for instance). Now try to strengthen your belief in it by considering either criticisms of that belief along with criticisms of the criticisms or by considering experiences that you think confirm that belief.

Which works best? You may, in some cases, be attracted to the belief after recalling experiences that seem to confirm it. But look more closely at these experiences. Why do you believe them to be veridical? Why do they hold sway in your mind? Most likely they are the kind of experience that others, too, would share were they in your presence when you had them. They seem veridical because they seem objective, and they seem objective because they are intersubjectively valid. The belief that "He, too, would be convinced that the experience is veridical, were he to witness it" does the work of convincing us.

The Scientist's Cognitive Anchor: Positivism and the Verification Principle

As intuitions about verification go, so do beliefs. If we think that only statements about the measurable and the observable have any meaning, then we will theorize only about quantities for which we have established measurement criteria. But suppose we discover, by logical analysis, that there is no verification principle—or principle that distinguishes between sense and nonsense on the basis of the connectedness of a statement to something we can observe. Then we are again left in a world where the boundaries between hallucination and reality are always dimly perceived, even as our stake in perceiving these boundaries grows.

But we *have* discovered, by logical analysis, that there is no verification principle lying around—no definitive way to distinguish between sense and nonsense on the basis of reference to empirical observations. The mind is far freer than thinkers had surmised during the years and decades that followed the rationalist century, and this freedom is terrifying, when finally beheld: Who will control the controllers? Who will observe the observers?

The verification principle played the same role for the scientific establishment of the nineteenth and twentieth centuries that dogmas had played for the founders of theological institutions in previous centuries. In the darker recesses of modern science, like the social sciences and biology, people still presume that a verification principle holds that can distinguish between sense and non-sense. We might look for hard data that can "prove" certain assertions to be true or false and defer in our decisions and judgments to the voices of people who can argue using phrases such as "studies have shown,"—that, for instance, certain chemicals are poisonous or that lay people in general are poor intuitive statisticians. From these "truths" we derive comfort, and we can well understand that the phrase "studies have shown" (whatever they purport to show) is supposed to help us anchor our minds in an idea. It gives us the comfort of "knowingness"—that state in which we believe our own stories.

But an idea cannot properly anchor our minds if we believe that there are many alternative beliefs to which we can instead commit: so we use the verification principle as a filter that selects the beliefs worthy of inductive generalization and use induction itself as a way of selecting among the remaining candidate beliefs. Or so it seems: for it may very well be that beliefs themselves use our false belief in a verification principle to entrench themselves in our minds and our false belief in inductive validation to polarize our minds even further.

Deceived About Deception? An Analysis of the Act of "Knowing"

Self-deception runs to the core of what we think it means to *know*. We are often deceived about the relationship we have with our own ideas, in particular about who is controlling whom: we, them or them, us. The alternatives feel menacing to the mind seeking shelter from the nameless. Skepticism can freeze us altogether. Fallibilism—the idea that our beliefs are likely to be false and that we should treat them only as approximate and tentative guideposts for action, to be discarded when they turn out to be refuted—is frightening, and we often confuse it with nihilism. So we live the lies of verificationism and inductivism because we are highly motivated to do so.

The capacity for self-deception makes it possible for our projects and hopes to become imprinted onto our ideas, onto our ways of viewing the world. Imagine being bereft of will. You neither hope nor fear for the realization of some future event. You may *prefer* one state of the world to another, but your awareness of this fact does not move you into immediate action aimed at bringing about the desired state. You are not apathetic or indifferent but simply do not seek to control or influence events in the world for your purpose. Will-less being contemplates without seeking to contemplate.

Consider your current projects, hopes, and fears. The same events that you were once perhaps merely observing now have a direction, an implication, and a purpose because of these entities. These events now lead you either closer to or further away from your future goal. It is just lazy or small-minded of you to think that there are some events that may not, after all, be relevant to your purpose. You would like to lose weight? Then why are you sitting down right now without doing something active? You would like to get ahead in your organization? Then why not use this time to network with some people higher up than you are, to research a topic that you know that your boss is interested in, or to go to your office now, in the middle of a weekend afternoon, to show your dedication? If you do not want to think of yourself as a "climber," you have many self-persuasion strategies to choose from: your work will be useful to the organization; in turn, it will benefit your customers and suppliers; besides, once you achieve a position of power, you will be able to put into practice all your current goals. Perhaps it is fatigue that is keeping you here? Then why not begin a new diet or start taking some fortifiers to wake you up? Why not orient all of your activities around the purpose that you know moves you and of whose failure you are ultimately afraid? And why stop at actions alone? Why not attempt to control and influence your thoughts, so that they, too, are aligned with your purpose? Why not visualize yourself incessantly as being in control or as having finally achieved your ends? Why not structure your thinking—while brushing your teeth or making love, say—

so that these activities come to provide time for rumination and planning and thinking through the consequences of every action that you will undertake? Why not do, in other words, what you have most reason to do, in view of your goals?

The man who "knows how to love himself"—as Shakespeare, via Iago, put it—knows no respite from the workings of his own mind. He has no weekend. He does not "go out" at night, except when he sees it to advance his greater purpose. His actions are all *means,* and he is constantly on the lookout for actions that are not means to some end so that he may replace them with "aligned" activities and for new possibilities for acting in ways that further his interest. He has definitively resolved the means-ends splitting of consciousness, in that all events, actions, objects, and people are means to the achievement of ever greater causal power, which itself is a means to the achievement of still greater power. His very ideas also become means—for getting himself to do what the attainment of his ends requires.

Here we come to the deep and subversive Nietzschean insight that ideas themselves are *actions:* they have deceived us for a very long time under the guise of atemporality or permanence, of essence and existence in a state of independence from the minds that have thought them, from the reality of the bodies associated with those minds. It is perhaps time to recognize—and cogitate on—the intentionality of believing, just as we have for so long recognized the intentionality of acting. Doing so, however, is a difficult task because we require language and concepts to refer to language and concepts. And the language and concepts that we have inherited—our joint Western and rationalistic heritage—are precisely those of laws, principles, and atemporal entities that implicitly deny the willfulness of thought. The language of the speaking, breathing, desiring, and suffering subject has been smothered—if it ever existed—by the impersonal language of the observer and the moralist. If, as Martin Heidegger pointed out, language is the house of being, then the search for a more personal, authentic, and connected being is, as well, a search for a more suitable and expressive language of the willing, sensing, and intending I.

9

The Moral Tyrant

If we have to use force, it is because we are America. We are the indispensable nation. We stand tall. We see further into the future.

—U.S. Secretary of State Madeleine Albright, 1998

[The] most fundamental problem of politics . . . is not the control of wickedness but the limitation of righteousness.

—Former U.S. Secretary of State Henry Kissinger, 1954

The Illusion That Clairvoyance Can Bring Peace of Mind

Seeing more deeply into the future does not always help us make our predicaments more decidable. The unknown lurks even as we think that we have acquired the ultimate weapon against it: the supercomputer. Cosmic predictability—the grasp of the laws of nature by the mind in such a way that the darkness of the next instant will be dispersed—does not soothe the moral doubter of her anxiety. Clairvoyants *can* be suffused with moral doubt. Consider:

A brain in a vat is at the wheel of a runaway trolley, approaching a fork in the track. The brain is hooked up to the trolley in such a way that the brain can determine which course the trolley will take. There are only two options: the right side of the fork, or the left side. There is no way to derail or stop the trolley, and the brain is aware of this. On the right side of the track there is a single railroad worker, Jones, who will definitely be killed if the brain steers the trolley to the right. If Jones lives he will go on to kill five men for the sake of thirty orphans (one of the five men he will kill is planning to destroy a bridge that the orphans' bus will be crossing later that night). One of the orphans who will be killed would have grown up to become a tyrant who made good, utilitarian men do bad things, another would have become John Sununu, a third would have invented the pop-top can.

If the brain in a vat chooses the left side of the track, the trolley will definitely hit and kill another railman, Leftie, and will hit and destroy ten beating hearts on the track that would have been transplanted into ten patients at the local hospital who will die without donor hearts. These are the only hearts available, and the brain is aware of this. If the railman on the left side of the track lives, he, too will kill five men—in fact, the same five that the railman on the right would kill. However, Leftie will kill the five as an unintended consequence of saving ten men: he will inadvertently kill the five men as he rushes the ten hearts to the local hospital for transplantation. A further result of Leftie's act is that the busload of orphans will be spared. Among the five men killed by Leftie is the man responsible for putting the brain at the controls of the trolley. If the ten hearts and Leftie are killed by the trolley, the ten prospective heart transplant patients will die and their kidneys will be used to save the lives of twenty kidney transplant patients, one of whom will grow up to cure cancer and one of whom will grow up to be Hitler. There are other kidneys and dialysis machines available, but the brain does not know this.

. . . Ethically speaking, what should the brain do? (Peterson 1998, p. 86)

Suppose *you* are the locomotive's engineer. You are a quick thinker and have weighed all of the possibilities. The point of no return is coming up. Choose now.

Now suppose you get another shot at your choice. Would you now choose differently? Are you doubtful of your imaginary choice? Do you seek solace in a cliché like "This is an impossible choice" or "Damned if you do, and damned if you don't"? If you knew that you would be able to find such solace no matter what you did, then why did you take the task of deliberation seriously? If you did not know this about yourself, then are you not self-deceived? And if you are deceived about yourself, then might you not be deceived about your choice? Now do you wish you had more time to decide? Or, rather, less? Moral doubt springs everywhere, like water leaks on the sinking ship of moral dogma. Like rats on that ship, minds flock to areas untouched by the flood, oblivious to the impending chaos. Moral certainty is the quickly sinking remnant of a shipwreck.

Knowledge of Fact and Knowledge of Value: The Instrumental Role of Morality

Time-bound creatures capable of reflection—humans, that is—are faced with a dilemma. On one hand, there is the need to act. Acting consciously means acting with an awareness of the irreversibility of the act and of many of its consequences. Actionable knowledge—the knowledge that makes action predicated on that knowledge possible—is in part knowledge of the consequences and in part knowledge that one will be able to live with the consequences. One must also deal with the incessant questioning that comes from awareness of moral doubt and moral conflict, from the need to be assured that we are about to do good and not just do well, to be assured that our goals and intentions rate highly on the cosmic hierarchy of values, that the means that we have chosen are matched to the goals by standards that would be accepted by someone else in our shoes.

Morality "furnishes a decided and decisive testimony as to who he is—that is to say—in what order the deepest impulses of his nature stand to each other," wrote Friedrich Nietzsche (1909–1913, p. 286). And, he continued, each of these impulses asserts itself in language and thought—that is to say, it philosophizes. These philosophizing impulses put words in our minds whose function and effect are to make us successful agents—unconflicted actors on a stage on which we are both observers and observed because we are conscious. Our consciousness is both the uncaused cause and the observer of our actions. And this observer has invented the myth of causation and determinism to exculpate itself from agency.

Thinking "Hot" and "Cool": The Raw Feels of Moral Deliberation

Whereas reasoning about what means are best suited to some ends can be a cool, detached process in which reasons and counterreasons execute a delicate dance, moral deliberation can open up as a chasm. The stakes for the individual are much higher: "What if I have been wrong all along?" he might ask? "What if I have not thought of something really important? Have I damned myself by my logical sloth or by my lack of sensitivity? What if my mind will by its own evil bent slight the most cherished values? How can I control my mind?"

Psychological studies suggest that we cannot—at least not reliably. But is not the ready availability of this excuse just a temptation? And is not his failure a failure of moral strength as well as one of cognitive prowess? Suppose it is. Can we know this beyond any doubt? Is doubting a sign of moral weakness or the messenger of freedom? Is freedom good in itself or only in view of the purposes that it enables us to pursue? What if we do not know whether our purposes will be achieved by a particular action? What if the search for such knowledge itself is misguided? What if there really is no single right answer—no matter how much information we have and no matter how long we think things over? If there is no single right answer, is all moral deliberation idle? Is the proper end of moral deliberation to try to decide whether moral deliberation is idle? What if we reach the conclusion that moral deliberation is indeed idle? Does that mean that any values will do to guide our actions? And if any values will do, then what is the point of searching for values in the first place? Why agonize over the choice? Why not trust ourselves to moral luck and obey our immediate instincts? If there is an element of chance in morality—if there is an objective chance that any particular principle is the wrong principle to act on (rather than a subjective chance that it is the wrong principle or an objective chance that we have *found* the wrong principle)—then won't the idea of a principle be radically compromised? Won't all principles, as probabilistic mixtures of right and wrong, be somehow tainted? And what good will any such tainted principle be? Can we use it to assign values ever again? If not, won't the idea of a value be compromised as well? Do not values rest on principles that, although within us, surpass our beings and particular circumstances? If the idea of value is compromised, won't it necessarily be true that our world "really" makes no sense? That *we* make no sense? That our lives *have* no sense because they have no value? Won't a valueless life come to nothing more than its existence? And is mere existence enough to tame the feeling of nothingness that takes us over?

If Rumination Is an Ocean, Morality Is a Buoy

Rumination is anxiety's fodder. Your automobile runs over a dog on a cold, wet fall night. Do you go out to see what happened to the animal? Suppose she is badly hurt. Do you take her to your home? But you are freshly married to a woman whose emotions are very fickle and who takes grave actions easily. You have an image of her leaving you over a spilled cup of coffee, and you feel morally responsible for her leaving you over a trifle you could have avoided and ending up in a relationship with someone who will exploit her anxiety to his advantage. What now?

Suppose you take the dog with you. Why have you done it? Is it not because of the fear of ruminating for the next days or months about what you should have done? Suppose you do not take the dog with you. Might it be because of your fear of ruminating over having caused the end of your unstable marriage—something you could have avoided by leaving the dog there? And suppose you now realize that your acts of generosity are no more than concessions to the looming guilt that holds up your emotions with the threat of rumination. What now? Are any of these feelings worth acting on?

Rumination is the weapon with which guilt, regret, and shame hold up your emotions. Moral conflict is conflict between two self-images we would like to hold up simultaneously but cannot because action forces us to choose between them. The self is split. We don't know who we are or what we are about, and we know that we do not know it. Logical contradictions loom everywhere.

You would like to be the person who saves the dog but would also like to be the person who can put personal guilt feelings aside when the larger issue of your relationship is at stake. The feeling that many values or many images are competing for your allegiance is similar to the feeling that no values are worth pursuing. Anxiety lurks in the incoherence that faces you. Nothing seems like it has value now because many things seem equally worth valuing. Relativism is threatening because the moral sense demands values that are absolute and universal—values that hold in all possible worlds that you can think of.

Fear of relativism is fear of the rumination it engenders. But why does rumination feel so bad? Consider an old story told by philosophers of rationality to make a point about the indeterminacy of preferences. A donkey searching for food comes across two haystacks in a field. One haystack is small but contains many strands of juicy green blades of freshly cut grass. The other stack is considerably larger and fluffier, but the cut grass in it has been dried out by the sun over the course of a few days, and so it is not as fresh as the grass in the first stack. The donkey ponders for a while and then makes for the green stack. Just before beginning to eat the hay, however, he thinks of the larger stack lying behind him that he will have to forego. The diaphanous glow of the larger, fluffier stack looms much larger in his eyes now that he has gotten this close to the greener stack.

Immediately he turns and makes for the fluffy stack. As he approaches it, he can already taste the golden brown strands of grass on his tongue. But as he gets closer, thoughts of the green stack start sprouting in his mind. Just as he is about to eat from the fluffy stack, thoughts of the green stack spring up in his mind and grow relentlessly: he can just see himself squeezing the green shoots of grass between his teeth and their sweet essence falling on his little tongue. Again he turns, just as suddenly as he did the first time, and makes for the green stack. The story has a sad ending: after many more oscillations between the two haystacks, the donkey dies of starvation.

The ruminating mind replicates—in thought—the actions of the donkey in real life. Rumination is a traveling back and forth of the mind, unconvinced of the true or ultimate value of any one option, belief, creed, or commitment. The mind oscillates between beliefs or commitments by bringing forth reasons and counterreasons for choosing one way or another at any one time. We reason with ourselves through choices among commitments. Rumination is deliberation pursued as if in a fever or a trance, without any leave to act before a *final* resolution has been reached, but with no glimpse into what such a resolution could look like.

To stay or to leave? He is so sweet at times, so happy in your presence, that you feel as if you could let yourself fall from great heights if he were next to you. But his moments of jealousy and sloth make that very happiness suspect. Is it a purely animal joy of having a secure mate at his side? Is it a deeper sentiment of comfort? Animal grin or sparkling, mindful glee: what will it be? One beckons the other. There is no hope for a quick resolution.

Justification as a Life Vest: The Dynamic of Accounting for Oneself

A definitive resolution might be one from which further deliberation cannot sway us. "What can I know without doubt?" asked René Descartes, in the first fully documented rumination of a human mind (Descartes 1990). "Cogito, ergo sum," he finally concluded—a conclusion, however, that had no implications for how he should act. Being is a precondition for rumination—for thinking of any kind, to be sure. That is why rumination about ultimate belief turns up being as the guarantor of certainty and thinking as the guarantor of being. But the fact that we simply are bears no implication for what we should do.

We are left without a justification for our actions, without some sort of guarantee that our actions—by fitting a narrative or story or model that places values on various actions and makes them right—will confer value on us and make us good. We are left doubting that our actions will take away the feeling of worthlessness that we dread: for they can only take away this feeling if we have no *doubts* about the fact that we have done *right*. We understand rightness as conformity to an ideal. We cannot have several ideals flying around because the existence of any other ideal undermines the standing and uniqueness of the ideal we hold. If an ideal is not unique, then it cannot confer on us the value we are seeking because we could be doing right by one principle and wrong by another. To cure the dread of falling short of the image, we must escape the ambiguity about the identity of the ideal.

The Search for Ideal Types: Creativity in the Service of Anxiety

The search for an ideal is motivated by the need to escape rumination and by the need to act in a justifiable way. We act justifiably when we have a justification for our actions that we believe to be true. "Tell me the truth so I can make up my mind whether or not to believe it," wrote Elizabeth I. Some beliefs let us act and live with the consequences of our actions: we call these beliefs "true." Others do not: we call them "false." Wisdom—which the queen was reputed to possess—consists in knowing the one kind from the other and in choosing accordingly.

There is no ultimate answer to a string of "Why?'s," but knowing that there is no ultimate answer—believing it fully and feeling the arbitrariness it engenders—can be paralyzing. We must have some answers, must have some moral principles that guide our actions, and must suppress (at the moment at which "the blade cuts into the flesh" and we must act irreversibly) the sneaking suspicion that Nietzsche is right—that our beliefs serve the purely instrumental function of making our predicaments actionable and of keeping us from rumination over what could have been. Acting consciously means acting in spite of being conscious.

Ideals as Inevitable Fictions: The Western Understanding of Cannibalism

Consider, as examples of Nietzsche's inevitable fictions, Michel Montaigne's interpretations of the subjective experience of the cannibals of his time, recently discovered in the New World—particularly in Brazil—and the counterinterpretations that they have stimulated. Montaigne argues that the cannibal is not prompted by hunger or the need for food. "The flesh of the prisoner who is to be devoured is in no way a food, but a sign," writes Frank Lestringant (1997, p. 102) in his study of perceptions of cannibalism. "Eating the body of another person does not provide nourishment or strength . . . ; in the last analysis it is a purely verbal transmission; or, as Montaigne himself wrote, 'They [the cannibals] require no other ransom of their prisoners, but an acknowledgment and confession that they are vanquished'" (p. 102).

The cannibal objectifies his prisoner before he eats her flesh. But (Nietzsche might ask) does he need to objectify his prisoner to eat her (which he wants to do to appease appetites that Montaigne might not deem human), or, rather, is the eating of the flesh itself a symbolic action, which the cannibal does *in spite* of himself, in spite of his immediate feelings? And (Nietzsche might want to know) does not Montaigne have some reason for salvaging the cannibal from his own image of the cannibal as a creature driven by nonhuman appetites?

Here, Nietzsche might gain the upper hand, for Montaigne does indeed seem to have a moral stake in saving the moral status of the cannibal:

Montaigne considers that the Nature of the New Indies is fundamentally good, and it is not the fault of that Nature if her children devour one another. A corollary of this is that the natural generosity of the "endless" continent is echoed by the "generosity" of an approach to warfare that involved no self-interested calculation. It is a notable contrast to the avarice of the first conquistadors. The Portuguese who made alliances with their former adversaries taught them another way to kill people, infinitely more cruel than simply eating them: "which was, to bury them up to the middle, and against the upper part of the body to shoot arrows, and then being almost dead, to hang them up." . . . Thus, the self-giving of the warrior, which extended even to his muscles and veins when he became his enemy's prisoner, seems as whole-hearted and willing as Nature's yielding of her fruits. . . .

Thus, Montaigne is finally able to save both the New World, in all its native goodness, and the Cannibal, whose appetites are moralized and endowed with a fully human meaning. (Lestringant, 1997, p. 102)

Lestringant points out, however, that the discovery that South America was an "island with limited food resources and practically devoid of herd animals" was to lend support to the hypothesis that cannibalism was concerned with food, a view, however, that was "inconceivable" in the Europe during the Renaissance: "it would have been inconceivable that cannibalism was a natural need, any more than the term could have applied to incest or homicide; all of them were human perversions inspired by Satan" (Lestringant 1997, p. 101). So just as the cannibal in one interpretation needs a fiction to perform the flesh-eating ritual, so Montaigne might seem to need a fiction—that of the noble cannibal—to carry on *his* philosophical activity.

But does Nietzsche then want to say that animal instinct itself is the master cause to which symbolism and morality are subordinated, making acting on one's instinct possible and unconflicted? This point was made by Girolamo Cardano in 1557, who wrote that the

Caribs, not content merely to devour enemies taken in war, do not shrink from eating children whom they have begotten upon their slaves. They are infamous enough to rip their own offspring from the womb and devour it, and then eat the mother as well. . . . [C]annibalism assumes the solemnity of a theatre of sadism for which there are no taboos. Anthropophagy accompanies infanticide and amorous dalliance lapses into an orgy of blood. The bonds of kinship, as well as those of blood, are scandalously transgressed for the sake of a stupid and bestial appetite, which alternates between sex and hunger: the victorious warrior fornicates with his female captives before devouring them along with their adulterous offspring. (Lestringant 1997, p. 117)

Nietzsche's instincts might now be aroused in the other direction: Could it not be that Cardano—a physician and mathematician—is trying to fuel his own world view in which raw and unprincipled appetites, fields, forces, and flows are the primary movers of the social world? Indeed, as Lestringant (1997, p. 118) points out, "Cardano cares little for ethnographical accuracy. He proclaims at the outset that he intends to treat the West Indies as a single whole, and blithely proceeds to confuse the sacrificial rites of the Aztecs, who tore the hearts from living victims and flung them, raw and quivering, upon the altar, with the vengeance cannibalism of the Tupinambas, as described by Thevet, Lery and Montaigne. . . . Cardano throws [these customs] on a disorderly heap which offers no foothold for symbolism." It is the self-proclaimed realist whose reality is in question; the truthfulness of the truthful seems doubtful, once we have even dimly perceived his purpose: for being able to act requires that his psyche be shaped by a cosmic model in which he has come to have a huge personal stake.

Moral Reasoning as Camouflage: The Dynamic of Proselytization

We seem to be engaged in a significant intrapersonal process of proselytization aimed at convincing ourselves of our own beliefs—and especially of the beliefs by which we place values on alternative possible worlds or states of the world. Doubt must be quelled so that rumination and regret do not turn life into a living nightmare. At least one chapter in the history of the mind has been written by the repeated salvage attempts of future-proof—read, doubt-free—moral dogma from inquiry, of moral certainty from doubt, and of self-righteousness from questioning.

The greater and the more irreversible the consequences of one's actions, the deeper and more comprehensive the dogma that one comes up with to salvage one's actions from the damnation of history. Killed hundreds of thousands of people with one nuclear bomb? Then we need volumes of analyses that show the cost—in human lives—of not bombing to be much higher than that of the bombing. Pulverized an entire army in the desert and turned human lives into acrid ashes over hundreds of square miles? Then we cannot just say, "It's about oil and dollars," but rather, "It's about national security, values, sovereignty, American jobs," and so forth. Need to destabilize a foreign government whose demise is essential for westward expansion? With Hitler, as with NATO, the answer remains the same: manufacture an ethnic crisis and intervene as the righteous liberator. The deeper the crime, the more unassailable the dogma has to be, and the more spotless the moral ground from which the dogma is launched. The world needs to be saved from its own righteousness, as Henry Kissinger noted.

The Anatomy of Political Scandal: Ideal Types at the Slaughterhouse of Public Opinion

Why did we care so deeply that the president of the United States gently inserted a cigar into the vagina of one of the White House interns? Does any evidence link executive incompetence with sexual hyperactivity and polygamy? According to recently documented incidence of illicit sex among U.S. executives, their night-time romps when away from home can turn into addictions that require treatment at recently opened specialized clinics. Yet shareholders continue to trade in the shares of the companies led by these sexual athletes. We seek not truth and validity, it seems, but rather confirmation of deeply held beliefs and stereotypes. No wonder that, since Watergate, every U.S. president has been hounded by Washington's scandal-mongering culture: we need to be very right and to stand very tall to take so many lives in conflicts abroad. The greater the crime, the taller the excuse, and the more noble the justification, as future events—we predict—will show.

Moral Intercourse: Interactive Moral Reasoning and the Ethics of the Torturer

The seeker of certainty tries to turn every sequence of experiences into a morality play in which good and evil are clearly and unambiguously represented in the protagonists. What is to be eliminated is moral doubt—and the proof of moral courage for the dogmatist is the violent destruction of the person cast in the evil role. Video replays of the Gulf War bombing raids on Iraqi facilities that found their way into the American media rooms were amazingly silent about the blood and suffering that the bombing raids caused on the raided. The "Pac-Man war" choreographers succeeded in caricaturizing what had to be destroyed, understanding how much easier it is for the American public to feel morally righteous for supporting the dismantling of a cartoon of evil than for dismembering breathing people. The moral dogmatist's views require—for their own sanctification—a public display and recognition of moral courage. Murdering or tormenting the evil ones in public sanctifies the dogmatist's unerring commitment with the blood of others.

It is perhaps illuminating to consider the moral intercourse of torturer and tortured to discover the anguish of the torturer about her own values in the tormented cries of the tortured. Imagine: you ask a young man who speaks the same language you do with the same accent to reveal some secret hideaway of his friends so you can trap them. You know that he belongs to a party that opposes—sometimes violently—the power of the party that pays for your meals and rent. You believe that the beliefs that he holds as true are the opposite of the beliefs you would recognize as true. You know that he has a wife, children, and parents and that he relates to them as you do to yours. You know that you, too, in his place would refuse to give the required information. You see the fear in his eyes—a fear of physical pain and of the unknown that awaits him.

The suspicion that he has already objectified you—cast you in the role of the evil one—propels you into action. You stretch him out on a bench, put a funnel into his mouth, and begin pouring water from a nearby drainage canal into him. Water pours out of his nostrils, tears come out of his eyes. He breathes out of his nose the water that you can barely stand to smell, and he coughs convulsively. "Where are they?" you blare in his ear but do not give him a chance to answer. Any refusal to answer would be like salt on your wounds. "And would *I* hold up for so long?" you ask yourself.

But what if he makes the conscious decision to tell? What then? Isn't it the case that he has then again placed himself above his predicament—above you, for that matter? He has confessed not because he *had no choice but to* confess but rather because he has decided on it rationally—and why? Could it not be that there is some denial of all values hidden in his implicit denial of his values? What if he has willingly renounced his values? Does that not make him a superior being to you, morally speaking? You, after all, feel that you *have no choice but to* soak him in the filth. But he has thought the matter over and made the conscious decision to renounce his values. He is above his values. Is he then not the Nietzschean superman, above all values? But what if he is lying? Then this charade has to start again from the beginning. You will have to again try and overcome his voice, his words, his calm composure that you can empathize with so much more easily than you can with his squeals.

So you keep pouring—one liter, five liters, eight liters. His stomach bulges; his pants are wet because you have filled him up. His eyes are swollen, and there is a streak of blood coming from his nose. You focus on it just as he screams "Fucker" in your face. You blare the question again and again start pouring the water just before hearing the answer. He is too conscious still. There is too much liberty for his consciousness to play its mind-awing tricks on you. You want a confession breathed through an animal gasp that he had no choice but to utter. This is the true test of your own value and weight in the universe—your world view poured out into living matter, just like the sewing machine that wrote out the judgment on prisoners' bare backs in Franz Kafka's "In the Penal Colony" (Kafka 1974). You want the confession to come as a catharsis—one that simultaneously recognizes your own position and the definitive destruction of his own morality.

Having no choice but to surrender the prized information would be a failure not only of his physique and physical stamina but of his moral being, now broken down by physical suffering: The idea that has lived in him could not (even) help him get over the ordeal. The moral principle that kept his consciousness above the pain could not save him: matter has triumphed over *this* mind, at least.

Opprobrium accrues to the one who confesses, in the torture room as on the streets. The opprobrium is not only for his shortcoming as a person: that would be immaterial if a person was only a collection of flesh and bones. It is rather for his failure as a moral entity—for the failure of his moral constitution to help his physical being rise above its pain. The torturer seeks to break down the voice of the tortured, to take away the agency that his voice gives him, by recognizing the selfhood of his I. Should the tortured freely decide to end the torture, the torturer has lost her stake.

"Intense pain,"—writes Elaine Scarry, "is world destroying" (Scarry 1995, p. 19). By "world" she means the inner world that language constructs out of perceptions. "In compelling confession—rather than merely coercing it—the torturer compels the prisoner to record and objectify the fact that intense pain is world destroying" (p. 31). That the world of the prisoner—the way in which he represents his life events—is destroyed is prima facie evidence that his world is destructible. This is the true evidence that the torturer is after. He will nonetheless accept an act of confession as partial relief from his moral anxiety if he believes that the prisoner has willingly renounced his moral commitment because he is motivated by an act of self-hatred. Where can this feeling come from?

Scarry writes, "Regardless of the setting in which he suffers, the person in great pain experiences his own body as the agent of the agony" (p. 35) and thus his palpable self as the proximate instrument of torture. The body intrudes savagely on the mind, and confession may be a fitting self-inflicted whipping of the tortured by the tortured—for it brings with it the viscerally sharp sensations of remorse, anguish, shame, and guilt. The confession comes as an act of self-punishment, which the torturer can interpret as a devaluation of the self of the tortured in his own eyes—of that same self who is the locus of the moral value that must be subverted.

To the anguished torturer, no detail is irrelevant, for any detail of the tribulation can be used to justify a declaration of "victory" in a moral war in which the stakes are high and the predicament risky—for the opponent may end up dead but unvanquished or unable to confer, by his actions, victory on his tormentor. The path to the confession is therefore all-important. Scarry writes, "Before destroying language, pain first monopolizes language, becomes its only subject: complaint, in many ways the non-political version of confession, becomes its exclusive mode of speech" (p. 36). The mind taken over by pain is a happy sight for the tormentor, for it can lead smoothly to the mechanical breakdown into confession that the torturer requires for her own moral calculus. The tortured's path through pain, then, is as important a "birthmark" of the confession as is the timing and gasping of the confession itself.

The game of deception is played out here on a grand scale. The torturer surely must have some notion that she is the paid hand of a large organization that may have no internal moral values to speak of—even by her own standards; that but for some circumstances of history that lie beyond her understanding, she and the prisoner might have changed places; and that the prisoner's confession is somehow causally related to her ordeal rather than to the relative standing of the tortured and the torturer in the grand scheme of values. Along the way, however, the minds begin to cooperate while the bodies clash. Both torturer and tortured come to see their battle as meaningful, to take on their roles as epic roles and not as the instantiations of a historical freak accident, to see the confession of the tortured as prima facie evidence of her moral weakness, and to see the moral value of the torturer as at stake in the game. In shouting savagely and refusing to confess to the last gasp, the tortured cooperates: confessing with a tired smile at some point would belie the entire spectacle as a farce.

As the pain of torture takes the tortured further toward the outer reaches of language and consciousness, the usual conscious motives for persevering in life, for striving to overcome the pain and go on living another day—such as a belief in a transcendental value—begin to waver. And as the pain of the tortured becomes more and more central to the language and consciousness of the torturer, her own reasons for persevering—for continuing to cause the pain—become stronger. While the two bodies snarl at each other, the two minds execute a delicate dance. The torturer's self-perceived moral value grows as a function of the recession of the moral force of the tortured, which duly recedes into the night and fog of nameless pain.

What subverts the tortured in torture is not pain but doubt. If pain can so overwhelm my mind, asks the tortured, how can the idea I embody have the transcendence that I have claimed for it? And if I resist, am I striking a pose for the benefit of an audience? Is my faith fake? If I am in the right, asks the torturer, then how can the idea I represent be dismembered by the resilience of a broken body? If I persist, have I yielded to fear? If I desist, have I fallen into doubt? Moral doubt undermines the value that both torturer and tortured claim and fuels the unfolding physical torment. Each is driven to persist by the hope that the doubt will be resolved in some way by the dance of their bodies.

Let's go back to the torment of the funnel. You are tired and slightly worried because the young man filled with ten liters of water gives no further sign of consciousness. Now you pounce on his chest and stomach with both fists and slap his face so hard that the right eye bounces around before the pupil closes—nothing! He seems peaceful. Even the tormented stream that was gushing from his nose is gone. He has a pulse, however. Suddenly his eyes light up, and he grins at you. There is unmistakable irony in his eyes. Now there truly can be no more peace—not for you, anyway. Where will you draw the boundaries of his consciousness? When will you ever be able to say, "He had no choice but to confess"? or "He had not the moral fiber to resist the pain"? Now your prospects for moral triumph—for overcoming the doubts in your own mind—are abysmal: murder him, and his silence will always remind you of your failure; accept his confession at some point, and remain haunted by his cruel irony: "Who knows what I really meant when I told you what you wanted to hear?'

Doubt is the tortured's torture, as it is the torturer's. For the tortured is also waging a battle—against his own consciousness. He asks, "Will you give way, feeble mind? And if you do, will *she* know it?" For the tortured has not truly succumbed until the torturer believes that he has succumbed to the pain—that the value that lies in his mind and conscious being has been taken over by the pain. He might indeed succumb, momentarily, and the torturer may not know it. Then all is not lost. Consciousness may be regained and with it the strength to resist until the next brutality—perhaps past it. Who knows? But what consciousness can survive the torturer's triumph? Won't the tortured infer his moral destruction from the torturer's surprised delight at his submission? Won't the battle then be over?

Moral Intercourse on the Corporate Ladder

We live in a corner of space-time—the twenty-first century Western hemisphere—where the ritual of torturer and tortured is played out, *sotto voce,* in corporate boards and offices, with people using words inscribed on sheets of papers entitled "Performance Evaluations" to inflict on each other the dances of condemnation, rebellion, contrition, resignation, and rebuttal that we might still see in torture chambers in the Eastern Hemisphere. For instance: You've been picked by the company board of managing directors to head your firm's turn-around in a large but generally sleepy European country. The regional manager—a polished, soft-spoken local who is several years older than you are—has consistently made you feel like an ignoramus. You feel, deep inside your bones, your lack of a classical education every time you see this articulate descendant of Aristotle. By contrast, your emotions seem now—and seem to have always seemed—a little too close to the skin. The redneck rears his ugly head every time you pose for the mirror: smart but uncouth, energetic but not smooth, strong as a bull but timorous like a dog about to urinate.

Alas, you get your big chance: the performance review. You get to bludgeon *him,* after all the time in which he has inflicted this silent disease on your self-esteem. The rubrics and headings come like blows of the whip: some impact on his creativity, some on his integrity, some on his intelligence, some on his wit, some on his energy, some on his strength of character, some on his sociability. The *holistic* approach to evaluation leaves no possible exit for the victim, no way he could tell himself a story that gets him off the hook. The people who came up with this set of procedures were men of genius, you now think with a smile. Under the guise of fairness and inclusiveness, they came up with a more comprehensive torture scheme than any one that had come before them: leave no stone unturned—or unsoiled, rather—all in the interest of being fair. You smile at the chuckle you choke back.

Ah, the performance review meeting! You see how he looks at you—what arrogant equanimity. He does not even show that he is nervous. Surely he knows that his bonus depends on this review! Does he not care that he will not be able to buy as much? But no, he won't show a hint of malaise or of worry. It's all part of the pose. "You did not do such a good job in getting those distributors motivated," you start matter-of-factly but knowingly touching on the most sensitive subject. No objection. He seems to look *through* you rather than *at* you, even when you address him directly. But perhaps he has realized that you are talking to yourself, rather than him. No, he cannot be that clever. Nevertheless, he clearly does not buy into your little show—yet. "And that meeting you put off until I had to intervene?" You've lost your temper (it happens all the time) and feel resentful of having lost it. But it seems to be paying off. He argues back. He has even sweated a bit. Look at the little alcoholic's nose getting all red! You've accused him of sloth, and he already sees himself, piglike, drinking beer when instead he could have gone and straightened out a difficult situation.

Ah, these company men and their value systems! All you have to do is chance on the right value that they are terrified of falling short of! Then you have their intestines in your pocket! You smile nondescriptly at his defending himself. He misinterprets your smile as understanding or sympathy. Perhaps he really is slothful—in his thinking as well as his doing! The smile is about your first little victory! You've found the little value that hurts him to fall short of. Now all you have to do is twist the knife a little bit more deeply into the wound. So you also tell him about the mediocre rapport with the rest of the sales staff: he is much too passive in his approach. You hope this variation on sloth should do the trick again—but horrors, he is looking out the window. Perhaps the proud son of Aristotle has not understood you, so you repeat your little jibe, only more clearly this time, using English, the universal language, spoken with a German accent that makes it seem even colder, even more detached from the intended recipient of the words that it has ever sounded to you.

No reaction. You cannot figure out why. Perhaps he is tired. Perhaps he does not think the charge worth refuting or has given up trying to communicate with you. So you cut to the chase and reveal his overall evaluation. This is supposed to be a grand total tally or average of all of the evaluations in the different areas in which he is being evaluated. Aha! Now he argues back! He brings up all of his past contributions, but in such a tone that you do not know whether he really cares! You begin to feel shaky and feel yourself beginning to sweat. Too much beer at lunch, perhaps. Is that a smile in the corner of his mouth, a sign of derision at the large half-moons of sweat under your arms?

Still, you are resourceful. You give him a slightly higher evaluation and tell him it is on account of your seeing the justice of his pleading. He smiles. Is he genuinely happy to have gotten a better rating? If so, then your domination over him is at last vindicated: he desired something that you have given him not for the reasons he thinks you have given it to him but rather to assert yourself. There is something sarcastic in his smile? Doubt is eating you again. This is what they mean when they talk of being eaten alive, perhaps. Has he gone back to his dear Aristotle? Has he written off the logic of the flesh and of money and of power as a mere diversion? Has he written you off as a fly on his wall? "Who is torturing whom here?" your teeth screech inside.

Making and Unmaking the World: Reflection on the Absurd

The moral sense helps consciousness make sense of the world. It helps *make* the world in the image of words—in the image of the metaphor that the creator's mind inhabits currently. Just as physical pain *unmakes* the creator's world by breaking down her language and her ability to express herself in language, grasping and living the absurd that lurks in the background of every word and action unmake the creator's world by rendering her mythology meaningless. The moral sense makes sense of perception by subsuming it in an image where good and bad are clearly labeled and transparent and where the predicament of the person who is bound by a particular morality is therefore actionable.

There is no ambivalence that plagues the world pictures of the addicted moralist. Her perceptions have penumbrae in her mind as one of the characters in a long narrative that organizes the life of the actor. Writes Jean-Paul Sartre (1956, p. 112), "This is what fools people: a man is always a teller of tales, he lives surrounded by his stories and the stories of others, he sees everything that happens to him through them; and he tries to live his life as if he were telling a story." "The falseness of an opinion is not for us any objection to it," echoes Nietzsche (1909–1913, p. 283), who is willing to renounce the search for truth—except for the truthful recognition of "untruth as a condition of life." But surely not even Nietzsche is willing to renounce the will to sense and implicitly to *some* morality—one based on lucidity.

Seeking sense—seeking "the way" to "the goal"—is as much part of our cultural ethos as is the belief that the world has a sense, that there *are* ways to universally worthwhile goals. The universality of "the way" and "the destination" is an anchor of the moral sense. It is by the uncanny frustration of this sense that Kafka (1974, p. 23) achieves his disquieting effect:

It was early in the morning, the streets clean and deserted, I was on my way to the station. As I compared the tower clock with my watch I realized it was much later than I had thought and that I had to hurry; the shock of this discovery made me feel uncertain of the way; I wasn't very well acquainted with the town as yet; fortunately, there was a policeman at hand, I ran to him and breathlessly asked him the way. He smiled and said: "You asking me the way?" "Yes," I said, "since I can't find it myself." "Give it up! Give it up!" said he, and turned with a sudden jerk, like someone who wants to be alone with his laughter.

The search for "the way" is itself "a way," one which, as Isaiah Berlin (1997, p. 37) noted, has anchored much of our Western imagination: "At some point I realised that what all these views had in common was a Platonic ideal: in the first place that, as in the sciences, all genuine questions must have one true answer and one only, all the rest being necessarily errors; in the second place that there must be a dependable path towards the discovery of these truths; in the third place that the true answers, when found, must necessarily be compatible with one another and form a single whole, for one truth cannot be incompatible with another—that we know a priori." This is the way that the policeman bids the man give up—give up the search for the "right" address, for the "right" tone in which to say something, for the "right" principle by which to act.

But what if not even coherence itself were one of the principles to which one strived to adhere? Then Kafka's howling policeman might bid us bid *it* good riddance—and then how should we understand Kafka's stories? How are we to understand his grammatical constructions, if not by the presumption that he trying to *be coherent,* to *make sense* to us by making sense to himself? Can he coherently advocate the abandonment of coherence? And, moreover, if there is no sense to be made of our experiences or of our search for making sense of our experiences, then how is this foregoing sentence to be understood? As a world ender? As a portal to a world in which language is a musical or visual form only, the faculty of understanding being relegated to a kind of secondary role (like musicology is to music)? As a portal to a new world that has "escaped language"? Where have we escaped "to"? And who are "we" who have escaped?

10

The Rational *Causeur*: The Subordination of Reason to the Passions

Sense—and this one ought to know—is always the nonsense that one lets go.
—Odo Marquard

Knowledge, also, is a form of power.
—Francis Bacon

The devil is the arrogance of the spirit, truth that is never seized by doubt.
—Umberto Eco, *The Name of the Rose*

Elaine Scarry (1995, p. 58) relates the following story about concentration camp guards in Nazi Germany, which she attributes to Bruno Bettelheim, one of the camp survivors: "Concentration camp guards, . . . repeatedly said to their prisoners, 'I'd shoot you with this gun but you're not worth the three pfennig of the bullet,' a statement that had so little effect on the prisoners that its constant repetition was unintelligible to Bettelheim until he realized that it had been made part of the SS training because of its impact on the guards themselves."

It is a clever construction. It objectifies the prisoner (by assigning him or her a monetary value). It masks the act of killing into a mechanical exercise—shooting with a gun (notice they did not say "*kill* you with this gun"). And it makes the guard's own actions seem like the outcome of a rational cost-benefit analysis (the loss of the three pfennigs was not considered worth the pleasure of the shooting). All of this meaning in one sentence that creates a semblance of normality and rationality around the death camp. The use of words, backed by the structure of logic, turns passions into reasons and makes it possible for one to live with oneself and to *go on.*

The pursuit of one's own desires is always in need of a story to back it up. Naked will is too frightening to oneself and others. "Can you stop the wind?" a devout smoker might ask when he is asked why he does not stop. "It's the four-year itch," says the executive who has just made love to a woman he met in a bar to his wife's attorney over the telephone. "Just give us the story, man," the layman pleads with the scientist. We cannot proceed in our pursuit of desire without the lines that make that desire seem reasonable.

Instrumental rationality is a penumbra that the future casts on our minds. The future is something that must be dealt with, possessed, reconnoitered, mapped, and controlled. Reason and science provide the tools for bringing the future into the present. How to get ahead? How to get a house? How to pay less for your mortgage? How to get into college? How to get into graduate school or professional school? How to make more money? These are the questions that eat away at most waking moments, turning all of living into an exercise in calculation on ever-longer time scales.

If you have invented means by which you can create wheat that flowers twice a year, would you not want to use your discovery to try creating wheat that flowers three or four times a year? Why stop there? If you can influence what a person eats for breakfast by selling her cheap grains, why not try to influence her dinner eating habits as well, particularly since you have in the meantime mastered the techniques of mass advertising to unprecedented degrees, and by inferring her preferences from her past behaviors you know that she will come to identify with your products? If you can monitor a person's reading habits by tracking his credit-card spending pattern, then why not use this information to tailor your advertisements to what you think are his personal tastes? If you have discovered a means by which you can spy on your boss's e-mails, why not use this power to make some suitable edits as well—especially as she cannot tell what is happening? The successes of instrumental reason point one toward its potential future uses, as ends become means. Instrumental reason is the tool by which passions can turn ends into means. We may underestimate, however, the power of instrumental reason to make means out of our minds and to establish itself as a dominant mode of looking at the world. "Who's whose master?" we might pause and ask.

Instrumental Reason as a Machine: The Emotional Structure of an Inference Engine

Before examining how instrumental reason is used to the end of increasing one's own causal powers or undermining the causal powers of others, let us examine the causal powers of reason itself. By a miraculous psychological feat, if you believe that all birds are mammals and that a robin is a bird, then you feel compelled to believe that a robin is a mammal. But who is *compelling you to believe*?

The logician replies, "The laws of logic—modus ponens, in particular. If I believe in the proposition 'If A, then B' and I also believe A, then I will necessarily also believe B." Her will to believe "not B" has been vanquished by the "force of logic." Ponder this bit of magic within yourself: your thoughts are stronger than you are; they have become, in fact, your master. And it is not you that uses logic to reason about the world, but rather it is logic that uses you to control your thoughts.

But wait! Why cannot we simply reject logic altogether and in particular declare our freedom from modus ponens? Well, how would we do this? We would make a proposition such as "I reject modus ponens," of course. The logician looks at us as if at an idiot. He might go about interpreting this proposition as follows: "She has just rejected modus ponens (proposition a), and she implicitly maintains that she-now is the same person as she-who-rejected-modus ponens (proposition b); therefore (by modus ponens), she has not only *assertively* rejected modus ponens but also performatively as well (proposition c). But hang on! She had *rejected* modus ponens, so surely her performative behavior is not necessarily bound by her assertive behavior. Therefore, she cannot assertively reject modus ponens in any way. Modus ponens is an a priori of communication. The only way in which modus ponens (or the law of the excluded middle, for that matter) can be rejected is by abandoning any sort of pretense of communicating—by abandoning the implicit purpose of language. But who would like to interact with someone who treats words as random collections of syllables?

There is a heavy price to pay for opting out of "language," and that is an abandonment of one's linguistic connection with others. This abandonment also entails the abandonment of many of one's causal powers over others. Consider a threatening pose, meant to cause someone to leave your neighborhood. If the pose is interpreted as a *communicative* act, then it stands a chance of being causally efficacious, since the intruder infers from the pose plus the assumption that the pose is meant to be communicative of the intent to strike or lash out at her if she does not leave. But if the pose cannot be interpreted as a communicative act, then it will not be associated with the intent to strike or lash out and cannot therefore be *causally* efficacious; if it is efficacious, it is so because, accidentally, the intruder interpreted it as a communicative action.

By *saying,* we aim to impose structure on experience. Logical structure helps us control our mind—and hence the world the mind creates—because it is predictable, reliable, and stable. When we use a tool for a purpose, we count on the stability of the tool, on its reliable response to our intentions and subsequent actions. Reliability makes a tool into what it is: it lets us use it to etch our wills into matter. Logic is such a tool; only now the matter in question is the sometimes incoherent stream of consciousness we experience, and the will is the will to believe rather than the will to act. Saying "This is a dog" about a set of images and sounds brings a potentially complex set of experiences together in a symbol that can be manipulated by our minds.

Logical structure, then, lends the contents of our mind the semblance of intelligibility. Intelligibility is what tames experiences by bringing them into the I system—the network of myths, stories, schemas, concepts, and ideas that make up the self's self-description. We use the rules of logic to rein in experiences to the self system. "I am clever," says one of the myths of the self system of beliefs, and the mind scours its memory for confirmatory experiences. The imposition of logical structure unto living memory parallels "man's search for meaning."

We search for meaning that helps us over the chasm of chaos, the anxiety of the dissolving self, the madness of the disillusioned who cannot deceive herself anymore about the senselessness of the world, the depression of the one who has exhausted his spiritual resources in the search for meaning, the metaphysical boredom of the aimless twentieth-century teenager. Logical form helps us create or re-create the meaning we yearn to discover.

Meaning depends on association and symbolism that are inherited and sometimes seem beyond our control. But association and symbolism can be manipulated with words and propositions. Scientific reasoning has taught us to relate to particulars as mere instantiations of generic entities. Logical atomism has taught us to break down complex propositions into conjunctions of simple propositions and has given us confidence that nature mirrors our minds in its behavior—that complex phenomena can analogously be broken down into simple phenomena and thus understood once and for all in their lawlike essence.

Paradox throws us into the nameless: this is why its presence is troubling. "Who shaves the barber who shaves all and only those who do not shave themselves?" goes the question. And the mind goes round and round in search of the answer. Alas, when we cannot find it (try it on yourself), we say that we cannot find it—not that there is no answer or that the question is meaningless. We dread to say, "MU!"—a term suggested by Douglas Hofstadter (1979) to mean "neither yes nor no, as I disagree with the premise of the question," when asked if we want our eggs fried or boiled this morning, when we do not in fact want any eggs at all. We dread to break the seamless interpersonal web of meaning from which stability itself emerges and glosses over mysteries and discontinuities.

Raw experience teems with mysteries. Mysteries are opportunities for falling into chaos and meaninglessness. They are reminders of the mystery from which we spend great energy seeking peace and shelter—the mystery of death. We call on reason to set us free from the anxiety these mysteries cause us, and we use reason to make believe that the structure of the world mirrors the logical structure of our theories about the world. This is the essence of the doctrine that identifies words with the experiences and objects that they refer to, that teaches an imperfect and reductive picturing of that reality in the mirror of language. By giving a name to an experience, we can control it by bringing it into logical contact with other names and propositions with which it can be made to cohere. But by making the word *stand for* the experience, we also lose the rich *raw feel* of the experience, its quality as a phenomenon.

Perhaps it is *because* raw feels are so informationally rich that we feel the need to control them by encoding experiences onto words. Using logic, we

bring the mystery of experience "home" into language. This is the great secret of the success of "diagnoses" in the modern era. The diagnosis is a
"bringing home" of something that is teeming with chaos—the experience
of illness. Give it a name, and already the experience has been tamed. It has
been made familiar. We have brought it under cognitive control. We have
pulled the raw experience into a symbol, which can now be manipulated. If
we manage to get ourselves to believe that the word *fully* captures the experience, then grammar and logic supply us with structures and levers that
seem to be attached to the world of experiences—not merely to the world
of words. Not just words but their referents, as well, appear structured and
controllable by the superstructures of language.

We can now *do things* with symbols that we simply cannot do with experiences. And logic is the equipment by which we wield our causal powers
on symbols. Modern scientific disciplines are full of nouns and proper
names. Each physical symptom has a name that makes it the proper domain of a particular expert. Each legal claim falls under a particular jurisdiction, a particular precedent that makes it the proper domain of some
paternal authority—a lawyer, a judge, a social worker, a legislature.
Nouns are the levers by which the professional handles our lives.

When Are Reasons Causes? The Fabric of Arguments and Its Understructures

Our use of language creates and preserves the semblance of a causal
nexus that links together social and psychological phenomena. If adherence to the rules of reason is a precondition for communicativity and
communicativity is a precondition for causal efficacy in the social realm,
then reason is a precondition for causal efficacy in the social realm. It
seems that to have causal powers over others through words and arguments, we must submit to the causal powers that reason holds over us. It
is a virtue, in modern Western society, to be a rational or reasonable person—to be a person whose actions and judgments are guided by the rules
of reason.

Reasons seem to be able to cause us to take certain actions. You think
that you will be unhappy if you stay in your current relationship, and you
leave your spouse of many years—in spite of your temporary yearnings for

another evening together and your fears of waking up alone tomorrow. How does this happen? Why does not your body do precisely the same as it has always done on many evenings before? Philosophers have puzzled over the miracle of mental causation for a long time and have come up with two equally silly solutions: they either deny that there are any physical events, or they deny that there are any mental events. We prefer to keep both and entertain the miracle of mental causation—although it is perfectly possible that there is no causation at all taking place but some other sort of relationship that we have not yet brought to language.

Our daily discourse suggests that we believe in the mental causation of actions by reasons. If reasons can cause actions (which in turn can cause other actions), then we have created a seamless causal web to describe the universe (including its consciousness-bearing inhabitants), in which reasons (which can be changed or modified only by rational arguments), cause actions, which in turn beget fresh grounds (such as reasons and arguments), for modifying previously held reasons, which in turn lead to new actions.

The "steering wheel" of our inner world is the set of principles of reasoning that we use to construct arguments. But for these principles, we could not appeal to reasons at all because we could get reasons to "talk to one another." Individual agency vanishes as reasons have turned into causes, which in turn provide reasons. The individual person is no longer free to decide among various reasons, to create new scenarios, to imagine new possible worlds, because were she reasonable she would already have *discovered* the reasons that bear on a particular situation. Thus, individual freedom—and with it the threat of chaos and anxiety—is curtailed by the adherence to reason in deliberation.

Alluring though it is, the dream is misguided because it assumes that the ways in which two or more people talk about an event they have witnessed in common will be identical. But while one may see a set of events as a revolution and interpret it as providing a reason to join in, another may see it as a debacle and see it as providing a reason to call the police. One man's revolution is another man's street brawl and yet another's carnival or spectacle. Mapping experiences to words is a slippery task. There are many experiences that one word can "point to" simultaneously, just as there are many words that can "stand in" for a particular experience. There is no theory-independent observation language because language already *is* a theory: our interpretation of action verbs contains specific attributions of causation, and our internal representation of nouns and adjectives is imagistic and metaphorical in nature. Speaking of a theory-independent observation language is therefore equivalent to (absurdly) speaking of a language-independent observation language or more simply of a language-independent language.

Propositions make sense (or can be said to amount to nonsense) only in the context of some overarching *metaphor* or imagery, as the work of psycholinguists like George Lakoff (1996) has shown. Lakoff uses the example of liberals and conservatives accusing each other of incoherence over their stands on different issues. To liberals, it seems like a contradiction that conservatives want to save the lives of unborn fetuses but are against increasing entitlements for children in poor families, which could the save the lives of children who have been born. To conservatives, it seems like a genuine contradiction that liberals on one hand oppose restricting the right to abortion and thus sanction the killing of unborn fetuses and on the other hand are ready to vote for large entitlements for poor families and thus now seem to be concerned to save the lives of the children they may have let die as fetuses. The contradiction goes away if we see society through the conservative imagery or metaphor—that of a family with a strict father who metes out rewards and punishments to children who are to be disciplined by experience. Through the conservative lens, the conservative opposition to abortion appears to be a straightforward application of a moral value placed on "living with one's mistakes" and "dealing with the consequences of one's actions" as does the conservative opposition to greater benefits for poor families. The liberals, on the other hand, according to Lakoff, implicitly buy into the metaphor of society as a family with a nurturant mother. In this metaphor, individual autonomy is nurtured from an early age and individual rights are cultivated. Through *this* lens, there is no contradiction in the liberal stance: a woman should be both free to choose to end her pregnancy *and* entitled to state help when times are hard.

The Cocoon of Reason: Metaphor and the Bounds of Sense

Metaphor embeds reason. When reasoning "from first principles," we reason within a metaphor or a universe of meaning. As John Searle (1996) has pointed out by his famous "Chinese room" argument, there is more to language than syntax. People sitting in a room and conjugating—correctly—Chinese verbs according to some rules that they follow algorithmically do not constitute Chinese speakers, and their expressions do not constitute linguistic expressions. Syntax is not enough to make logic, and, by the same token, reason and logic are not enough to make an argument.

Reason does not create a seamless causal nexus: there arise potential discontinuities every time that two people communicate. However, it is nevertheless true that the judicious use of reason bestows causal powers on its user, which she can amplify by hiding or masking the assumptions underlying an argument and then by relying on the causal powers that the rules of logic exercise on our minds to do the rest of the "causal work." If I can get you to buy into the metaphor of a person as a maximizing agent who more or less mechanically maximizes a constrained utility function, then I can, by the rules of logic, get you to accept a large number of explanations and predictions generated by economic science. If I can get you to buy into the "society as a family with a strict father" metaphor, then I can get you to accept many normative principles that underlie conservative thinking on social issues.

Almost two hundred years ago, Pierre-Simon Laplace invented a demon. He thought the demon could be real but is highly unlikely. The Laplacian demon registered in its memory the positions and momenta of all of the particles in the universe, and—using Newton's three laws of classical dynamics—computed the momenta and positions for all of the particles in the universe for all times thereafter. The demon turned out to be impossible to achieve but promptly turned into a metaphor for structuring our understanding of the world. And this metaphor has colored much of scientific imagination ever since.

This apogee of mechanical determinism seemed feasible for a long time—at least until the discovery of quantum and chaotic phenomena a century later. The marvel is not, however, that the machine was proved to be *in principle* unrealizable—all the more so since the discovery of chaotic phenomena in dynamical systems. The marvel, rather, was that the machine was *thought possible* in the first place. And it is a marvel of the human mind—or rather, of the power of a metaphor to shape our perceptions or of the power of reason to shape our deepest intuitions. From the necessitarianism implicit in logic we—perhaps unconsciously—inferred a necessitarianism implicit in the workings of the universe.

Necessitarianism dies hard, and there is a good reason for it. If I can persuade you that *necessarily* the world will be in a particular way in the future, then I have acquired great powers over you. If you cannot but believe that the capitalist system will end in bloodshed and that a dictatorship of the proletariat is the only viable alternative, then you will be motivated to help me bring that revolution about. Any other aim that you may personally have will be counter to the "iron laws of history." If you believe that a market is the most efficient means of organizing production and will, in the foreseeable future, come to dominate all other forms of organization, then you will curtail efforts to create alternative forms of organization. Such is the power of structuralist theories of social action, such as Marxism or neoclassical economics—a power that rests on the "necessitarian illusion." "We can explain anything," the modern biologist says with a smile. "But can you predict?" the thinker retorts.

In the modern classroom, teacher and student alike succumb wholeheartedly to the need to "make sense" of a situation or a text. "What makes sense for this woman to do next?" asks the instructor, awakening you from a private musing. "This woman" is the vice president of a large brokerage house in a populous, ethnically diverse U.S. city. A broker who works in the same firm has asked her for his own private office on the same floor—something that other brokers do not have. "Or else, I'll leave," he says in his Chinese-accented English. But he is not just any broker. Over the past year, he landed a $1 million account without any leads from anyone else in the firm.

He has, however, requested her indulgence in all sorts of little quirks that he declares necessary for courting the local Asian community—like spending not much of his time in the office and even no time at all, on many occasions. His boss at first looks on him with suspicion ("What kind of broker wanders about all day long?") and then with condescension aimed at masking her awe over his achievements ("Ethnic tricks"). How hard it is to deal with the achievements of another! Now comes his request, backed by an ultimatum. And this young professor with his "What makes sense . . . ?" is about to justify the VP's firing of the broker for his request. Which she does. How could she not? Was she not the first woman VP in the history of this office? And did she get there by giving in to male ultimatums? How easily these men are taken in by the metaphor of battle and subjugation when they deliver an "or else"! Now a student puts up his hand and argues that "or else" should be let go. "It's unfair to the others," he squeals.

Right. "Just show me a $1 million account, and I'll give you my office," is what the woman VP should be saying to any of these conscientious objectors. The student is not arguing for fairness on moral grounds (he does not think that will work in the M.B.A. classroom, especially when the discussion is not about ethics). No, he is arguing on grounds of rational self-interest. A riot in the office might lead to lost opportunities, lost profits, lost something or other. So it is rational to be fair, in this case at least. But it would not be fair to be rational. Has he thought of that? The instructor dutifully jots down the prescription of the student. Others nod. The next slide reveals that the VP indeed fires "Or else, I'll leave" but manages to keep his $1 million account. Smiles all around: she must have done the right thing.

The Challenge of the Absurd

The loops of justification and the building blocks called *certainty* and *truth* are so rarely in question in everyday discourse that we call geniuses those who succeed in keeping us attentive to their words while introducing us to the undercurrents of reason, through the medium of the absurd. Franz Kafka's (1974, p. 120) predilection for the absurd that lurks in the everyday can make us feel that we are about to lose our bearings because our common sense has gone mad:

There are four legends concerning Prometheus:
According to the first he was clamped to a rock in the Caucasus for betraying the secrets of the gods to men, and the gods sent eagles to feed on his liver, which was perpetually renewed.
According to the second, Prometheus, goaded by the pain of the tearing beaks, pressed himself deeper and deeper into the rock, until he became one with it.
According to the third, his treachery was forgotten in the course of thousands of years, forgotten by the gods, the eagles, forgotten by himself.
According to the fourth, everyone grew weary of the meaningless affair. The gods grew weary, the eagles grew weary, the wound closed wearily.
There remained the inexplicable mass of the rock. The legend tried to explain the inexplicable. As it came out of a substratum of truth it had in turn to end in the inexplicable.

That the truth is inexplicable may be acceptable to some: words cannot fully capture our experiences. But that something is inexplicable *by virtue* of its being true is a new and unexpected twist: for what is the point of trying to *express,* to capture reality in language and paint the image of the world in words? What is the point of seeking a *sense* in our experiences?

"There remained the inexplicable mass of the rock." He had already set us up for the cold bath by setting forth the fourth myth as a plausible alternative to any of the other three. Everyone grew weary of the situation. Perhaps they had all started out enthusiastically—the gods with moral indignation, the eagles with voracious appetites egged on by godly threats for nonperformance, Prometheus by what he had imagined to be his fate on the earth. But few can outlive sleeplessness and hunger and boredom and a monotonous diet—so now version 4 becomes plausible, in spite of the fact that it contradicts our feeling that myths make sense, that they tell of what could not have been otherwise. We feel the same malaise when we hear four equally plausible versions of an entrenched myth that we feel when we hear modern complexity theorists talking about "playing the tape" of the history of life on earth again from the beginning and ending up with very different results, or when we hear them shoot down the age-old notions of equilibrium and of the informational efficiency of hierarchical forms of organization: "It could be otherwise. Just let yourself think it." They echo Kafka, in the language of mathematical symbols.

That it could be otherwise is psychologically painful because nothing follows from a story with many possible endings and meanings, no prescriptions for thought and action. What conclusions can we now draw from the myth? That Promethean knowledge is paid for dearly, as we are bid to believe by the modern mythology of the glorious entrepreneur? That the gods are not to be denied in their unbending wills, as we are bid to do by the modern scientific picture of the world? Hardly. Kafka suggests a world that might grow weary of itself and throw over not only its old knowledge and values but also its criteria for what qualifies as knowledge and values. It is a world that might randomly throw up all over its heroes, for no good reason. It is a world of people who are free to decide, not only among their actions but also among their beliefs.

Darkness at Noon: Modernism and the Twilight of Instrumental Rationality

Real decisions happen—when they do—at the level of choosing commitments of the mind to a metaphor that makes sense of a situation or to an ideology that disposes of a particular predicament. "I don't approve of mixing ideologies," says Arthur Koestler's (1941, p. 128) ambivalent executioner Ivanov in *Darkness at Noon:*

> There are only two conceptions of human ethics, and they are at opposite poles. One of them is Christian and humane, declares the individual to be sacrosanct, and asserts that the rules of arithmetic are not to be applied to human units. The other starts from the basic principle that a collective aim justifies all means, and not only allows, but demands, that the individual should in every way be subordinated and sacrificed to the community—which may dispose of it as an experimentation rabbit or a sacrificial lamb. The first conception could be called anti-vivisection morality, the second, vivisection morality. Humbugs and dilettantes have always tried to mix the two conceptions; in practice, it is impossible. Whoever is burdened with power and responsibility finds out on the first occasion that he has to choose; and he is fatally driven to the second alternative. . . . In times of need—and politics are chronically in a time of need—the rulers were always able to evoke "exceptional circumstances" which demanded exceptional measures of defense. Since the existence of nations and classes, they live in a permanent state of mutual self-defense, which forces them to defer to another time the putting into practice of humanism.

The inquisitioner's goal is to get the old revolutionary (Rubashov, who helped Number One come to power) to confess to a crime against the state that he did not commit—in the interest of the revolution, the continuing revolution, and the one true revolution. Why "one true"? Because this time, the revolutionaries are not self-deceived about the aims of the revolution: "Look at the Gracchi and Saint-Just and the Commune of Paris. Up to now, all revolutions have been made by moralizing dilettantes. They were always in good faith and perished because of their dilettantism. We for the first time are consequent" (p. 129).

So entrapment of the mind by logic and its harness to a world cause appears to be the goal of the rational revolution—the one true goal because the others, such as greater prosperity and freedom, seem to have been laid aside temporarily:

> "So consequent, that in the interests of a just distribution of land we deliberately let die of starvation about five million farmers and their families in one year. So conse-

quent were we in the liberation of human beings from the shackles of industrial exploitation that we sent about ten million people to do forced labor in the Arctic regions and the jungles of the East, under conditions similar to those of antique galley slaves. So consequent that, to settle a difference of opinion, we know only one argument: death, whether it is a matter of submarines, manure or the party line to be followed in Indo-China. . . . Those are the consequences of our consequentialness."
(p. 130)

And does this matter? "What of it?" answers Ivanov. "Don't you find it wonderful? Has anything more wonderful ever happened in history?" (p. 130). And now, the mesmerizing metaphor: "We are tearing the old skin off mankind and giving it a new one" (p. 130). But the metaphor does not work on someone who has once seen past it, as Rubashov has: "I see the flayed body of this generation: but I see no trace of the new skin." Ivanov also has seen beyond the metaphor—although he may not yet know it. Back in his office, he finds Gletkin, whose adherence to party ideology is so tight that he does not even believe in persuasion by argument: to argue a point is to admit that it can be defeated, even in principle. So Gletkin believes in persuasion by physical torture: and with every fresh scream from the tortured, a little personal myth grows up in his tiny mind: were *he* the one tortured, he would not give in: "I have a backbone, which he hasn't." "But you're an idiot," comes Ivanov's knee-jerk reaction. "For that answer you ought to be shot before him" (p. 141).

Meanwhile, Rubashov's private thoughts (perhaps Koestler's thoughts as well) are trapped in the cage of a Newtonian metaphor—the same Newtonian metaphor that animates mechanistic thinking in biology today: history's laws of motion can be discovered, for history is the motion of a gigantic mechanical swing:

A hundred and fifty years ago, the day of the storming of the Bastille, the European swing, after long inaction, again started to move. It had pushed off from tyranny with gusto; with an apparently uncheckable impetus, it had swung up towards the blue sky of freedom. For a hundred years it had risen higher and higher into the spheres of liberalism and democracy. But, see, gradually the pace slowed down, the swing neared the summit and turning point of its course; then, after a second of immobility, it started the movement backwards, with ever-increasing speed. With the same impetus as on the way up, the swing carried its passengers back from freedom to tyranny again. He who gazed upwards instead of clinging on, became dizzy and fell out. Whoever wishes to avoid becoming dizzy must try to find out the swing's law of motion. We seem to be faced with a pendulum movement in history, swinging from absolutism to democracy, from democracy back to absolute dictatorship" (p. 143)

The law-of-motion metaphor propagates all the way to the representation of the mind: "As to the Fatherland of the Revolution, the masses there are governed by the same laws of thought as anywhere else. If these laws be the stuff of reality, then all that happens happens necessarily: only what must happen happens, and therefore it is pointless to inquire into anything other than causes: 'Woe to the fool and the aesthete who only ask how and not why'" (p. 147).

The machine metaphor is also at work in Gletkin's description of "normal procedures": "You have the right to make a statement or to refuse. In your case a refusal would amount to a disavowal of the declaration of willingness to confess, which you wrote two days ago, and would automatically bring the investigation to an end. In that eventuality I have the order to send your case back to the competent authority, which would pronounce your sentence administratively" (p. 148).

The language of "logical consequentiality" finds an echo in a 1938 paper of Paul Samuelson, where he claims that people's observed choices "reveal" their preferences: if you are observed to choose an object X when an object Y is also available and you are a rational person, then you will not be observed to choose Y when X is also available. If you choose an apple when you could have had an orange, then you should not choose the orange when you could have had the apple. Never mind that you chose the apple to go with some poems by Rilke about late autumn that you chose to remember and the orange to go with some memories of a past lover. "How can you do the opposite of what your (past) actions logically imply?" asks the freshly minted doctor in economics, citing the insight behind the Weak Axiom of Revealed Preference. "But you're an idiot," echoes Ivanov from across many miles and (not so many) years. Actions *don't* imply anything—only their interpretations do.

Like in so many show trials—in so many presidential impeachments and CEO sackings—in this show trial too it is important that the logic of the judgment be tight, that it be itself unimpeachable. We understand why it is so important to Number One that the logic be tight and the accused be revealed to be actual criminals—and Rubashov understood this as well:

"It is necessary to hammer every sentence into the masses by repetition and simplification. What is presented as right must shine like gold; what is presented as wrong must be black as pitch. For consumption by the masses, the political processes must be colored like ginger-bread figures at a fair" (p. 150). Number One is worried about preserving the image that he has carefully built up in his own eyes and believes that by stomping out doubters he is stomping out *doubts* themselves.

But why is it also important for the bureaucrat Gletkin? What mileage does the apparatchik get out of the seamless working of the apparatus? Well, for one thing, Gletkin's promotion depends on the smoothness with which the "trial" goes off. His job is not to inquire into facts but to direct a mise en scène of the facts. The better the mise en scène, the more indistinguishable the story is from what seems like reality. But how good does the mise en scène have to be at a minimum? Good enough to allay Number One's doubts: "I know thee, Stalin" is always lurking in the shadows, and Number One's sleep is harrowed by the nocturnal "I know thee's." But what if the story is "too good"? That is also dangerous: Number One could become suspicious that the aparatchik is being ironic or sarcastic with him.

There is another reason for the aparatchik's play addiction to rigor: he is himself a believer: "You know what is at stake here. For the first time in history, a revolution has not only conquered power, but also kept it. We have made our country a bastion of the new era" (p. 152). He has himself accumulated too many crimes, too many false confessions obtained under torture, which could be justified only by a belief strong enough to overcome any doubts about the ultimate purpose of the enterprise: "The leader of the Party had the wider perspective and the more tenacious tactics. He realized that everything depended on surviving the period of world reaction and keeping the bastion. He had realized that it might last ten, perhaps twenty, perhaps fifty years, until the world was ripe for a fresh wave of revolution. Until then we stand alone. Until then we have only one duty: not to perish" (p. 153). There is, alas, a *duty* associated with survival: no longer is survival the animal instinct of any man alive, but rather the survival of the revolution constitutes the duty of the enlightened revolutionary, one that justifies anything: "The bulwark must be held, at any price and with any sacrifice" (p. 153).

The bureaucrat has his own doubts and fears to allay—the fear of perishing as an individual in the churning of the revolutionary machine, the doubt that the revolutionary story really hangs together as he was taught that it does, the doubt that his own actions are ultimately justified, and the fear of the consequences of having been no more than a petty torturer for an arbitrary cause for most of his life. For him, justification is all-important: "The party's line was sharply defined. Its tactics were determined by the principle that the end justifies the means—all means, without exception" (p. 155).

This is one of the keys to Gletkin's thought: no atrocity can be spared in theory because no atrocity *has* been spared in practice, and *all* imaginable atrocities are allowable as means to the end of the survival of the revolution. For Gletkin, the conviction that the story is true is a naked babe constantly in peril: it needs to be nurtured, fed, defended—sometimes with ferocity—against those who would raise doubts. But with every new atrocity, the need to believe that the story is true grows—and hence the motivation and propensity to commit new atrocities grow. For Gletkin, the purpose of each atrocity is to convince *himself* that the stories extorted under duress offer confirming evidence for the myths of the revolution. But since they were extorted under *duress,* giving them any evidential support is clearly an example of self-deception. In the end, Gletkin himself appears to have some doubts about the power of the revolution's ideas to move someone to confess: "I congratulate you on your success, Comrade Gletkin," his secretary smiles at him. Gletkin turned the lamp down to normal: " 'That,' he said with a glance at the lamp, 'plus lack of sleep and physical exhaustion. It is all a matter of constitution' " (p. 155).

11

Soliloquies of the Candid Villain: Catharses of the Master Passions

'Tis in ourselves that we are thus or thus.
Our bodies are gardens, to which our wills are gardeners . . .
—Iago, in William Shakespeare, *Othello,* act 1.

But I'll set down the pegs that make this music as honest as I am.
—Iago, in *Othello,* act 2.

Good night, honest Iago.
—Cassio, in *Othello,* act 2.

Shakespeare's Iago *is* honest: he is true to himself and to his audience. His aim is easy to understand to begin with, but he makes it explicit: drive his military superior (Othello) into a fatal stroke of jealousy over a purported liaison between Othello's wife (Desdemona) and his lieutenant (Cassio), whom Iago is trying to eliminate for his own purposes. He pursues his plan through its twists and turns without once feigning the pursuit of a purpose that is larger than his own life. Iago is the *lucid* villain—truthful without seeking to impress by his truthfulness and honest about the fact that he is being deceitful: "I am not what I am."

Iago's soliloquies are *cathartic.* They let what he feels come to the light of words—shamelessly but candidly—and here lies Shakespeare's art in letting his will speak for herself. Catharsis is not only illuminating but liberating. It frees the subject from his own value judgments: "What do you really want?" the cathartic moment asks. "To get my friend fired so I can get her office and job," you might answer as if under a spell. And then you might shudder. You might try to punish yourself. Many of the rituals that contort obsessive-compulsives are reported by them to be *penitentiae* for "horrible thoughts." But are you justified in forcing yourself to forget your impulse or desire and to deny its magnetic force? You cannot unlive what you have just lived by repeating it, as the obsessive-compulsive does. You cannot erase what you have thought about undressing your boss once you have indeed thought about it. And acting on your urge might only produce *greater* anxiety. Catharsis is not about letting loose with animal emotions—acting out on the most destructive instincts we have—and thus acting out is very rarely cathartic. Catharsis is rather about bringing these emotions *as* emotions before consciousness—becoming conscious of their sway on the body and hold on the mind. It is therefore about awakening to greater self-knowledge, and this is why Iago—and Richard III and Napoleon—are *awake*. Their utterances—and perhaps their actions—are *cathartic:* you can let them speak from within you and feel truthful while echoing them, thus letting words mirror your mood—if only for an instant.

Only in cathartic moments do we become fully conscious of the workings and powers of the passions. But for catharsis, the passions would remain the *silent* directors of our actions, which we would engage in while offering up excuses, rationalizations, and moralizations. Only in moments of catharsis does the intelligence of the passions—the cunning of feeling—become evident. "For my next act, I will have my brother locked up in prison and killed—watch me," beckons Richard III in his asides—and he *does it,* as Al Pacino points out, mesmerized and mesmerizing, in his documentary. Watch, first, as envy comes out of the image that Richard has seen of himself in others' eyes:

I, that am rudely stamped, and want love's majesty
To strut before a wanton ambling nymph;
I, that am curtail'd of this fair proportion.... (1.1.16–18)

Then as the envy turns to reproach and resentment toward a *fate* that seems to be bent on creating cosmic harmony and justice:

Cheated of feature by dissembling nature,
deform'd, unfinish'd, sent before my time
into this breathing world scarce half made up
And that so lamely and unfashionable
That dogs bark at me as I halt by them;
have no delight to pass away the time,

Unless to spy my own shadow in the sun,
And descant on mine own deformity . . . . (1.1.19–27)

And then again as the revolt turns into the pronouncement of a *curse* against fate itself—which is at the same time a *determination* of his own life:

And therefore,—since I cannot prove a lover
To entertain these fair, well-spoken days,
I am determined to prove a villain,
And hate the idle pleasures of these days. (1.1.28–31)

So he will act in accordance with what his fate has fated him to be and do: he will carry out his fate *with intention:*

Plots have I laid, inductions dangerous,
By drunken prophecies, libels and dreams,
To set my brother Clarence and the king
In deadly hate the one against the other
And, if King Edward be as true and just
As I am subtle, false and treacherous,
This day should Clarence closely be mew'd up
About a prophecy which says that G
Of Edward's heirs the murderer shall be. (1.1.32–40)

Richard lends his will to his fate—or at least that is what Shakespeare has him tell us he is doing. But we see something else as well: we see him fashioning his fate according to his true nature, by *choosing* to be what he *feels* that he is.

"Figure out what you are and be that," is the advice of a psychiatrist to an indecisive smoker in Kenneth Branagh's movie, *Dead Again.* Most of us stumble into engagements, training programs, relationships, marriages, contracts, and careers. *Things happen to us. We* happen as well—to those whom we are in touch with. We have reasons for most of the actions we have taken but almost never take the actions that we have most reason to take (Abelson 1986). Reasons consequently have no *cutting power.* They do not slice through the darkness of the coming moments in the way in which we think they do—although our beliefs that they *are* indeed causally potent are critical for our confidence to take action. We need to feel as if we are acting for a reason even though we will change our minds many times into the future about those reasons.

Not so with Richard: he does not grope into the labyrinth of time because he, unlike us, is not self-deceived. He has seen into the future, and *his* reasons will become *causes* of his actions. Herein lies the overwhelming power of the cathartic moment: you just *know* what it is you are going to do and *why* it is that you are doing it. "I just realized that I hate you—that I have never felt close and intimate to you," a woman writes to her husband of many years after seeing a stranger with her husband's build model a pair of Lederhosen she wanted to buy him in a German shop while on a trip to Europe. This character in Haruki Murakami's short story "Lederhosen" writes these lines from Japan, where she has gone immediately on seeing the stranger come out of the dressing room: no words, no good-bye's—just the cathartic moment that bade her leave, immediately and irrevocably.

Catharsis as the Restoration of Self-Agency

The cathartic mind is no longer a machine for producing justifications: now you have real agency, real causal powers. You are *free*—perhaps not in the sense of doing what you freely will but in the sense of *wanting* what you are about to do. The feeling of freedom is exhilarating. It is the feeling of being unconstrained by the fear of consequences and mores that we find in Iago and Richard, who *embrace* their destiny rather than fight it—like most mortals—and thereby make destiny seem to be bent according to their wills.

Think of a long and painful relationship that you perhaps wanted to leave—possibly because you did not feel "together" or because you did not feel the "fatedness" of your bond. You have turned back many times at the last moment. How else could it have been? How can you say, "You know (and I know you don't know), I want to leave and to be alone." Time and again you shrink from the words that, once spoken, cannot be taken back. But Richard *says* such words and *can* take them back and *does not*. He follows his mind down the path of his destiny. "Europe, as we know it, will cease to exist," echoes Adolf Hitler across the centuries, and again, mesmerizingly, he follows through. His actions—and the world's fate—are true to his words.

Catharsis as Penitence and Renewal

But not only master villains have had their consciences illuminated by the cathartic moment. Their moments of light are just more transparently cathartic than those of others: why would one admit to such wishes if they were not true? It is also the catharsis of the common man—the apparently *exemplary* man, the seeming saint—that can unleash thoughts into feelings with equally striking results, as it does for Albert Camus's (1956) judge-penitent who takes *The Fall:* here the light shines briskly but fleetingly on the soul because for Clamence there is always a chance that catharsis itself is a pose: "After prolonged research on myself, I brought out the fundamental duplicity of the human being. Then I realized, as a result of delving in my memory, that modesty helped me to shine, humility to conquer, and virtue to oppress."

At first one feels in the presence of a confession of a life spent misleading others for the purpose of making Clamence look better in his own eyes:

The feeling of the law, the satisfaction of being right, the joy of self-esteem, cher monsieur, are powerful incentives for keeping us upright or keeping us moving forward. . . . I was truly above reproach in my professional life. I never accepted a bribe, it goes without saying, and I never stooped either to any shady proceedings. . . . I even had the luck of seeing the Legion of Honor offered to me two or three times and of being able to refuse it with a discreet dignity in which I found my true reward. Finally, I never charged the poor a fee and never boasted of it. Don't think for a moment, cher monsieur, that I am bragging. I take no credit for this. The avidity which in our society substitutes for ambition has always made me laugh. I was aiming higher; you will see that the expression is exact in my case.

To be set *above*—here is the intention that Clamence recognizes in his life, to which all has been subordinated: "I have to admit it humbly, mon cher monsieur, I was always bursting with vanity. . . . I conceived at least one great love in my life, of which I was always the object. . . . I, I, I is the refrain of my whole life, which could be heard in everything I said. . . . I could never talk without boasting, especially if I did so with that shattering discretion which became my specialty." Not boasting has become a form of boasting, then. Now we begin to suspect that sincerity itself—our own, perhaps—can also be a pose, a vehicle for self-promotion. But Clamence's own conscience is powerless to grant the ultimate approval of his actions:

I could live happily only on condition that all the individuals on earth, or the greatest possible number, were turned toward me, eternally in suspense, devoid of independent life and ready to answer my call at any moment. . . . For me to live happily it was essential for the creatures I chose not to live at all. They must receive their life sporadically, only at my bidding. I haven't changed my way of life. I continue to love myself and to make use of others. Only, the confession of my crimes allows me to begin again lighter in heart and to taste a double enjoyment, first of my nature and secondly of a charming repentance.

Catharsis splits off consciousness into two circles and strands. One savors the slothful pleasure of the vain. The other savors the athletic pleasures of engaging in a confession that cuts through one strand of conscious being after another—recounting one's lies and poses, recounting the poses and lies of recounting one's lies and poses, recounting the poses and lies of recounting the poses and lies of recounting one's lies and poses, and so on, in a never-ending ascent that looks like a descent to the unsuspecting listener, who, alas, is informed of Clamence's intentions: "Admit . . . that today you feel less pleased with yourself than you felt five days ago? Now I shall wait for you to write me or come back. For you will come back, I'm sure."

Cathartic Self-Consciousness: The Raw Feel of "I"

Let us picture the social animal's awakening into a cathartic moment. You are in front of a mirror. You've put on your best clothes and now have a last look at yourself before going out to a party where all of your friends and colleagues will show up to offer you their congratulations. You have done it, at last, just as you said you would and in spite of their doubts and ironic smiles. One last look in the mirror. And just as you are about to break off eye contact with the mirror, you hear laughter just behind you— a laugh of genuine amusement at something ridiculous, ironic but honestly amused. You blanch and turn. No one.

You look at the mirror again. No sign of the jitters that have started up like ants in your stomach. And now the laughter comes on again, right behind you, the same as last time, perhaps a little louder and more vehement this time. You keep looking at the mirror. The right corner of your lip is twitching nervously, your eyes do not have the proud sparkle that you thought that you had seen in them (and how so-and-so will like those looks). Your cheeks are falling, your chin has overgrown the taut look of youth.

You take off your clothes, still in front of the mirror, and feel that there stands a large piece of meat and also feel the *me*ness of that piece of meat. That your body can be desired now seems like a joke perpetrated on a certifiable idiot. To each of your witticisms you can think of a reply that would have humiliated you had *they* thought of it in time—but you never gave them the time to think about your words. A quick wit, you are—quick as a worm in the land of snails, that is. For you cannot stand to be around anyone more beautiful, sharper, taller, and quicker than you are.

Your smiles are aimed to please and to impress. Even your walk has been faked according to what you think would be a "cool" pace: you are currently aiming for the detached pose. Your own laughter could never match the crystalline peals you have just heard: it is always contrived to respond quickly and predictably to the jokes of your superiors and those on whom you feel your career depends.

And your love life: all in all, you would rather not spend any more time with your current lover. There has not been any true understanding between you in almost five years. Just parallel monologues and silences that do not even seem meaningful. You have not truly been behind the smiles you put on in the morning for each others' sakes. The flesh is still standing there in front of you. But now the laughter is gone. The recognition of your poses has brought quiet to your mind, and there is no need to go to a party ever again, perhaps.

Catharsis of Logos Turned on Itself: The Critical Turn in Philosophy

Friedrich Nietzsche (1910–1913, p. 285), too, once stood in front of such a mirror:

What provokes one to look at all philosophers half suspiciously, half mockingly, is not that one discovers again and again how innocent they are—how often and how easily they make mistakes and go astray; in short, their childishness and childlikeness—but that they are not honest enough in their work, although they all make a lot of virtuous noise when the problem of truthfulness is touched even remotely.

They all pose as if they had discovered and reached their real opinions through the self-development of a cold, pure, divinely unconcerned dialectic (as opposed to the mystics of every rank, who are more honest and doltish—and talk of "inspiration"); while at bottom it is an assumption, a hunch, indeed a kind of "inspiration"—most often a desire of the heart that has been filtered and made abstract—that they defend with reasons they have sought after the fact.

Nietzsche's is the catharsis of the anxiety that predates wishful thinking and self-deception: Is not living estimating, preferring, being unjust, being limited, wanting to be different? But these are precisely the states of being that morality is called on to guard us against: morality construed as a rigid set of principles is a denial of life and the life instinct. It is in the spirit of any principle that speaks through us that it represents a claim to truth and validity. Therefore, it is in the spirit of the principles and reasons that we consciously subscribe to that they *shackle* us. Catharsis of the fear that makes us cling to them is liberating, if only for an instant: for then the *idea* of the escape, the *myth* of the catharsis itself, becomes an idea that shackles us.

Catharsis and the Search for the Authentic Moment

Catharsis therefore cannot be an *idea* or a cognition, just as it cannot be a mere *emotion*. It is, rather, a phenomenon peculiar to consciousness, whereby an emotion comes to the foreground of conscious awareness in a way that *discloses it* as the emotion it is. This, at least, is the subjective feeling of the catharsis. The liberating feeling of the cathartic state does not come merely from the *recognition* of the emotion but rather is the feeling that accompanies the disclosure of the emotion. The most satisfying catharsis is one that has infinite *depth*—wherein we know, we know that we know, we know that we know that we know, and so forth. This is because there is no doubt left over or lurking around that all this letting go of the comfortable levers of cognitive control of the emotions may be a show of candor put on for the benefit of some audience.

Think of an excruciating pain, one that does not leave you the space to reason—perhaps from breaking an arm or from burning your flesh with a hot iron. You might scream involuntarily, and if you feel that the scream is entirely *caused* by the pain, if it is an outward expression that does not exaggerate or understate the pain, then the scream feels good: it helps make the pain go away, at least for a short period of time. Your expression was *congruent* to your sensation—it fit—and this fit between thought and feeling makes for the cathartic experience.

Of course, you cannot have aimed for the fit, just as you cannot *aim* to be spontaneous. You cannot say, "If only I cry a little bit more softly, then the expression will match the sensation," then cry more softly, and then actually feel that the expression matches the sensation. *Planning* kills cathartic experiences. The suspicion that someone is putting on shows for our benefit or is acting out her pain to get attention shuts down our emotional access to that person's expressions. We are no longer *there* for her. We move away. On the other hand, when we sense that every one of her expressions is cathartic, that *she* is wholly and nonstrategically *behind* her expressions, then we have the feeling that we are dealing with an *authentic* person— one who does not wear fake smiles.

Reasonable Doubts: How Do We Know We Are Not Faking It All?

But how do we know whether an expression is cathartic? How do we know how to feel about someone else's tears? We do not. Herein lies the great gamble of authenticity. We can be deceived by other members of our own species. We can be taken in, but the joke is not on the one who has been taken in but rather on the one who has done the taking in. And this is not because of some latter-day salutary judgment of the authentic but rather because of the inauthentic's own feelings: having made a screenplay out of his feelings, he has sullied them. Like Clamence in Camus's story, he can never feel those feelings again *cathartically* without a painful splitting of his consciousness into one duplicitous part that is forever stuck into a pose and another part that expresses the "real" self. The mask, it turns out, cannot be taken off at will: after a while, it gets stuck to the skin and comes off only by taking a layer of skin with it and leaving part of itself burned into the flesh. While the mask may seem like it has come off, the *maskhood* of the mask's wearer and the maskedness of her feelings remain.

The chameleon's catharsis is almost always an exercise in absurdity, for who is the speaking subject? The deceiver or the deceived? If the deceiver talks, then what he is saying can be subsumed in the sentence "I am now uttering a lie." This sentence, if true, must be false; if false, then it must be true. Its truth value is not calculable. What if the deceived is talking? Then what she is saying can be subsumed by the sentence "This sentence is a lie I have been told." The same trip into the absurd ensues. Thus, the chameleon who simulates the cathartic experience has tainted not only the trust of the witness but also his own relationship with truth. The very *idea* of truth has been dissolved because of the splitting of the consciousness of the speaking subject into deceiver and deceived.

Catharsis and the Demand for Dramatic Productions

But what if certain emotions cannot be subjected to catharsis without the expectation of major socially imposed penalties? Are we forever fated to hide ourselves and to live in the lukewarm light of slighted authenticity? You may feel the urge to rip off a person's ear and feed it to her dog or to have unconventional sex with your manager or to pour hot coffee in a secretary's lap. What do you do with all those feelings? Where do you let them speak, when letting them speak will shut you out forever?

In the theater. The gigantic movie industry in the United States, Canada, and Europe is a purveyor of vicarious cathartic experiences. Murder and mayhem run rampant on the screen. They are in demand as lightning rods for cathartic experiences that would otherwise be sought on the streets and in the bedroom. As moviegoers, we use the violent ends of the on-stage villains as vehicles for our own destructive instincts toward those whom *we,* in our turn, vilify in our lives. By watching videotapes of couples mating in various roles of masterhood and slavery—the standard roles of what we call pornographic films—we express, virtually, our own desires to be enslaved or to enslave. By one interpretation of the movie experiences, then, the theatergoer lets herself loose by letting go of the idea of the bloodshed that she might crave, and she lets go by letting it be played out on screen.

This favorite theory of Hollywood producers turns out, on closer examination, to be only partly right. The movie does produce a catharsis: seeing Jimmy kiss Jane under the desert moon after years of anguish trying to escape Jane's oppressive mother and uncle who are trying to marry her off provides a release for the oppression we feel in *our* lives, where we are also trying to escape oppressive spouses, in-laws, and parents and be on our way to happiness. But at the same time, the celluloid produces an *objectification* of persons that makes *real-life* cathartic experiences of bloody destruction easier to pursue. Once you see Jimmy torture Jane with a blade tied to the end of a car's antenna, it is easier to snap into the Jane role when you see someone who fits the Jimmy role. Roles are easier to cut up with blades than are people because there is no empathetic link that needs to be broken between a person and an object. Unsurprisingly, serial killers borrow from one another's rituals, as each ritual contains a story that turns the murdered into a mere image or an idea. Thus, the violent movie produces not only a catharsis in the sense of letting be or expressing what you in fact feel but also an objectification that undermines the link that we have in real life to other people.

The cathartic experience provided by the celluloid is increasingly degenerate: the imperative for market success dictates that the movie appeal to the common denominator in the ocean of emotions of the moviegoers. Emotions on the screen become increasingly simple, raw, coarse. Think it through: don't villains blowing up with regularity and spilling their blood on the screen leave you increasingly cold? And is that because you can never quite fit your own fantasies into the simple-minded rituals that take place onscreen? Your imagination may, of course, degenerate to the point where you take the director's suggestions seriously. But you know (as you always already have known) that the fear you feel is not *your* fear. Surely it is not your fear for yourself in the situation of the heroine about to be stabbed; it is too transparently your fear for *her* getting stabbed. When the celluloid has shut down, you will be left with *your* fears—and with your cannibalistic instincts toward *your* boss, with *your* urges to enslave *your* secretary by tying her to the tree that sits outside your office, and with *your* longing to escape *your* marriage to a vast blue unknown hatched in the crevasses of your mind.

The mineness of the cathartic experience makes catharsis the experience it essentially is. To these mysterious urges the false catharses of the celluloid are but diversions; although what keeps you going back to the big screen is the *hope* (and *their promise*) that *this time* you really will be taken over by someone else's emotions: "a movie that will move you to (something or other)" is what many film ads promise the prospective moviegoer.

And what does *moving* you entail if not a *takeover* of your body by an emotion that you will be able to *see* played out in front of your eyes—precisely the cathartic experience, except that the I has been faked.

The theater brings the vicarious experience of another's emotions closer to a cathartic experience. Here it is more difficult to objectify a person, for here she is, breathing and trembling right in front of you. If she collapses unpredictably and in a way that does not seem like it is part of the script, you will rush to her aid. If she suddenly undresses, you will be awkward and find it difficult to look into her eyes, even though you have seen many women undress in front of a camera. It's just that you have been on the other side of the impregnable celluloid, behind which all is fake. But the breathing being on the stage is not fake, so cathartic experience stands a better chance of unfolding.

With the actor in flesh and blood mounted on a live stage we are closer to realizing the preconditions for a cathartic experience because the actor's emotions are "live" and therefore subject to the same fluctuations and responses that we are subject to. The being-there of the stage actor's actions is of a different quality than that of the actions of the actor on the screen, where nothing could happen other than what has already happened in the filming process. A fire in the movie theater, for instance, will not produce panic in the actors on the screen: we of the audience will be the only ones fleeing. In the live theater, we and the actors are together in our susceptibility to at least some future events—such as the fire in the theater or tomorrow's weather in the city.

Master playwrights use this insight to bring us and the live actor even closer together. Nothing "happens" in Samuel Beckett's *Waiting for Godot,* and once we "get it," we are together in the nonhappeningness of the cosmos with the characters and the actors. *A Midsummer's Night's Dream* contains a play within a play, and we (the audience) observe the observers. Our attention is directed thereby to *our* observers: we may not be the final observers in the chain, even though it certainly *feels* as if we are. But then it feels the same way to the actors on the stage as well; they are oblivious of their obliviousness, but *we* are not. So we are together with them in our ignorance of being observed, just as we would be in our awareness of being observed. Wherever we go, there we are—together.

In the theater, a power of abstraction can work to bring us closer to the emotions of the protagonists—unlike the goings on at the cinema, where the trend toward typifying villains and heroes as morally pure, one-dimensional characters takes us away from empathy. We abstract from the plight of Friedrich Dürrenmatt's (1964) *Romulus the Great* the situation of the man who has married a vain woman for reasons of career advancement (she was the emperor's daughter), found the bargain wanting years later, and now is getting out to pursue other interests while he still has life left in him, even though he is the current Roman emperor and everyone is looking to him to save the Roman empire from the barbaric Teutons. Part of what helps us grasp his predicament is the susceptibility of this Romulus to the same future that may await us. Even if, as an emperor, he is a figurehead and a figment of the imagination, as a man on the stage he is a portal to our understanding him as a bored husband.

Now let's move one more step on the scale of phenomena that aim to see us through cathartic experiences. In the psychoanalyst's office, catharsis is perhaps the happiest outcome of the interaction, the prize for the analyst's hard work. When it occurs, the analysand is brought face to face with her own emotional commitments, which she brings to language and thereby in some way masters. "The fault, dear Brutus, is not in our stars, but in ourselves," and turning into a detective looking for clues in the crimes against our own sanity and consciousness is one way of looking at the psychoanalytic project. The "captaincy of the soul" is by no means a foregone conclusion: it is as ephemeral as the cathartic experience itself.

As Jonathan Lear (1997) has pointed out, psychoanalysis presupposes the "revelation principle": "The analysand was not allowed to try out a debating position, but had to bring his own commitment to the inquiry. If the inquiry led to contradiction, it was not the reductio of an abstract position with no . . . owner, but of the analysand's own commitments." We see, then, that the psychoanalytic experience—in its ideal embodiment as a Socratic dialogue—is always already supposed to be cathartic in nature. There is no psychoanalytic path to catharsis, for true psychoanalysis is already cathartic in nature. This insight does not square well with intuition: escaping prevalent inauthenticity and self-deceit seems to be the prima facie purpose of psychoanalysis, not the precondition for it. As with the theater, there are actors and audiences in psychoanalysis, but the analysand is both at the same time—or more precisely, both reside in the same psyche, for she is the audience for her own emotions. The cathartic experience comes with consciousness of this observership but can come only with some detachment from the feeling I whose emotions are the apparent movers and shakers.

The Silence of the Actor: Creating the Cathartic Moment

Contemplation (and the cathartic experience that sometimes comes with it) presupposes that you can remain unmoved by the feelings that you are about to feel—precisely the ability that is in doubt for the analysand. Achieving the standing of an audience in the theater of her own emotions is what the analysand seeks in the psychoanalytic experience—The cathartic experience, cannot come so long as we connect to emotions such as love, hate, anger, and contempt *anxiously*—in a way that makes our actions prey to direct emotional causes. Anxiety is the broth wherein our feelings live. It is a hot broth. That we can feel without doing is unthinkable while we are submerged in the broth. Action—including actions aimed at repressing certain affect-laden thoughts—is to the anxious what a breath of fresh air is to the drowning. Like the drowning person who is unconscious of being able to hold her breath or to breathe under water or of the fact that taking deep breaths makes her susceptible to the next wave, the anxious actor is oblivious to the addictiveness of acting out of anxiety. Catharsis of the emotions requires that, even if for a brief instant, we escape anxiety: otherwise it is as unthinkable as is breathing underwater. Therefore, the escape to catharsis must simultaneously be an escape *from* anxiety.

Words can help bring catharsis on, not *as* words but *as* actions. Assertions such as "I am free" and "I love you" are not only *indications* but also *actions* that we live through. As such, the experiences they refer to are genuine and authentic only if the action of asserting itself feels genuine and authentic. What if, say, you stopped feeling free halfway through uttering "I am free"? If you stick to your plan of finishing the sentence (something most people would expect you to do), then, obviously, you truly *are* no longer free—because you felt compelled to finish uttering "I am free" in spite of not feeling free. So your prima facie "feeling of not being free" has been borne out by your experience: you have become what you feel your-self to be. Becoming unfree did not *cause* your feeling unfree but rather was in some way *caused* by it—or, more exactly, by the objective state of un-freedom that was caused by your feeling unfree.

Words can lead to cathartic experiences only insofar as they do not fal-sify the emotions they seek to capture. The path to catharsis through words is fraught with the dangers of incoherence. A catharsis of deceitful-ness ("I am telling a lie") is paradoxical, but the *feel* of the paradox *is* the catharsis of the lie. It is essential, then, to see words as *actions*—to which we may be moved by anxiety and thus to expose the ever present duality of our selves as actors and observers. Words are not mere observers of our in-ner turmoils; they have their own roles to play. Observing the observers—and the observers of the observers, as Dürrenmatt (1988) put it—and so forth up (down?) the spiral of consciousness is always *within* the realm of the cathartic mind, which *is*, and *sees what is*, and *sees that it is*, all at the same time.

Laughter is perhaps the purest cathartic experience because it is so sud-den and unambiguous when it is authentic. Laughter sneaks up on us: it is unplanned, unpremeditated. You're in line with your groceries at the su-permarket, when you look into the eyes of the check-out clerk, and sud-denly you both laugh. For an instant, you have both escaped your roles: you have escaped your concerned look and outward respectability, and he has escaped his habitual boredom. You have both peeked at each other, ever so subtly, from behind the masks that—you discover—have not be-come quite burned into your faces.

Umberto Eco (1983, p. 477) brought the point of conflict between cathartic laughter and moral dogma into sharp focus in the confrontation between two monks—William, an erudite archaeologist of knowledge, and Jorge, a staunch defender of the pillars of dogmatic faith. Says William:

You are the Devil. . . . They lied to you. The Devil is not the Prince of Matter; the Devil is the arrogance of the spirit—truth that is never seized by doubt. The Devil is grim because he knows where he is going and, in moving, he always returns whence he came. . . . I would like to smear honey all over you and then roll you in feathers, and take you on a leash to fairs, to say to all: He was announcing the truth to you and telling you that the truth has the taste of death, and you believed, not in his words, but in his grimness.

Jorge wishes to drive out laughter from the world because "laughing through fear" curbs fear's power to move people to his truths:

Laughter frees the villein from fear of the Devil because in the feast of fools the Devil also appears poor and foolish, and therefore controllable. But [Aristotle's book on laughter] could teach that freeing oneself of the fear of the Devil is wisdom. That laughter is proper to man is a sign of our limitation, sinners that we are. But from this book many corrupt minds like yours could draw the extreme syllogism, whereby laughter is man's end. Laughter, for a few moments, distracts the villein from fear. But law is imposed by fear, whose true name is fear of God. This book could strike the Luciferine spark that would set a new fire to the whole world, and laughter would be defined as the new art, unknown, even to Prometheus, for conciling fear. (p. 474)

The mind's Apollonian pleasure in perceiving the comical is mirrored in the body's Dionysian pleasure in living laughingly. And it is the temporary uncontrollability of the laugh—the feeling of "letting oneself go" freely—that gives laugh's pleasure its sparkle. And it is the uncontrollable pleasure of laughter that makes laughter cathartic. More so than sexual orgasm—which can be recruited by the mind to signify control or the assertion of power—pure, crystalline laughter cannot be seized and captured by a word. It just is. And we just are, when we laugh.

The moral dogmatic is horrified: how can living out uncontrollability and letting incongruence tickle your neurons be allowed to go on freely in a world where the fear of losing control or of dissolving into the unknown is supposed to bring man into the bosom of the law? Laughter makes the devil appear inoffensive by making the uncontrollable appear and feel pleasurable. Now fear of the uncontrollable will not determine the fearful to seek shelter in the house of dogma: she might just laugh instead of shaking. Laughter laughs, and fear fears. Sternness quells fear but is overcome by laughter, which in turn can be swallowed by fear. From this emotional trialectic spring the battle cries of the dogmatic: give fear a chance to make us stern and grim; squash laughter.

By reifying fear ("whose true name is fear of God") the moral dogmatist makes a desperate attempt to make the divine palpable. Knowledge of the divine—he thinks—is felt first and foremost as a bodily knowledge, as a primeval fear. The body's trembling—the aversion to fear, to the fear of fear—makes the body yearn for the womblike security of dogma. Hints and hunches that the dogma is fallible or just plain wrong are destabilizing:

they bring to the forefront the grim prospect of fear's spirals. Doubt, then, must be suppressed. But how is this done in a world where seeing is believing? No one has ever seen an idea or a dogma, no matter how much personal experience she has had with it.

If you only believe it when you see it, then doubt can never be far away, for even if you think you have seen, you may be experiencing an illusion. Moreover, if you admit that more often than not you need to believe it to see it—as much of cognitive psychology shows—then you never know quite what it is that you have seen. The eye of the beholder does not merely mirror. It creates. Dogma can never be a perfectly safe home from the fear of refutation, but its beckon is the strongest in the times of greatest fear. The situation looks desperate for those who seek authentic experiences. But from behind the sordid mask of the man who takes himself seriously, there sometimes sprouts an ironic smile. If consciousness can act as a sort of mirror that catches the smile, then the liberating curls of laughter—and with them the cathartic experience of laughing at oneself—can never be far off.

12

Escape from the Master Passions

A Tantric ritual: during the initiation ceremony, you are given a mirror in which you see your own image. Contemplating it, you realize you are nothing but that, i.e. nothing. To what end, so many pretenses, so many airs and graces, when it is so easy to comprehend one's insignificance?

—Emil Cioran, *Drawn and Quartered*

To see what is, is the ending of that which is.

—J. Krishnamurti, *On Fear*

To be is to be cornered.

—Cioran, *Drawn and Quartered*

The Seamlessness of the Passions

We have until now examined passions and desires in pure forms. But we live in impure states—though not the less passionate on account of their impurity. We might desire to create a new enterprise, a new poem, a new novel, and go about it feverishly—but become racked by guilt toward those who are trapped by fear of rejection and loneliness in jobs that bore them and families they feel nothing toward, people whom we used to know and now must use for our purpose and leave them behind once we are ourselves free. We might experience the wish for what "might have been"—for writing the poem while we are working on starting the enter-prise or for making love to a friend while trying to write the novel. We might experience the envy of those who have achieved in the past what we do not truly hope to achieve in the future; an overwhelming feeling of not being able to match the combination of insight and energy of a Tolstoy, a Rilke, or a Michelangelo. We might experience the fear of losing our position or our identity—the loyalty of our friends, whose regard for us is often conditional on our wallowing in a state of mediocrity comparable to theirs and who will not forgive our foray into the breathless unknown. We might experience all of these states at different times, each taking us along its own path, each combining thought and feeling so perfectly that affect and cognition seem to enhance each other and feed on each other to create a seamless web of motive, feeling, and belief that amounts to a life story.

Wherever we try to go—emotionally speaking—we may already be in the grip of *some* passion. There is no separation between the feeler and the felt, as everyday language usage would seem to indicate. The thoughts that come may fuel our doubts and suspicions that our being comes to nothing—a feeling that we can escape through the pursuit of desire. We could seek to escape in the unrestrained pursuit of distraction and pleasure—in hedonic sex, drinking, or eating. We might try to escape in running marathons, in acting out feverishly, in letting our ambition lead us forward and following it blindly. We might seek escape in numbing compulsions, in turning a light on and off repetitively until the image in our mind is just right. We might seek escape from self-doubt and rumination in the putting down of others, in the destruction of physical and mental objects associated with those whom we envy or whom we may jealously guard ourselves against.

Self-Consciousness as a Trap and the Idea of the Escape

Consciousness of being in a particular state does not always facilitate our escape from that state. Consciousness, rather, presents the conscious with many paradoxes and impossibilities. We cannot successfully *try* to forget our former lovers. We cannot successfully *try* to be spontaneous. Indeed, merely *wishing* to be spontaneous can make us self-conscious and inauthentic. We cannot will ourselves to think a certain thought on command and then recall it in the same form at will, unencumbered by the noises that time makes while passing through our minds. We cannot successfully will a thought away or keep it from coming on. We are, in fact, often caught in the mesh of our own passions, in the sense that our awareness of being caught cannot help us free ourselves from the passions. Moreover, we can never be sure that our thoughts and reasons—the way we see the world—

have not themselves been taken over by one passion or another—that we really *would* see everything differently if we were in the grips of some other passion, even though our thinking seems to be quite objective for the moment.

Attempts to escape the master passions are attempts to escape oneself— the idea and feel of the self. The I—posited as a physical entity, a chain of causally connected events, a soul, a story, a myth, a narrative—grounds envy, ambition, and jealousy, in the sense that these passions spring from the idea and feel of the self, of identity, of self-sameness, of the temporally enduring I. The impulse to fight for increasing causal powers presupposes the doing, acting I, in which the uncaused cause must reside. The I, in turn, escapes its awareness of its temporal boundedness in the fight for more power, greater recognition, and more control over others.

On the Apparent Impossibility of the Escape: The Self as a Problem

The impulse to *compare* oneself to others and to place values on the results of the comparisons often presupposes the mythological I—a self made up of stories and narratives and images that can be related to the stories and narratives and images of other I's. Without the narrative and image of the I, no comparison is possible. Without comparison, no relative value judgment is possible. Without a relative value judgment, no desire is possible. Without desire, no action *seems* possible.

But there is no such thing as nonaction. We have annihilated the idea of not acting in our minds. Indeed, *not acting* has come in our civilization to be seen as a form of action: the body still exists, cells within it still *secrete* their juices inside your various cavities, we still have *consciousness* and therefore still have agency. What difference can it possibly make that we have not decided to act rather than deciding to not act? We cannot rub our I out.

Even if the I effaces itself by just *watching,* the others will construct it in their own image and we will re-internalize it. Mesmerized by the looks of the others, the I reemerges and lives, breathes, compares, judges, and desires. If envy and jealousy—the passions most closely associated with comparisons—were somehow to be eradicated from a person through deep prayer, psychoanalysis, or a new psychopharmacological agent, they would be immediately resuscitated from the contact with others in society, who want to see the I in him.

We come to the following statement of the problem: one possible escape from the master passions can be carried out by escaping the self—the thought and image of selfhood and identity. But this is a difficult task since the self may be at the core of what we currently know as culture: in the language that picks out individuals from a crowd and assigns possessions, characteristics, rights, and properties to these individuals; in the legends that sing of individual passions and conquests and achievements; in the system of laws and rules that assign agency, property, and responsibility to persons; in the tacit rules of coordination that make the self the basic unit of interaction; in the sciences that make individuals the basic units of analysis of large-scale social phenomena; in the arts that glorify the sensuous qualities of personhood; in the words of the poets that make the subjective feels of selves *qua* selves the fabric of their ballads; in the private thoughts that turn to the image, the appearance, and the impression of the self on the other.

Just try escaping yourself! You will instantly become aware of your physical limits—of your spatial boundedness, of the limitations that your attempts to flee your own body come up against. You will become aware, more acutely than ever, of your *identity*—precisely what you were trying to escape. How, after all, can you try to escape something without knowing *what* it is that you are escaping? That would be akin to trying to leave a country without knowing what the boundaries of the country are. Trying to escape into the not-I therefore requires an even deeper engagement with the I. You will become aware of the dependence of the feel of the I on the idea of the I—letting go of any of the memories or narratives that the I participated in will destroy the feel of self-identity and self-sameness. The I will no longer be the same I. But since self-sameness is a critical part of identity (I need someone to be identical to in order to conclude that I am the same through time), cutting off I-in-the-past from I-in-the-present results in cutting off the umbilical cord that had fed my I-hood.

You may become aware of the *desires* of the I because I and his desires are mutually reinforcing. I desires, and I's desires make I into what, essentially, I is. You might try then to escape your desires by repressing them, by inflicting some severe physical punishment on yourself every time temptation comes into your mind, or by trying to replace your undesirable desires with more desirable desires. But what are these acts, if not acts of desire— the desire to desire differently or not at all? It takes desire to act to squelch your desire. Once again, you come up against an infinite regress, wherein consciousness seems to hurt your chances of escape.

You might become aware of the inescapability of the master passions. Once the envious thought about your friend's wife has sucked you in, your reasoning mind will fly to make a rendezvous with her the most natural occurrence at the end of the day. Once the will to write has entered your veins, you will find imminently good and independent reasons to leave your all-too-demanding wife. Once the fear of losing your best friend has tried you, you will jealously guard her every step, pretending the whole time that she "cannot take care of herself." And you might find that being aware of the inescapability of the passions is itself no help in making them escapable, just as an awareness of the futility of trying to be spontaneous is no help in your actual attempt to be spontaneous.

Break-outs: A Brief History of Metaphysical Innovations

There have been many escape attempts that have defied heavy odds and come close to loosening the bonds of selfhood on the I. There is the Nietzschean escape attempt—to imagine living the same predicaments in our lives over and over again, in eternity. Physically, the scenario is possible if it is a possible world consistent with empirical evidence and some background assumptions. What does it mean for us? We would not have any memory of past predicaments—not, in any case, any memory to offer us guidance as to "what to do" to make things come out well for us "in the end." We simply believe that our lives will be played out again and again, for eternity to come. Each action, look, and word, once engaged, becomes part of eternity. One should then live as if every moment would be revisited over and over again, as if each moment would come again and again and again in the future.

And are there moments that you would like to live through over and over again, infinitely? What would you do differently if this Nietzschean conception really were true? Each moment has within it the sprouts of infinity—indeed, only through constant change and through constant becoming can one "cleanse" oneself of what is impure and habitual and lethargic in the past. Thus, the idea of selfhood, of self-sameness, of identity, is a burden to the Nietzschean time traveler. It needs to shrugged off at every new moment. Each of us is an Atlas whose burden is his or her own past.

The myths we use to think of as our past freeze us in a pose, a gesture, a self-concept that is temporally stable and therefore closed to further change. But the world may be different on every new pass of the self through the world. So the mythological self needs to be discarded with each new moment so that its projection into infinity will be *open* and forever *becoming*. The *moment* should be reduced to the point of nonexistence, such that even the smallest division of time—the fastest stroboscope of our lives—finds our spirits *moving*.

In a Nietzschean cosmos, the physical I is also shown up to be an illusion, for the I's physical being or identity is related to its persistence through a linear time. Each new moment *finds* us there, passes *through* us, or *passes by* us. The I *endures* the flow of time. That is precisely what the "eternal return of the same" denies; for time does not visit us and flow past us, but rather *we* visit and flow past time. The physical I is an illusion of the flow of consciousness through time that turns out to split off into as many parallel universes as are required by the various actions we freely take.

Through will we can create a new universe every conscious instant. We must consider, however, this question: "Is this a universe we want to create (here and now)?" How do we go about answering this question? Surely the answer we give must be true or good or best in all possible worlds—and there is an infinite number of them. Should we reflect forever—forever dreaming up new possible worlds? This is the project of the poetic imagination across the millennia. Should we try to ground our knowledge of *this* world into such certainty that we can be absolutely sure that no possible world has escaped us? This has been the (failing) project of logicians, positivist scientists, and epistemologists for the past hundred years. Should we try to make our inner moral beings immune to any outside influence—perhaps by distilling optimal being to a set of immutable principles to which we arrive by reason alone? This is the project of Kantian moral philosophers, who usually succeed only by failing to take into the account the crucial details that condition and sometimes determine our predicaments.

In none of these cases is a single I up to the task. In all of these cases the evolution of consciousness is a collective process. The poetic *imagination,* the scientific *method and spirit of inquiry,* and the moral *project* grow through time and through the dialogue of many different conscious minds. Once again, the I as the seat of reasoning and deliberation is dissolved— and becomes a historical nonentity in the light of eternity.

The Always-Already-There Nature of Subjective Being: A Heideggerian Escape

Heidegger (1962) proposes that we think of the being of persons as a particular form of existence, in particular one that is conscious of having been thrown toward death. Spatiality, temporality, and identity are not—as they are with Descartes or with Kant—primitives, a prioris of *any* experience, or *enablers* of any kind of experience. Rather, the way in which a person constructs spatiality, temporality, and the I will be related to his ways of being, such as being in, being with, being for, or being toward death. What *exists,* therefore, is not a set of objects, persons, minds, or disembodied souls floating around a material universe and investing matter with will but rather ways of being, of which the way of being toward death conditions the experience that persons have of the world.

There is nothing essential about the self. There *exist* only ways of being that can become embodied in what look like different physical persons at different times. The appearance of identity, of selfhood, of self-sameness as *essential* is a phenomenon of our conscious being toward death, of our conscious being in the world, and of our conscious being toward time. Just as this escape undermines the identity of the physical, temporally enduring I, it also undermines the identity of the mythological I, which must rest on some *story* or some set of *axioms* that are definitive of the I's ways of being. But the mythologizing I is itself a way of being, one that tries to enshrine into eternity the being of a being that is headed for an end. It springs, therefore, from the being toward death that is constitutive of people's ways of being.

A Gentle Farewell to Language: Krishnamurti's Escape Attempts

Krishnamurti (1991) puts us face to face with the being of fear and leaves us there. He does not feel the need to *counsel* or to guide. His proposal is perhaps bolder than Heidegger's and gentler at the same time: "To see what is, is the ending of that which is." Just see it. Feel it. Feel your fear— not *that* you are afraid and not *what* you are afraid of. See your fear itself.

"Virtue is clarity"—not clarity of propositional thought, to be sure. On the contrary, thinking—and in particular thinking in the way we have become accustomed in the West—brings us into an iron circle of fear and desire from which there is no escape: "Nobody wants to be free of pleasure, but we all want to be free of fear; we can't see that both go together; they are both sustained by thought."

We need consciousness to fear, just as we need consciousness to escape fear. We need, in particular, the image of the feared—the image of the object of our fear: "I am afraid of my wife. She has an image about me, and I have an image about her. There is no actual relationship except, perhaps, physically." It is the image that divides, and the I-hood of the I that creates the images. It is necessary to partition the world into separate I's—the fear and anxiety of the I that gives birth to its I-hood, and the division created by the image that increases the I's fear of annihilation: "If we have no relationship with one another, there is fear. One dominates the other, and either they separate or come together only in bed. So we live a brutal life with one another."

Face fear, says Krishnamurti, and you will also face the source of the I. You will also stare I-hood down. By seeing yourself, you will escape yourself. But you will not escape in a mirror: the face has been trained to hide, the eye to distort, the mind to obfuscate, the word to lie. You will not escape in the eyes of the others: they have stories to spin, projects to pursue, strategies to implement, fears to overcome, lies to tell. And you will not escape in your stories and images, for they are have been manufactured under the inspiration of fear and sing the I-hood of the I. Consciousness liberates, not in the same way that slapping a word onto an experience liberates but in a way that no longer depends on past and future events. Krishnamurti never says, positively, how it liberates, for how could he? To say is to entrap into the word. To entrap is to yield again to fear. Forgo the stories, man; forgo the press; forgo the models and the magic glass balls; forgo the avid stare into the future and the watchful gaze toward the past; forgo living according to your image and projects. Freedom from the I is freedom not only from fear but from time as well because it is only through the I that time appears as the devastating sequence of events leading to the nameless.

Foray into Timelessness: A Popperian Escape

There is also a Popperian escape from I-hood. Karl Popper (1979) proposes that there exist at least three worlds. The first world is the world of physical events and objects, such as atomic phenomena, automobiles, and door knobs. The second world is the world of perceptions, feelings, and emotions. These are direct and visceral responses that people and animals have to their environments. The third world is the world of ideas and scientific theories and musical works. The three worlds are interconnected, and people *exist* in all three worlds at the same time. It may be said, then, that persons *are* the interstices that bring together the three worlds.

But how are the three worlds brought together? By the impulse to truth. Whereas worlds one and two are temporally bounded and ephemeral, world three is not bound by time. Ideas are timeless. Not surprisingly, most logics are tenseless. "There exists X" or "X exists" is usually taken to mean that X exists for all time henceforth. X has been called into existence, and miraculously *we* have done it, with our own wills. Hence, when we accept our world-three life, we acquire the power to create *ex nihilo:* we create ideas and works of art and literature that escape temporality and exist in an atemporal space.

To acquire this power and to create atemporal entities, we must give up something—but what? Precisely the mineness of the idea, the poem, or the musical score. The proposition "X is P" will endure if it is truthlike or maximally close to the truth. The *Art of the Fugue* will endure if it finds *resonance* with other beings living in world three. We do not know of any theory that is certifiably true in all possible future worlds, nor do we know of any way of writing a musical piece that will guarantee that future generations will resonate with it for all times to come. Therefore, we must settle for *imperfection* and, implicitly, for *perfectibility* of our ideas and art forms.

Einstein was a great thinker: that is perhaps true. But his ideas are probably mistaken: they will likely be shown to be mistaken by future minds. Had Einstein, however, kept his ideas to himself or written them in a language that was his and his alone—an Einstein-language—then he would have kept *ownership* of these ideas, would have imprinted his *identity* on them in a way that cannot be reversed or modified. The price he would have paid, however, is that his ideas would have disappeared once his life in worlds one and two was over. His ideas would have died along with him. Instead, we have ideas that have come from Einstein, which we can interact with, modify, refute, or reinterpret in terms of our growing knowledge of the mathematical ideas that Einstein himself interacted with.

Thus, we can exist in world three, but in so living we sacrifice our identity. We become part of something much larger, of an unfolding collective process by which *a* consciousness of the world grows, without it necessarily being *our* consciousness of the world. To escape time, we give up identity. To escape death, we give up ownership. To escape passage into nothingness we give up the commonly held idea of what it means to exist and to be something or someone.

The Dissolution of Being: A Skeptic's Solution

The I can also be escaped by a concerted effort along the lines of the skeptic's argument. The skeptic does not think he is justified in believing any statement describing his sense experience except if he is *antecedently* justified in believing that he is not dreaming up his own perceptions—indeed his whole past experience. It is a tricky escape route, for the skeptic's argument may lead to solipsism, wherein only the thinking I exists, the rest of the world being figments of her imagination. Here, the I becomes most prominent and becomes the *cogito* of Descartes let loose into the latter-day anomie of a twentieth-century teenager. Indeed, the skeptic desiring to rid herself of a self must go further. She must claim that, indeed, her thoughts and perceptions of the external world—even the most vivid ones—are figments of *an* imagination, which may not be only hers. There is no I that is experiencing the supposedly dreamlike experiences of the skeptic. There is, similarly, no I that is imagining or dreaming or that is dreaming that she is dreaming, and so forth.

This is a straightforward extension of the skeptic's argument, since identity and self-sameness require a grounding in a continuous, or continuously existing, I. In turn, the presumption of this continuity requires a grounding in *fact*—in the very outside experiences that the skeptic denies to be real. Thus, once the skeptic wants to say that she may very well be dreaming all of her experiences, she will be hard-pressed to say what I (the dreamer) means when she says "I." The skeptic therefore proceeds to I-less solipsism, wherein the dreaming and imagining are done not by anyone in particular but rather by *anyone* at all.

A Simple Plan: "Letting" and the Dissolution of Desire

There may be many more ways of escaping the I, and many more thinkers will be pushed to heights of ingenuity by the flight from themselves. Those that we have described, however, require a retraining of the senses and the emotions by the mind—a leap of the imagination that is *immediately* followed by an emotional leap. You cannot acquire an *acquired pleasure* overnight, and thus you cannot wake up tomorrow humming *The Art of the Fugue,* having thus far listened only to Rachmaninov. To the unwilling, these leaps seem like impossible tasks, and the philosophers proposing them seem like lunatics who cannot possibly practice what they preach. The passions are left behind by the leaps that the imagination can make; and the imagination, looking back and finding no passion coloring the new landscape, shrivels back into apathy.

In this spirit we might be wise to seek ways of escaping the self that are simple, that speak directly to the experiences of obsession and repression and aggression that we share toward thoughts, images, objects, and people; a way of escaping desire that speaks directly to the phenomenology of desire. As selves caught up in desires, goals, and projects, we can ask, What makes us helpless to abstain from acting in certain situations or from thinking certain thoughts? What determines our being toward the world? The answer we suggest is: anxiety. Our desires are anxious desires: we are anxious to fulfill them, in the sense of being afraid of not having fulfilled them. Our goals are anxious goals, in the sense that we are afraid of failing to accomplish them. Our ideas and thoughts and images are anxious because we are afraid that they will turn out to be false or illusory. Our attempted escapes from anxiety—through ambitious desire and conquest, jealous desire and envious resentment—are themselves anxious. They are impetuous and do not admit of questioning or analysis. Doubt must be suppressed, for doubt, like time, is corrosive of our beings, as Emil Cioran (1972) has suggested.

We need, then, a counterweight to desiring, to Eros, in the realm of the mind, and that counterweight is *letting*—letting come, letting be, and letting go. Letting is a form of being, just as desiring is, but it is a form of being that does not presuppose or require the idea and feel of the I that wants, acts, and sweats. It does not exclude the idea of the I, to be sure, and it certainly does not repress the idea of the I.

You *let thoughts come* that, when in the desiring state of being, you might repress—thoughts that your partner may secretly at times crave sex with another, that your stomach has gotten very large over the last year, that you may die on your next plane trip, that your boss has pretended to be able to help you all of these years when in fact he is himself in a tight spot in the organization; that the world is not as predictable as some scientists portray it to be, that it is in doubt whether your life up to now has been a sham or not, that perhaps your moments of authenticity were your greatest stage acts yet, that your children's love for you is really quite animal-like and rests on their material dependence on your physical person.

Let the thoughts be as they are, as they have always been, for they may be true just as well as they may be false, they may be evil just as well as they might be good. Let be the thoughts and the objects and persons that they represent. You do not act on the urge to ask your wife about her fantasies (she will deny them), to ask yourself about your poses (you will start concocting some defensive ritual or defensive story), or to ask your boss about the extent of his influence (you will tempt him to dissimulate his or her real feelings). You resist all attempts to escape your thoughts through the levers of desire but do not resist by *fighting* (that is already the kernel of desire springing up inside of you) but rather by *letting be*. If you let be whatever is—as Heidegger wrote—then you are free to witness the truth—free, in other words, to let come the thoughts that are coming to you.

You let go of the thoughts, the objects, the people, the time of your life. You do not hang on to your serenity even though you are astounded that you have found it. You do not linger or look back, doubting, like Orpheus did Hades, the presence of the kind light with which you might see the world. You let go of the best and the worst, of the ugly and the beautiful, of the malevolent and the kind. You let go of your thoughts, of your perceptions, of your memories. You let go of the people that are *going* from your life, of the objects that you are about to abandon, of the cities that are about to take their leave of you, of the languages that you once spoke and mastered, of the countries that are disappearing under your airplane. You let go of your lovers, wives, children, friends, slaves, masters, and husbands. You let go and let them go.

Once you've let go, you do not *move on*. That is again the kernel of desire sprouting to repress the about-to-become-past in your mind. Rather, you let come again new thoughts, new feelings, new gestures, and new actions. With them, the feelings of a new I are born. But it is an I that defies definition, an I that comes into being in spite of itself because its essence is in letting rather than wanting. The letting I does not will itself to be in a particular way. It does not will the world or other people to be in a particular way. It does not want to see the world in a particular way. It lets come, lets be, lets go, and frees itself from itself continuously.

13

Postlude: Explaining How an Explanation Explains in the Social Sciences

According to a standard view of explanation in the social sciences, individuals or groups of individuals are the units of analysis that figure in our beliefs about the world. In sentences like "John married Jane," subject-persons do things with or to object-persons. Thoughts occur to subject-persons, who may be persuaded or not persuaded by reasons and moved or unmoved by emotions. Events happen to object-persons, who can be the objects of illusions, delusions, and psychotic visions and who may be the objects of desire, hatred, jealousy, and envy of subject-persons. Subject persons engage in behaviors that can be observed by others, for whom they become object-persons.

Observers can test various cause-and-effect hypotheses on their observations. Social scientists say, for example, that people are motivated to work harder by the promise of material rewards, that they are not motivated to work harder by material rewards, that all such relations depend on the institutional and cultural context of the interaction, that all people are moved by fear, that some people are not moved by fear, and so forth. From these basic intuitions, social scientists build theories that aim to explain the observed phenomena. From these theories, they build models of particular phenomena.

Models are theories to which initial and boundary conditions have been specified. Hypotheses are theorems that follow by self-evident logical steps from the models they rest on. They are tested against observation statements that the model builder has deemed relevant and informative to the model in question. The model is said to be corroborated if the hypotheses are confirmed by the observation statements and to be refuted if they are disconfirmed. This strategy mirrors that of natural scientists, and the stature and prestige of the social scientist often turn on the degree to which the process of inquiry in the social sciences matches that of the natural sciences.

However, most people are not as confident of the predictions made by psychological and social models as they are of the predictions made by models from the natural sciences. "The human element" is inherently unpredictable, the saying goes. Dostoyevsky even claimed that unpredictability is a characteristically human trait: for even if a man knew what he had to do to achieve his end, he may still decide not to do it, just to show that he is human.

Social psychological studies have added some support to the general pessimism—for it is the situation, argue psychologists, rather than the characteristics of the actor, that is more likely to influence people's behaviors. No general typology of situations has been unambiguously articulated. Indeed, the way in which people construe situations is so tightly coupled with their personal biases, culture, and mythology that the project of constructing a typology of situations that transcends cultures may be a hoax, akin to that of constructing a view of scientific rationality that cuts across all possible metaphysical world views.

Absent such a comprehensive family of constructs and concepts, the problem of predicting behavior seems radically underdetermined. No sooner do we have a model that seems reasonably competent to predict behavior in a particular set of situations than something else becomes relevant to the actors by virtue of their being actors and therefore hidden from us as observers. Are these limitations intrinsic to any process of explaining behavior, or are we as scientific observers systematically missing something in our inquiries?

The work that you have just read is an attempt to build explanations of behavior that use the *first-person access* that we have to other people's motivational and preactional states. Personhood and access to first-person experiences are assets that have been heavily underutilized by the social scientist, for fear that his or her biases and interpretations will damage the objectivity of his or her reports. As people, we have the ability to simulate internally the predicaments of other people, whereas we do not have an equal ability to simulate the predicament of electrons or genes. Introspection is a tool of inquiry about others. Self-analysis, thought experiments, the exploration of cognitive maps, and criticism of the results of introspection are the instruments by which introspective inquiry proceeds. Comparison with the predictions that others would make in similar situations is a regulative mechanism that functions in the same way in which it operates in the natural sciences. Transpositional objectivity need not be *replaced* by introspection, just as introspective inquiry does not preclude the possibility of comparing our experiences among ourselves and of working harder at introspection and analysis when we end up with different beliefs and predictions about the same phenomenon.

Can the evidence of introspection and introspective report count for the validation of a theory in the same way that transpositionally objective or intersubjective observations do? Alvin Goldman (1997) has recently put forward an argument that the requirement that only public evidence of the kind we normally assume to be invariant under changes in the identity of the observer can be relaxed to include evidence from introspection and introspective reports. He does so by loosening our confidence in the belief that scientific evidence is only of the public kind. He defines an intersubjective method for producing evidence by the requirements that two or more investigators "can severally apply the method to the same questions" and that the method, if actually applied, would induce the same beliefs in the investigators. When we talk about how scientific a particular belief is, we at least have in mind its *responsiveness* to observation statements produced by the method satisfying such conditions.

What is wrong with introspective reports in view of this dominant approach to social science? Well, for one thing, one person cannot bear witness to another's internal psychological state, which means that introspective statements cannot be intersubjectively verified. But wait! says Goldman. The definition says nothing about requiring two or more scientists actually to have observed it already. We could not do new science if only past observations are to count; the definition stipulates only that there be a possible world in which one could introspect another's internal psychological state. And there is: he gives the example of Siamese twins joined at the brain—perhaps not (yet) capable of survival until the age when states can be linguistically interpreted but arguably capable of mutual introspection, and the time may come when such introspection can be linguistically interpreted.

Goldman also argues that the conditions that we place on scientific knowledge are unwarrantedly harsh: they exclude as being unscientific some observations that we definitely want to have access to as part of science: he gives the example of observations carried out by observers in different space-time "corners" of the universe, whose light cones do not intersect during their lifetimes but who carry out the same experiment and have the same cognitive and perceptual capacities. Here the fact that we now think it is physically impossible for them to reach intersubjective agreement should not preclude their observation statements to qualify as scientific. But this is precisely what the (standard) definition requires. Therefore, argues Goldman, the standard definition should be abandoned or modified; at the very least, there is no a priori reason for excluding introspective reports from the realm of observation statements.

We have yet to say, of course, what conditions should apply to guide the production of scientific evidence. Is it the case that anything goes? Surely we can recall instances of fraud or self-deception in which the criticism of others has made a crucial difference to the integrity of our beliefs. Cannot these instances suggest a general method for the production of evidence that permits introspective statements into the scientific picture of the world? Start with the realization that seemingly objective statements like "That is green" require an act of introspection: producing language requires consciousness, and "That is green" requires a separation between subject and object and an interpretation of a raw feel that only a conscious being is aware of. So all scientific and public observation statements are introspective in nature.

When you say, "Yes, it is," to someone who says "That is green," thus conferring publicity on her statement, you are not saying, "I know how you feel," but rather, "I am conscious of how I feel." When, on the other hand, you are empathically understanding—by appeal to introspection—someone's anger or folly, you seem to be saying, "I know how you feel."

But—retorts the scientific psychologist—you cannot *know* how she feels. Even in the case of watching a green butterfly, her internal psychological state of green may feel like your internal psychological state of red. Empathic understanding is elusive, and claiming to have access to it is presumptuous. If you are satisfied with this account, then you are probably like most people of science today. This view, however, is unfair: for all you are saying when you say, "I know how you feel," is really, "I know how I feel, having simulated in my mind the conditions that you are describing to me." That is, we do have first-person access to others' descriptions, and this first-person access is *essential* to the investigation of the claims to validity of these descriptions.

What would you do if you point to a leaf; say, "It is green"; and then hear your friend say, "Are you nuts? That is red"? Presumably you would point to some other object to see how far your disagreement goes. Do you both agree that the sky is blue? Do you both agree that the sun shines yellow? If you register fresh disagreements, then what? You would probably go to a third person, who will be the adjudicator of your misunderstandings. But what if the third person agrees with one of you sometimes and with the other on other occasions? Then your temptations to take both friends to an asylum notwithstanding, you might consult a fourth person. Fresh disagreements might prompt you to start building theories that explain your differences and are testable by observation statements that you all agree on—the relative lengths of rods or of musical tones, perhaps. And on you would go down the path of mutual constructive criticism.

The same protocol can be followed with more complex introspections. Understanding another's jealousy can be the outcome of simulating the conditions that seem to have produced that feeling in him or her, which may be easily done if the language he uses to describe his predicament is sufficiently vivid. "I understand," you tell him. Only now, instead of *disagreements* producing crises of legitimation, *agreements* produce them as well: "What do you mean, 'I understand'?" your friend says. Then he proceeds to query you on the meanings that you have attached to various elements in his story: How did you think he related to her smile? What do you think he thought she thought? And so forth.

Your understanding grows with every question. But it is not only understanding of what is the case, but it is understanding of what is not the case. "I understand" quickly becomes "I thought I understood," "Here are the ways in which I misunderstood," and "Here is what it takes to improve my understanding." You do not need a friend to carry out the criticism: you can simply turn your own criticism inward and realize that all private understandings are ultimately fallible and perfectible, by the method of conjuring up possible worlds to test the interpretations that we give to various images and propositions. Thus, the method of criticism—applied with some candor and integrity—can yield scientifically satisfactory evidential reports based on introspection. Criticism entails advancing as many relevant alternative interpretations as we can think of and choosing from among them. A relevant alternative interpretation of a particular understanding of a statement is often a claim that the initial explanation was a *misunderstanding* of it, along with a reason that explains why the initial understanding is amiss.

Of course, there is no given or predetermined end to this process: our beliefs at any point in time are as good as the number of relevant alternatives that we have critically considered. Suppose you want to interpret a squeal of laughter in the darkness of a cave as a theatrical act. You might then generate and test hypotheses about the circumstances that surrounded the eerie sound (was the person under the impression that she was being heard?), and you might generate and test hypotheses about alternative motives (was it the bittersweet rejection of a lover's advances?). Your final beliefs will depend not only on how diligent you have been in checking through your hypotheses but also on the types of relevant alternative explanations that you have put forth. Not only what we currently think of as evidence but also the kinds of conjectures that we put forth will determine the beliefs that you would end up with.

What is the *best* belief that you could end up with here? It is the explanation of the squeal of laughter in the dark that the squealer, in a quiet and reflectively introspective mood, would agree was the best translation into language of her psychological state. But what makes *her* the authority, even in the quiet, reflexive mood? Could it not be that she is self-deluded or that she is trying to *convince herself* of something by convincing you of it? So, she, too, should engage in criticism, this time of her own state when she squealed. If you can interact with her, your analyses—carried out with critical intent—can help discipline both actor and observer, and together you will be able to rule out more of the *incorrect* interpretations of the laughter in the dark than will any of you acting separately. Thus, inquiry about other persons proceeds through a watchful *dialogue* between subject and object. This is an unusual dialogue, to be sure, for no sooner does the speaking subject speak his mind than his words become the object of the other's criticism and his own analysis. The subject-object dialectic gets played out both intrapersonally (as my ideas become the object of my own analysis and criticism) and interpersonally (as your ideas become the object of my analysis and criticism based on my own introspection of their meaning).

A second feature of this work is a new ontology for thinking about social and psychological phenomena. What exist, according to this view, are not necessarily individual people and social structures comprising individuals and evolving in time according to individuals' wishes and desires but rather embodied emotions that can amplify each other into burgeoning spirals or quietly die out, according to the conditions that characterize a particular group or society. Current thinking in the social sciences posits the thinking, feeling, desiring I, either implicitly or explicitly. Having postulated selfhood, however, most of the social sciences hasten to construct explanatory models that deny agency, adducing cause-and-effect explanations of a biological, psychological, or sociological nature to explain how people act given what they think, feel, or perceive. Freedom of will of the individual would be an unmitigated disaster for theoreticians who try to come up with necessary and sufficient conditions for particular individual actions.

Consider the interplay between different scientific models of humans in a hypothetical courtroom argument:

Prosecuting attorney: He did it slowly, deliberately, and smilingly, your honor. What he did was to kill his cousin with a hatchet.

Defense lawyer: In a moment of delirium, under the influence of alcohol, provoked by discovering that she had joined a religious cult whose precepts went against everything that he had been brought up to respect.

Prosecutor, wielding the hatchet: Just imagine it, folks. I come up to you, hatchet raised, and know what I am about to do. The young woman is in a corner of the fenced garden, her eyes wide open. She understands my intent. And I too now realize what she thinks. Drunk, yes, but all of a sudden jolted awake by her terror. Blinded by vengeful passion, yes, but all of a sudden aware that what I hate is a figment of my own imagination, which has cast her in the role of a blasphemer.

Defense lawyer: Do not be taken in by images worthy of a cheap novelist. The hatchet was on the table. She was chiding him, laughing at his weak physical disposition, making fun of his fruitless pursuit of sexual relations with women. And now she wielded her own hatchet—a psychological one—and slashed at him with that snide remark about his creed that had kept him from becoming what he really is, that has effectively castrated him. All of a sudden he saw *her* as the embodiment of all of his pain—her depraved morals, her sickly laughter and nihilist disposition. He saw her through a lens, darkly—the embodiment of evil, if ever he knew it. He picked up the closest thing at hand and whacked her—not with the *intent* to kill, no, with the intent of *shutting down* her voice within him, a voice that he hears now, that he will always hear. He was not motivated by his fury. No, he *acted out* his fury. He was *gripped*. Good people, have you never been gripped by an idea or an emotion before? Consciousness is a feeble swimmer in the cauldron of the passions. And you need to establish *consciousness* in order to convict. But can you? Introspect, good people, introspect.

Social scientists and biologists often generate *exculpations from causal agency* for individual people, such as genetic traits, moral upbringing or lack thereof, education, lack of education, innate dispositions, character, personality, endogenous preferences, cognitive limitations, cognitive biases, social forces such as the pressure to conform, and so forth. Thus, the role of the I is that of a billiard ball, responding more or less passively (read: predictably) to the forces acting on it. The scientist's task is to figure out all of the forces and their interactions—and then all social phenomena will become predictable. This is the Newtonian project of social science, first dreamt up by Auguste Comte (1974) a century and a half ago and having reached an apogee in the dogmatic Marxism of the twentieth-century dictatorships and the structuralist and analytical models of the economy in contemporary North America. The foundation (or, perhaps, the end goal?) of such program of inquiry is a view of the I as constrained by laws of behavior to take certain actions in the same way as electrons are constrained by the laws of physics to move along certain trajectories. Recent experimental work suggests that the explanatory successes of this project are *illusory:* people act *as if* they are obeying laws of behavior because they *see themselves* as being determined by those laws: consciousness mocks science by impersonating zombiehood.

If we stray from the path to the mechanistic fallacy, we are at once confronted with a choice—to keep or not to keep the I as a basic ontological entity for scientific explanations of individual and social behavior. Some philosophers—like Derek Parfit (1984, p. 275)—have argued that identity, construed as *sameness* or self-similarity, is untenable: "The existence of a person just consists in the existence of [a] brain and a body... and the occurrence of many other physical and mental events." If you are destroyed here on Earth and replicated on Mars by a teletransporter, there is a sense in which you have died: your replica really *is* a replica, even though she thinks that she is really you. She will have all of your memories, physical and cognitive attributes and capabilities, and fears, phobias, and desires, but she will not be identical to you in the way in which you hold yourself today to be identical to yourself tomorrow.

If you are taken with this account, then you are in for a surprise: for Parfit proceeds to argue that when pressed to say *what exactly* are the differences between the two situations (of, respectively, continued existence and destruction followed by teletransportation), you are bound to come up empty. If you adopt *causal connectedness* as the criterion of personal identity, then you are forced to grant your selfhood to any connected series of events involving parts of your body—to all of the recipients of your organs or blood, for example. If you are committed to the continued physical existence of a brain in the body of a person as the criterion of identity, then you are forced to abandon it in the case of partial brain cell transplants or physical alterations of the brain that shut down consciousness. If you are committed to the continued presence of memories in a person that were causally related to that person's experiences, then you are forced to abandon the person's identity in the case of amnesiacs or people who have undergone partial brain damage that prevents them from recalling events.

Parfit is led to conclude that "identity is not what matters. What matters is . . . psychological connectedness (holding of particular direct psychological connections) and psychological continuity (presence of overlapping chains of connectedness), with the right kind of cause" (p. 279). Any cause will do. There is no significant difference, in this view, between normal survival and teletransportation. There is also no major stake in the answer that we give to the question "Am I about to die?" which turns out to be impossible to answer coherently by any standard views of identity.

We are left with a view of the I that does not presuppose or require physical personhood. We have agency but no physical agent. It is an I that can be instantiated in many different physical bodies, sequentially or simultaneously and one that causes them to take particular actions—the ambitious I, the jealous I, the envious I, the anxious I. Psychological connectedness of the I that appears in bodies and causes them to act means that it emotes within a particular mythology or representation of the world: one that assigns causal powers to various people and objects, that assigns values to various objects and actions, and that assigns various roles and relationships to objects, people, and places. The representation contains *objects* of desire and *objects* of resentment, which are *created* rather than discovered. The envious I creates objects of envy that then serve to fuel more envy. The ambitious I creates objects of desire that further stimulate ambition. The jealous I constructs situations that further fuel his jealousy.

The emoting I is *the* psychologically connected I: we speak of people as being possessed by envy, blinded by ambition, or consumed by jealousy. The gripped individual is a new unit of analysis that the foregoing text polishes and sets forth. Freed from the constraints of having to slice up the world into different, separate people with identities, goals, and desires, we can speak of *envy* as possessing, of *ambition* as blinding, and *jealousy* as consuming. It is not the jealous, ambitious I that is doing; rather, it is the passions that are doing, through the I's in their grasps. Individual agency is of course in danger, unless the master passions can themselves be escaped. It is the role of consciousness to reestablish agency, sometimes against heavy odds. It is the role of philosophical thought to rescue consciousness from the grips of emotions so powerful that they shape reality for those in their grasp, to the extent that the external world ceases to supply a point of reference, criticism, and correction for the inner psychological world.

Social history can be reconstructed as a set of emotional dynamics, of struggles games and dialectics played out by embodied feelings. Embodied envy, as we have shown, can amplify itself within a single person, recruit other people to its cause, and consume an entire society, inspiring people to take actions driven by resentment and fear of each other's envious retribution. Ambition, in turn, can lead to dialectics of master and slave, of sadist and masochist, of desiring and desired, of entrepreneur and bureaucrat, in which individual roles evolve according to different dynamics and give rise in turn to new dialectics as the mythology that underlies a culture grows to fill the need for a universe of discourse and action in which the contest over causal powers can be played out. The "thrill of the kill" that characterizes the Hegelian dialectic of master and slave is replaced by the game of seduction, revelation, and retreat of the desirous-desired dialectic; by the games of seduction, manipulation, control, submission, and rebellion; by the master-slave dialectic played with chips, dollars, and feelings of self-esteem or self-debasement instead of blood in the financial markets, in hierarchies and in families; and by the dynamic interplay between power and knowledge by which new institutions create their own bases of knowledge to increase the reach of their teachings and the causal powers of their incumbent practitioners in the lives of lay people whose intuition is subjugated to the judgment of the experts.

Master passions can generate dialectics that consume eons on the canvass of history. Their embodiments can fuel each other intrapersonally and interpersonally: envy stokes envy, masterhood attracts and begets opposition, sadists prey on masochists even as they are themselves drawn to masochism, the masochist's renunciation stimulates the sadist to new acts of cruelty, each entrepreneurial success feted by the press creates the desire for greater successes in the future, each increase in causal powers highlights the possibility rather than the achievement and causes one to want more causal powers. Thus, in the realm of embodied passions, myself and I at different times can be far more different than you and I are at any one given time. You could be the closest continuer to my being—since your emotional state most closely approximates my emotional state, whereas I have left my former emotional state behind me. The act of *leaving* one's feelings behind can open the windows of consciousness. The self—an image concocted by an emotional state—is negated, even as the I—the witness of that state—is reestablished.

References

Preface

Hume, D. *Treatise of Human Nature*. Oxford: Oxford University Press, 1960.

Solomon, R. *The Passions*. Indianapolis: Hackett, 1993.

Chapter 1

Camus, A. *The Fall*. Trans. Justin O'Brien. New York: Knopf, 1956.

Cioran, E. *Oeuvres*. Paris: Gallimard, 1996.

Crook, J. H. "The Socio-Ecology of Primates." In J. H. Crook, ed., *Social Behaviour in Animal Societies*. London: Routledge, 1970.

Hirschman, A. *Exit, Voice and Loyalty*. Cambridge: Harvard University Press, 1974.

Rosetti, D. G. "Sudden Light." *Oxford Anthology of Poetry*. Oxford: Oxford University Press, 1981.

Snow, C. P. *The Two Cultures*. Cambridge: Cambridge University Press, 1963.

Chapter 2

Abelson, R. "Beliefs Are Like Possessions." *Journal for the Theory of Social Behaviour* (October 1986): 223–250.

Bargh, J., and T. Chartrand. "The Unbearable Automaticity of Being." *American Psychologist* (July 1999): 462–479.

De Sousa, R. *The Rationality of the Emotions*. Cambridge: MIT Press, 1987.

Elster, J. *Alchemies of the Mind*. New York: Cambridge University Press, 1999.

Fischhoff, B. "Hindsight Does Not Equal Foresight: The Effects of Outcome Knowledge on Judgment Under Uncertainty." *Journal of Experimental Psychology: Human Perception and Performance* 1 (1975): 288–299.

Fisher, H. *The Anatomy of Love*. New York: Basic Books, 1992.

Frank, R., T. Gilovich, and D. Regan. "Does Studying Economics Inhibit Cooperation?" *Journal of Economic Perspectives* (Spring 1993): 159–171.

Gilovich, T. *How We Know What Isn't So*. New York: Free Press, 1993.

Hawkins, S., and R. Hastie. "Hindsight: Biased Judgments of Past Events After the Outcomes Are Known." *Psychological Bulletin* 107, no. 3 (1990): 311–327.

Hirschman, A. O., *The Passions and the Interests*. Cambridge: Harvard University Press, 1984

James, W. *The Principles of Psychology*. New York: Holt, 1890.

Langer, E. *The Psychology of Control*. Hillsdale, NJ: Erlbaum, 1975.

Loewenstein, G. "Behavioral Decision Theory and Business Ethics: Skewed Trade-offs Between Self and Other." In D. Messick and A. Tenbrunsel, eds., *Codes of Conduct*. New York: Russell Sage, 1996.

McAdams, D. *The Stories We Live By*. Evanston, IL: Northwestern University Press, 1993.

Nisbett, R., and L. Ross. *Human Inference*. Englewood Cliffs, NJ: Prentice Hall, 1981.

Sartre, J.-P. *The Emotions: Outline of a Theory*. Trans. Bernard Frechtman. New York: Philosophical Library, 1948.

Searle, J. *The Mystery of Consciousness*. New York: Basic Books, 1996.

Singer, J., and S. Schachter. "Cognitive, Social and Physiological Determinants of Emotional States." *Psychological Review* 59, no. 5 (1962): 379–399.

Solomon, R. *The Passions*. Indianapolis: Hackett, 1993.

Taylor, C. "Interpretation and the Sciences of Man." In R. Martin and J. McIntyre, eds., *Philosophy of the Social Sciences*. Cambridge: MIT Press, 1992.

Van Maanen, J. "Fear and Loathing in Organization Studies." *Organization Science* 5, no. 3 (1995): 687–692.

Chapter 3

Asch, S. "Opinions and Social Pressure." *Scientific American* 193, no. 5 (1955): 31–35.

Bruner, J., and L. Postman. "On the Perception of Incongruity: A Paradigm." *Journal of Personality* 18 (1949): 206–223.

Festinger, L. *A Theory of Cognitive Dissonance*. Englewood Cliffs: Prentice Hall, 1957.

Frost, R. *The Road Not Traveled and Other Poems*. New York: Dover, 1993.

Heidegger, M. *Being and Time*. 1927. Trans. M. MacQuarrie and Edward Robinson. Oxford: Blackwell, 1962.

Hume, D. "Enquiry Concerning Human Understanding." In *The Empiricists* New York: Doubleday, 1974.

Kierkegaard, S. *The Concept of Anxiety*. Trans. Reidar Thomte and Albert Anderson. Princeton: Princeton University Press, 1963.

Maio, G. R., and J. M. Olson. "Values as Truisms." *Journal of Personality and Social Psychology* (1998) 74: 212–218.

Searle, J. *The Construction of Social Reality*. New York: Free Press, 1996.

Chapter 4

Boorstin, D. *The Image: A Guide to Pseudo-Events in America*. New York: Harper and Row, 1983.

Foucault, M. *Power/Knowledge: Selected Interviews and Essays, 1972–1977*. New York: Norton, 1981.

Friedman, M. "The Methodology of Positive Economics." In M. Friedman, ed., *Essays in Positive Economics*. Chicago: University of Chicago Press, 1953.

Girard, R. *Deceit, Desire and the Novel*. 1961. Trans. Yvonne Frecerro. Baltimore: Johns Hopkins University Press, 1965.

Hegel, G. W. F. *The Phenomenology of the Spirit*. 1807. Trans. A. V. Miller. Oxford: Oxford University Press, 1977.

Heilbroner, R. *The Nature and Logic of Capitalism*. New York: Norton, 1985.

Lewis, D. "Counterfactual Dependence and Time's Arrow." in David Lewis, *Philosophical Papers*. Vol. 2. Oxford: Oxford University Press, 1986.

Marx, K. *Capital*. 1872. Vol. 1. Trans. Ben Fowkes. New York: Penguin Classics, 1975.

Marx, K., and F. Engels. *The German Ideology*. Ed. R. Pascal. New York: International, 1939.

Schelling, T. "The Intimate Contest for Control." In T. Schelling, *Choice and Consequence*. Cambridge: Harvard University Press, 1984.

Volkogonov, M. *Stalin: Triumph and Tragedy*. London: Weidenfeld and Nicolson, 1991.

Weber, M. *The Protestant Ethic and the Spirit of Capitalism*. London: George Allen & Unwin, 1930.

Chapter 5

Bakunin, M. *Bakunin's Writings*. Trans. and Ed. Guy A. Aldred. New York: Kraus Reprint, 1972.

Boudon, R. "Envy" In J. Elster, ed., *Rational Choice*. London: Routledge, 1981.

Engels, F. *The Origin of the Family, Private Property and the State*. New York: Doubleday, 1933.

Engels, F. "Socialism: Utopian and Scientific." In J. Somerville and R. E. Santoni, eds., *Social and Political Philosophy*. New York: Doubleday, 1963.

Freud, S. "Group Psychology and the Analysis of the Ego." In *Collected Works*. Vol. 18. Trans. Alix Strachey. London: Hogarth, 1955.

Hitler, A. *Mein Kampf*. 1931. In J. Somerville and R. E. Santoni, eds., *Social and Political Philosophy*. New York: Doubleday Anchor Books, 1963.

Kant, I. *Grounding for the Metaphysics of Morals*. trans. James W. Ellington. 1785. Indianapolis: Hackett, 1985.

Lenin, V. I. "State and Revolution." In J. Somerville and R. E. Santoni, eds., *Social and Political Philosophy*. New York: Doubleday Anchor Books, 1963.

Marx, K., and F. Engels. "Manifesto of the Communist Party." English Edition, 1888. In J. Somerville and R. E. Santoni, eds., *Social and Political Philosophy*. New York: Doubleday Anchor Books, 1963.

Murdock, G. P. *Social Structure*. New York: Free Press, 1960.

Pipes, R. *The Russian Revolution*. New York: Knopf, 1990.

Proudhon, J. *General Idea of Revolution in the Nineteenth Century*. 1851. Trans. John Beverly Robinson. London: Freedom Press, 1923.

Scheler, M. "Resentment in the Make-up of Morals." 1955. In H. Schoeck, ed., *Envy*. Indianapolis: Liberty Fund, 1969.

Schoeck, H. *Envy: A Theory of Social Behavior*. 1966. Indianapolis: Liberty Fund, 1987.

Chapter 6

Camus, A. *The Myth of Sisyphus*. Trans. Justin O'Brien. London: Hamilton, 1960.

Chapter 7

Cioran, E. *A Short History of Decay*. 1949. Trans. Richard Howard. New York: Arcade Books, 1972.

Nietzsche, F. *Beyond Good and Evil: Prelude to a Philosophy of the Future*. Trans. Helen Zimmern. In *The Complete Works of Friedrich Nietzsche*. London: Foulis, 1909–1913.

Chapter 8

Abelson, A. "Beliefs Are Like Possessions." *Journal for the Theory of Social Behaviour*. (October 1986): 223–250.

Lakatos, I. "Falsification and the Methodology of Scientific Research Programmes." In I. Lakatos and A. Musgrave, eds., *Criticism and the Growth of Knowledge*. New York: Cambridge University Press, 1970.

Miller, D. *Critical Rationalism*. Illinois: Open Court, 1994.

Milton, J. *Complete Poems*. Harvard Classics Vol. IV. New York: P. F. Collier, 1909–1914.

Oksenberg Rorty, A. "Explaining Emotions." In A. Oksenberg Rorty, ed., *Explaining Emotions*. New York: Cambridge University Press, 1988.

Popper, K. R. *Knowledge and the Body-Mind Problem*. London: Routledge, 1979.

Sartre, J.-P. *Being and Nothingness*. Trans. H. E. Barnes. New York: Philosophical Library, 1956.

Chapter 9

Berlin, I. "The Pursuit of the Ideal." In I. Berlin, *The Proper Study of Mankind: An Anthology of Essays*. New York: Farrar, Strauss and Giroux, 1997.

Descartes, R. "Discourse on Method." In *Descartes' Selected Writings*. New York: Penguin Classics, 1990.

Kafka, F. *Collected Short Stories*. Trans. Willa and Edwin Muir. Hammondsworth: Penguin Books, 1974.

Lestringant, F. *Cannibals*. Cambridge: Harvard University Press, 1997.

Nietzsche, F. *Beyond Good and Evil: Prelude to a Philosophy of the Future*. Trans. Helen Zimmern. In *The Complete Works of Friedrich Nietzsche*. Edinburgh: Foulis, 1909–1913.

Peterson, J. *Maps of Meaning. The Architecture of Belief*. London: Routledge, 1998.

Sartre, J.-P. *Being and Nothingness*. New York: Philosophical Library, 1956.

Scarry, E. *The Body in Pain*. Cambridge: Harvard University Press, 1995.

Chapter 10

Hofstadter, D. *Godel, Escher, Bach: An Eternal Golden Braid*. New York: Basic Books, 1979.

Kafka, F. *Collected Short Stories*. Trans. Willa and Edwin Muir. Hammondsworth: Penguin Books, 1974.

Koestler, A. *Darkness at Noon*. New York: MacMillan, 1941.

Lakoff, G. *Moral Politics*. New York: Free Press, 1996.

Samuelson, P. "A Note on the Pure Theory of Consumer's Behaviour." *Economica* 5 (1938): 61–71.

Scarry, E. *The Body in Pain*. Cambridge: Harvard University Press, 1995.

Searle, J. *The Mystery of Consciousness*. New York: Basic Books, 1996.

Chapter 11

Abelson, R. "Beliefs Are Like Possessions." *Journal for the Theory of Social Behaviour* (October 1986): 223–250.

Camus, A. *The Fall.* Trans. Justin O'Brien. New York: Knopf, 1956.

Durrenmatt, F. *An Angel Comes to Babylon and Romulus the Great.* New York: Grove Press, 1964.

Durrenmatt, F. *The Assignment, or, On Observing the Observers of the Observers.* Trans. Joel Agee. New York: Random House, 1988.

Eco, U. *The Name of the Rose.* Trans. William Weaver. San Diego: Harcourt Brace Jovanovich, 1983.

Lear, J. *Open Minded.* Cambridge: Harvard University Press, 1997.

Nietzsche, F. *Beyond Good and Evil.* Trans. Helen Zimmern. In *The Complete Works of Friedrich Nietzsche.* London: Foulis, 1910–1913.

Shakespeare, W. *Othello.* In *William Shakespeare's Complete Works.* London: Gramercy Books, 1990.

Shakespeare, W. *Richard III.* In *William Shakespeare's Complete Works.* London: Gramercy Books, 1990.

Chapter 12

Cioran, E. *A Short History of Decay.* 1949. Trans. Richard Howard. New York: Arcade Books, 1972.

Heidegger, M. *Being and Time.* 1927. Trans. John MacQuarries and Edward Robinson. Oxford: Blackwell, 1962.

Krishnamurti, J. *On Fear.* San Francisco: Harper, 1995.

Popper, K. R. *Knowledge and the Body-Mind Problem.* London: Routledge, 1979.

Chapter 13

Comte, A. *The Essential Comte.* Ed. Stanislav Andreski. New York: Barnes and Noble, 1974.

Goldman, A. "Science, Publicity and Consciousness." *Philosophy of Science 64,* no. 4 (1997): 525–545.

Parfit, D. *Reasons and Persons.* Oxford: Oxford University Press, 1984.

Index